The Poems
of
Henry Wadsworth
Longfellow

BLACK'S READERS SERVICE COMPANY

NEW YORK, N. Y.

CONTENTS

INTRODUCTION

Poets are, according to tradition and numberless historical examples, an unhappy race of men, cursed by their sensitivity, plagued by their imagination, victimised by their emotions, and incapable of adjustment to the requirements of a prosaic world. But against the examples that sustain the rule we may set others, though less numerous, which notably and nobly contradict it; and prominent among these is the singularly serene, successful, and happy life of Henry Wadsworth Longfellow. He was happy in his ancestry, which on his mother's side led back to John and Priscilla Alden; in the accident of birth that brought him into a home made pleasant by sufficient means, gentle breeding, and unaffected culture; and in the natural surroundings amid which his early and late years were spent. Throughout his life he was happy in his friends, such friends as Nathaniel Hawthorne, James Russell Lowell, and Charles Eliot Norton; and he was happy in both his wives, although the manner of his losing them was sad in the first case and shockingly tragic in the second. He was happy at home and abroad, in his children and in his contacts with the great world. He was, too, almost continuously happy in his work both as professor and as poet, even if the claims of academic routine irked him a bit before he stepped free of them after eighteen years of service. The path that he followed to popularity and eminence, that led from the shores of Casco Bay to the place that he occupies, in effigy, in the Poets' Corner of Westminster Abbey, ran straight and clear; it was innocent of pitfalls and stumbling-blocks, and it was haunted by no demons of doubt. Longfellow knew what he wished to do with his life, did it supremely well according to the judgment of his generation, and was amply rewarded. In short, exceptional good fortune was his lot.

Born in Portland, Maine, on February 27th, 1807, in the same year as Whittier and two years before Poe. Longfellow was a high-spirited, intellectually inquiring lad—"a lively boy," wrote his brother, "with brown or chestnut hair, blue eyes, a delicate complexion, and rosy cheeks; sensitive, impressionable; active, eager, impetuous, often impatient; quick-tempered, but as quickly appeased; kind-hearted and affectionate" —who proved a ready scholar and was prepared to enter Bowdoin College before he was fifteen years old. His awakening to literature came through Irving's "Sketch Book," which he read with mounting excitement as it was published number by number; and his own literary debut was made, in lumbering metre, with "The Battle of Lovell's Pond," which was printed in the Portland *Gazette,* in November, 1820. Graduation from Bowdoin meant the choice of a career, and he thought for a time of following his father as a lawyer, but when his college invited him to become its first professor of modern languages he did not hesitate; and the summer of 1826 saw him boarding the packet-ship *Cadmus* bound for Havre. Three years were spent abroad, in France, Spain, Italy, and Germany, acquiring the knowledge of languages essential to the position he would occupy, and in soaking up a multitude of romantic and colorful impressions that were later to find a place in his poetry. Indeed, as Louis Untermeyer has said, "The rest of his life, and the greater part of his poetry, was an effort to translate the background of those years into the language of his own times." Returning to Bowdoin, his days were filled with lecturing, teaching, the making of textbooks, and a little original writing; in 1831 he married Mary Storer Potter, and the future seemed to promise him only domestic happiness and the studious pleasures of an academic career. As yet the poet had not emerged. Professorial advancement came in 1835, when Harvard offered Longfellow the Smith Chair of Modern Languages, and again he decided that study abroad was essential before he assumed the responsibilities of the proffered position. This time his chief interest was in the Scandinavian tongues, and he went first to Denmark and Sweden, later visiting Holland and Germany. It was in Rotterdam that his wife fell ill and died; and, after a winter of study at Heidelberg, he returned to America to take up his residence in Cambridge alone.

The period of his Harvard professorship corresponds with his first period of poetic fecundity. "Voices of the Night" was published in 1839. "Ballads and Other Poems" in 1841, "Poems

INTRODUCTION

on Slavery" in 1842, "The Belfry of Bruges" in 1846; "Evangeline" in 1847, and "The Golden Legend" in 1851. Anthologies,
a drama in verse, and various prose pieces swelled the total
of Longfellow's production during these years. After his retire-
ment from Harvard, in 1854, the story of his life is—apart
from the tragic death of his second wife, Frances Elizabeth
Appleton, who was burned to death in 1861; and his final visit
to Europe, when Cambridge made him a doctor of laws, and
Queen Victoria received him at Windsor—largely the story of
his writings. "Hiawatha" extended his popularity in 1855,
"The Courtship of Miles Standish" confirmed it in 1858; and
from then until his death, on March 24th, 1882, Longfellow
continued to produce volume after volume, rising steadily
towards the same position in America that Tennyson was
approaching in England,—that of a National Institution.

Longfellow's reputation has suffered, like Tennyson's, from
the excessive adulation of his contemporaries, and from the
fact that succeeding generations of school children have had
his verses thrust upon them to be memorized; the verses, as
they conclude, of a solemn, preachy old gentleman with a
beard. It is hard to repair this kind of school-room damage;
but I would suggest to the prejudiced reader that, if he returns
to Longfellow, he approach him by way of the chatty, amus-
ing, and very human letters that he wrote home during his
first visit to Europe. The Longfellow that they reveal is not
a bearded moralist, but a young man who had a keen eye for
the beauty of Basque girls, and who was "absolutely thunder-
struck" but at the same time delighted "to find an old friend
in Paris," when he discovered in the Louvre a Venus that was
"an exact portrait of Miss K——." But the unprejudiced
reader can, if he has any faculty of appreciation, turn straight
to the poems themselves, and, separating the wheat from the
chaff, find wheat enough to reward his winnowing. Literature
does not have to be of the first and greatest rank to be
enjoyable.

BEN RAY REDMAN.

EVANGELINE.

A TALE OF ACADIE.

1847.

THIS is the forest primeval. The murmuring pines and the
hemlocks,
Bearded with moss, and in garments green, indistinct in the
twilight,
Stand like Druids of eld, with voices sad and prophetic,
Stand like harpers hoar, with beards that rest on their bosoms.
Loud from its rocky caverns, the deep-voiced neighboring
ocean
Speaks, and in accents disconsolate answers the wail of the
forest.

This is the forest primeval; but where are the hearts that
beneath it
Leaped like the roe, when he hears in the woodland the voice
of the huntsman?
Where is the thatch-roofed village, the home of Acadian
farmers,—
Men whose lives glided on like rivers that water the wood-
lands,
Darkened by shadows of earth, but reflecting an image of
heaven?
Waste are those pleasant farms, and the farmers forever
departed!
Scattered like dust and leaves, when the mighty blasts of
October
Seize them, and whirl them aloft, and sprinkle them far o'er
the ocean.
Naught but tradition remains of the beautiful village of
Grand-Pré.

Ye who believe in affection that hopes, and endures, and is
patient,

1

Ye who believe in the beauty and strength of woman's devotion,
List to the mournful tradition still sung by the pines of the
forest;
List to a Tale of Love in Acadie, home of the happy.

PART THE FIRST.

I.

IN THE Acadian land, on the shores of the Basin of Minas,
Distant, secluded, still, the little village of Grand-Pré
Lay in the fruitful valley. Vast meadows stretched to the
eastward,
Giving the village its name, and pasture to flocks without
number.
Dikes, that the hands of the farmers had raised with labor
incessant,
Shut out the turbulent tides; but at stated seasons the flood-
gates
Opened, and welcomed the sea to wander at will o'er the
meadows.
West and south there were fields of flax, and orchards and
cornfields
Spreading afar and unfenced o'er the plain; and away to the
northward
Blomidon rose, and the forests old, and aloft on the mountains
Sea-fogs pitched their tents, and mists from the mighty At-
lantic
Looked on the happy valley, but ne'er from their station
descended.
There, in the midst of its farms, reposed the Acadian village.
Strongly built were the houses, with frames of oak and of
chestnut,
Such as the peasants of Normandy built in the reign of the
Henries.
Thatched were the roofs, with dormer-windows; and gables
projecting
Over the basement below protected and shaded the door-way.
There in the tranquil evenings of summer, when brightly the
sunset

Lighted the village street, and gilded the vanes on the chimneys,
Matrons and maidens sat in snow-white caps and in kirtles
Scarlet and blue and green, with distaffs spinning the golden
Flax for the gossiping looms, whose noisy shuttles within
doors
Mingled their sound with the whir of the wheels and the songs
of the maidens.
Solemnly down the street came the parish priest, and the
children
Paused in their play to kiss the hand he extended to bless
them.
Reverend walked he among them; and up rose matrons and
maidens,
Hailing his slow approach with words of affectionate welcome.
Then came the laborers home from the field, and serenely the
sun sank
Down to his rest, and twilight prevailed. Anon from the
belfry
Softly the Angelus sounded, and over the roofs of the village
Columns of pale-blue smoke, like clouds of incense ascending,
Rose from a hundred hearths, the homes of peace and contentment.
Thus dwelt together in love these simple Acadian farmers,—
Dwelt in the love of God and of man. Alike were they free
from
Fear, that reigns with the tyrant, and envy, the vice of
republics.
Neither locks had they to their doors, nor bars to their
windows;
But their dwellings were open as day and the hearts of the
owners;
There the richest was poor, and the poorest lived in abundance.

Somewhat apart from the village, and nearer the Basin of
Minas,
Benedict Bellefontaine, the wealthiest farmer of Grand-Pré,
Dwelt on his goodly acres; and with him, directing his household,
Gentle Evangeline lived, his child, and the pride of the village.
Stalworth and stately in form was the man of seventy winters;

Hearty and hale was he, an oak that is covered with snow-
    flakes;
White as the snow were his locks, and his cheeks as brown as
    the oak-leaves.
Fair was she to behold, that maiden of seventeen summers.
Black were her eyes as the berry that grows on the thorn by
    the wayside,
Black, yet how softly they gleamed beneath the brown shade
    of her tresses!
Sweet was her breath as the breath of kine that feed in the
    meadows
When in the harvest heat she bore to the reapers at noon-
    tide
Flagons of home-brewed ale, ah! fair in sooth was the maiden.
Fairer was she when, on Sunday morn, while the bell from its
    turret
Sprinkled with holy sounds the air, as the priest with his
    hyssop
Sprinkles the congregation, and scatters blessings upon them,
Down the long street she passed, with her chaplet of beads
    and her missal.
Wearing her Norman cap, and her kirtle of blue, and the
    ear-rings
Brought in the olden time from France, and since, as an
    heirloom,
Handed down from mother to child, through long generations.
But a celestial brightness—a more ethereal beauty—
Shone on her face and encircled her form, when, after con-
    fession,
Homeward serenely she walked with God's benediction upon
    her.
When she had passed, it seemed like the ceasing of exquisite
    music.
Firmly builded with rafters of oak, the house of the farmer
Stood on the side of a hill, commanding the sea, and a shady
Sycamore grew by the door, with a woodbine wreathing
    around it.
Rudely carved was the porch, with seats beneath; and a
    footpath
Led through an orchard wide, and disappeared in the meadow.
Under the sycamore-tree were hives overhung by a penthouse,
Such as the traveller sees in regions remote by the road-side,

Built o'er a box for the poor, or the blessed image of Mary.
Farther down, on the slope of the hill, was the well with its
    moss-grown
Bucket, fastened with iron, and near it a trough for the horses.
Shielding the house from storms, on the north, were the barns
    and the farm-yard.
There stood the broad-wheeled wains and the antique ploughs
    and the harrows;
There were the folds for the sheep; and there, in his feathered
    seraglio,
Strutted the lordly turkey, and crowed the cock, with the
    selfsame
Voice that in ages of old had startled the penitent Peter.
Bursting with hay were the barns, themselves a village. In
    each one
Far o'er the gable projected a roof of thatch; and a staircase,
Under the sheltering eaves, led up to the odorous corn-loft.
There too the dove-cot stood, with its meek and innocent
    inmates
Murmuring ever of love; while above in the variant breezes
Numberless noisy weathercocks rattled and sang of mutation.

  Thus, at peace with God and the world, the farmer of
    Grand-Pré
Lived on his sunny farm, and Evangeline governed his house-
    hold.
Many a youth, as he knelt in the church and opened his
    missal,
Fixed his eyes upon her, as the saint of his deepest devotion;
Happy was he who might touch her hand or the hem of her
    garment!
Many a suitor came to her door, by the darkness befriended,
And as he knocked and waited to hear the sound of her
    footsteps,
Knew not which beat the louder, his heart or the knocker of
    iron;
Or at the joyous feast of the Patron Saint of the village,
Bolder grew, and pressed her hand in the dance as he whis-
    pered
Hurried words of love, that seemed a part of the music.
But, among all who came, young Gabriel only was welcome;
Gabriel Lajeunesse, the son of Basil the blacksmith,

Who was a mighty man in the village, and honored of all
    men;
For since the birth of time, throughout all ages and nations,
Has the craft of the smith been held in repute by the people.
Basil was Benedict's friend. Their children from earliest
    childhood
Grew up together as brother and sister; and Father Felician,
Priest and pedagogue both in the village, had taught them
    their letters
Out of the selfsame book, with the hymns of the church and
    the plain-song.
But when the hymn was sung, and the daily lesson completed,
Swiftly they hurried away to the forge of Basil the black-
    smith.
There at the door they stood, with wondering eyes to behold
    him
Take in his leathern lap the hoof of the horse as a plaything,
Nailing the shoe in its place; while near him the tire of the
    cart-wheel
Lay like a fiery snake, coiled round in a circle of cinders.
Oft on autumnal eves, when without in the gathering darkness
Bursting with light seemed the smithy, through every cranny
    and crevice,
Warm by the forge within they watched the laboring bellows,
And as its panting ceased, and the sparks expired in the ashes,
Merrily laughed, and said they were nuns going into the
    chapel.
Oft on sledges in winter, as swift as the swoop of the eagle,
Down the hill-side bounding, they glided away o'er the
    meadow.
Oft in the barns they climbed to the populous nests on the
    rafters,
Seeking with eager eyes that wondrous stone, which the
    swallow
Brings from the shore of the sea to restore the sight of its
    fledglings;
Lucky was he who found that stone in the nest of the swal-
    low!
Thus passed a few swift years, and they no longer were
    children.
He was a valiant youth, and his face, like the face of the
    morning.

Gladdened the earth with its light, and ripened thought into
   action.
She was a woman now, with the heart and hopes of a woman.
"Sunshine of Saint Eulalie" was she called; for that was the
   sunshine
Which, as the farmers believed, would load their orchards
   with apples;
She, too, would bring to her husband's house delight and
   abundance,
Filling it full of love, and the ruddy faces of children.

II.

Now had the season returned, when the nights grow colder
   and longer,
And the retreating sun the sign of the Scorpion enters.
Birds of passage sailed through the leaden air from the ice-
   bound,
Desolate northern bays to the shores of tropical islands.
Harvests were gathered in; and wild with the winds of Sep-
   tember
Wrestled the trees of the forest, as Jacob of old with the
   angel.
All the signs foretold a winter long and inclement.
Bees, with prophetic instinct of want, had hoarded their honey
Till the hives overflowed; and the Indian hunters asserted
Cold would the winter be, for thick was the fur of the foxes.
Such was the advent of autumn. Then followed that beau-
   tiful season,
Called by the pious Acadian peasants the Summer of All-
   Saints!
Filled was the air with a dreamy and magical light; and the
   landscape
Lay as if new-created in all the freshness of childhood.
Peace seemed to reign upon earth, and the restless heart of
   the ocean
Was for a moment consoled. All sounds were in harmony
   blended.
Voices of children at play, the crowing of cocks in the farm-
   yards,
Whir of wings in the drowsy air, and the cooing of pigeons,

All were subdued and low as the murmurs of love, and the
    great sun
Looked with the eye of love through the golden vapors
    around him;
While arrayed in its robes of russet and scarlet and yellow,
Bright with the sheen of the dew, each glittering tree of the
    forest
Flashed like the plane-tree the Persian adorned with mantles
    and jewels.

Now recommenced the reign of rest and affection and
    stillness.
Day with its burden and heat had departed, and twilight
    descending
Brought back the evening star to the sky, and the herds to the
    homestead.
Pawing the ground they came, and resting their necks on each
    other,
And with their nostrils distended inhaling the freshness of
    evening.
Foremost, bearing the bell, Evangeline's beautiful heifer,
Proud of her snow-white hide, and the ribbon that waved
    from her collar,
Quietly paced and slow, as if conscious of human affection.
Then came the shepherd back with his bleating flocks from
    the seaside,
Where was their favorite pasture. Behind them followed the
    watchdog.
Patient, full of importance, and grand in the pride of his
    instinct,
Walking from side to side with a lordly air, and superbly
Waving his bushy tail, and urging forward the stragglers;
Regent of flocks was he when the shepherd slept; their pro-
    tector,
When from the forest at night, through the starry silence, the
    wolves howled.
Late, with the rising moon, returned the wains from the
    marshes,
Laden with briny hay, that filled the air with its odor.
Cheerily neighed the steeds, with dew on their manes and
    their fetlocks,

While aloft on their shoulders the wooden and ponderous
saddles,
Painted with brilliant dyes, and adorned with tassels of
crimson,
Nodded in bright array, like hollyhocks heavy with blossoms.
Patiently stood the cows meanwhile, and yielded their udders
Unto the milkmaid's hand; whilst loud and in regular cadence
Into the sounding pails the foaming streamlets descended.
Lowing of cattle and peals of laughter were heard in the
farm-yard,
Echoed back by the barns. Anon they sank into stillness;
Heavily closed, with a jarring sound, the valves of the barn-
doors,
Rattled the wooden bars, and all for a season was silent.

In-doors, warm by the wide-mouthed fireplace, idly the
farmer
Sat in his elbow-chair, and watched how the flames and the
smoke wreaths
Struggled together like foes in a burning city. Behind him,
Nodding and mocking along the wall, with gestures fantastic,
Darted his own huge shadow, and vanished away into dark-
ness.
Faces, clumsily carved in oak, on the back of his arm-chair
Laughed in the flickering light, and the pewter plates on the
dresser
Caught and reflected the flame, as shields of armies the sun-
shine.
Fragments of song the old man sang, and carols of Christmas,
Such as at home, in the olden time, his fathers before him
Sang in their Norman orchards and bright Burgundian vine-
yards.
Close at her father's side was the gentle Evangeline seated,
Spinning flax for the loom, that stood in the corner behind
her.
Silent awhile were its treadles, at rest was its diligent shuttle,
While the monotonous drone of the wheel, like the drone of
a bagpipe,
Followed the old man's song, and united the fragments to-
gether.
As in a church, when the chant of the choir at intervals ceases,

Footfalls are heard in the aisles, or words of the priest at the
    altar,
So, in each pause of the song, with measured motion the clock
    clicked.

  Thus as they sat, there were footsteps heard, and, suddenly
    lifted,
Sounded the wooden latch, and the door swung back on its
    hinges.
Benedict knew by the hob-nailed shoes it was Basil the black-
    smith,
And by her beating heart Evangeline knew who was with him.
"Welcome!" the farmer exclaimed, as their footsteps paused
    on the threshold,
"Welcome, Basil, my friend! Come, take thy place on the
    settle
Close by the chimney-side, which is always empty without
    thee;
Take from the shelf overhead thy pipe and the box of to-
    bacco;
Never so much thyself art thou as when through the curling
Smoke of the pipe or the forge thy friendly and jovial face
    gleams
Round and red as the harvest moon through the mist of the
    marshes."
Then, with a smile of content, thus answered Basil the black-
    smith,
Taking with easy air the accustomed seat by the fireside:—
"Benedict Bellefontaine, thou hast ever thy jest and thy
    ballad!
Ever in cheerfullest mood art thou when others are filled with
Gloomy forebodings of ill, and see only ruin before them.
Happy art thou, as if every day thou hadst picked up a
    horseshoe."
Pausing a moment, to take the pipe that Evangeline brought
    him,
And with a coal from the embers had lighted, he slowly
    continued:—
"Four days now are passed since the English ships at their
    anchors
Ride in the Gaspereau's mouth, with their cannon pointed
    against us.

What their design may be is unknown; but all are commanded
On the morrow to meet in the church, where his Majesty's mandate
Will be proclaimed as law in the land. Alas! in the meantime
Many surmises of evil alarm the hearts of the people."
Then made answer the farmer—"Perhaps some friendlier purpose
Brings these ships to our shores. Perhaps the harvests in England
By the untimely rains or untimelier heat have been blighted,
And from our bursting barns they would feed their cattle and children."
"Not so thinketh the folk in the village," said, warmly, the blacksmith,
Shaking his head, as in doubt; then heaving a sigh, he continued:—
"Louisburg is not forgotten, nor Beau Séjour, nor Port Royal.
Many already have fled to the forest, and lurk on its outskirts,
Waiting with anxious hearts the dubious fate of to-morrow.
Arms have been taken from us, and warlike weapons of all kinds;
Nothing is left but the blacksmith's sledge and the scythe of the mower."
Then with a pleasant smile made answer the jovial farmer:—
"Safer are we unarmed, in the midst of our flocks and our cornfields,
Safer within these peaceful dikes, besieged by the ocean,
Than were our fathers in forts, besieged by the enemy's cannon.
Fear no evil, my friend, and to-night may no shadow of sorrow
Fall on this house and hearth; for this is the night of the contract.
Built are the house and the barn. The merry lads of the village
Strongly have built them and well; and, breaking the glebe round about them,
Filled the barn with hay, and the house with food for a twelvemonth.

René Leblanc will be here anon, with his papers and inkhorn.
Shall we not then be glad, and rejoice in the joy of our
    children?"
As apart by the window she stood, with her hand in her
    lover's,
Blushing Evangeline heard the words that her father had
    spoken,
And as they died on his lips the worthy notary entered.

III.

BENT like a laboring oar, that toils in the surf of the ocean,
Bent, but not broken, by age was the form of the notary
    public;
Shocks of yellow hair, like the silken floss of the maize, hung
Over his shoulders; his forehead was high; and glasses with
    horn bows
Sat astride on his nose, with a look of wisdom supernal.
Father of twenty children was he, and more than a hundred
Children's children rode on his knee, and heard his great
    watch tick.
Four long years in the times of the war had he languished a
    captive,
Suffering much in an old French fort as the friend of the
    English.
Now, though warier grown, without all guile or suspicion,
Ripe in wisdom was he, but patient and simple, and childlike.
He was beloved by all, and most of all by the children;
For he told them tales of the Loup-garou in the forest,
And of the goblin that came in the night to water the horses,
And of the white Létiche, the ghost of a child who unchris-
    tened
Died, and was doomed to haunt unseen the chambers of
    children;
And how on Christmas eve the oxen talked in the stable;
And how the fever was cured by a spider shut up in a nut-
    shell,
And of the marvellous powers of four-leaved clover and horse-
    shoes,
With whatsoever else was writ in the lore of the village.
Then up rose from his seat by the fireside Basil the black-
    smith,

Knocked from his pipe the ashes, and slowly extending his
   right hand,
"Father Leblanc," he exclaimed, "thou hast heard the talk in
   the village,
And, perchance, canst tell us some news of these ships and
   their errand."
Then with modest demeanor made answer the notary
   public:—
"Gossip enough have I heard, in sooth, yet am never the
   wiser;
And what their errand may be I know not better than others.
Yet am I not of those who imagine some evil intention
Brings them here, for we are at peace; and why then molest
   us?"
"God's name!" shouted the hasty and somewhat irascible
   blacksmith;
"Must we in all things look for the how, and the why, and
   the wherefore?
Daily injustice is done, and might is the right of the
   strongest!"
But, without heeding his warmth, continued the notary
   public:—
"Man is unjust, but God is just; and finally justice
Triumphs; and well I remember a story, that often consoled
   me,
When as a captive I lay in the old French fort at Port
   Royal."
This was the old man's favorite tale, and he loved to repeat it
When his neighbors complained that any injustice was done
   them.
"Once in an ancient city, whose name I no longer remember,
Raised aloft on a column, a brazen statue of Justice
Stood in the public square, upholding the scales in its left
   hand,
And in its right a sword, as an emblem that justice presided
Over the laws of the land, and the hearts and homes of the
   people.
Even the birds had built their nests in the scales of the
   balance,
Having no fear of the sword that flashed in the sunshine
   above them.
But in the course of time the laws of the land were corrupted;

Might took the place of right, and the weak were oppressed,
    and the mighty
Ruled with an iron rod. Then it chanced in a nobleman's
    palace
That a necklace of pearls was lost, and ere long a suspicion
Fell on an orphan girl who lived as maid in the household.
She, after form of trial condemned to die on the scaffold,
Patiently met her doom at the foot of the statue of Justice.
As to her Father in heaven her innocent spirit ascended,
Lo! o'er the city a tempest rose; and the bolts of the thunder
Smote the statue of bronze, and hurled in wrath from its left
    hand
Down on the pavement below the clattering scales of the
    balance,
And in the hollow thereof was found the nest of a magpie,
Into whose clay-built walls the necklace of pearls was in-
    woven."
Silenced, but not convinced, when the story was ended, the
    blacksmith
Stood like a man who fain would speak, but findeth no
    language;
All his thoughts were congealed into lines on his face, as the
    vapors
Freeze in fantastic shapes on the window-panes in the winter.

    Then Evangeline lighted the brazen lamp on the table,
Filled, till it overflowed, the pewter tankard with home-
    brewed
Nut-brown ale, that was famed for its strength in the village
    of Grand-Pré;
While from his pocket the notary drew his papers and ink-
    horn,
Wrote with a steady hand the date and the age of the parties,
Naming the dower of the bride in flocks of sheep and in
    cattle.
Orderly all things proceeded, and duly and well were com-
    pleted,
And the great seal of the law was set like a sun on the margin.
Then from his leathern pouch the farmer threw on the table
Three times the old man's fee in solid pieces of silver;
And the notary rising, and blessing the bride and the bride-
    groom,

Lifted aloft the tankard of ale and drank to their welfare.
Wiping the foam from his lip, he solemnly bowed and de-
    parted,
While in silence the others sat and mused by the fireside,
Till Evangeline brought the draught-board out of its corner.
Soon was the game begun. In friendly contention the old
    men
Laughed at each lucky hit, or unsuccessful manœuvre,
Laughed when a man was crowned, or a breach was made in
    the king-row.
Meanwhile apart, in the twilight gloom of a window's em-
    brasure,
Sat the lovers, and whispered together, beholding the moon
    rise
Over the pallid sea and the silvery mist of the meadows.
Silently one by one, in the infinite meadows of heaven,
Blossomed the lovely stars, the forget-me-nots of the angels.

Thus passed the evening away. Anon the bell from the
    belfry
Rang out the hour of nine, the village curfew, and straight-
    way
Rose the guests and departed; and silence reigned in the
    household.
Many a farewell word and sweet good-night on the door-step
Lingered long in Evangeline's heart, and filled it with glad-
    ness.
Carefully then were covered the embers that glowed on the
    hearth-stone,
And on the oaken stairs resounded the tread of the farmer.
Soon with a soundless step the foot of Evangeline followed.
Up the staircase moved a luminous space in the darkness,
Lighted less by the lamp than the shining face of the maiden.
Silent she passed through the hall, and entered the door of
    her chamber.
Simple that chamber was, with its curtains of white, and its
    clothes-press
Ample and high, on whose spacious shelves were carefully
    folded
Linen and woollen stuffs, by the hand of Evangeline woven.
This was the precious dower she would bring to her husband
    in marriage,

Better than flocks and herds, being proofs of her skill as a
    housewife.
Soon she extinguished her lamp, for the mellow and radiant
    moonlight
Streamed through the windows and lighted the room, till the
    heart of the maiden
Swelled and obeyed its power, like the tremulous tides of the
    ocean.
Ah! she was fair, exceeding fair to behold, as she stood with
Naked snow-white feet on the gleaming floor of her chamber!
Little she dreamed that below, among the trees of the orchard,
Waited her lover and watched for the gleam of her lamp and
    her shadow.
Yet were her thoughts of him, and at times a feeling of
    sadness
Passed o'er her soul, as the sailing shade of clouds in the
    moonlight
Flitted across the floor and darkened the room for a moment.
And as she gazed from the window she saw serenely the moon
    pass
Forth from the folds of a cloud, and one star follow her
    footsteps,
As out of Abraham's tent young Ishmael wandered with
    Hagar!

IV.

PLEASANTLY rose next morn the sun on the village of Grand-
    Pré,
Pleasantly gleamed in the soft, sweet air the Basin of Minas,
Where the ships, with their wavering shadows, were riding at
    anchor.
Life had long been astir in the village, and clamorous labor
Knocked with its hundred hands at the golden gates of the
    morning.
Now from the country around, from the farms and the neigh-
    boring hamlets,
Came in their holiday dresses the blithe Acadian peasants.
Many a glad good-morrow and jocund laugh from the young
    folk
Made the bright air brighter, as up from the numerous
    meadows,

Where no path could be seen but the track of wheels in the
    greensward,
Group after group appeared, and joined, or passed on the
    highway.
Long ere noon, in the village all sounds of labor were silenced.
Thronged were the streets with people; and noisy groups at
    the house-doors
Sat in the cheerful sun, and rejoiced and gossiped together.
Every house was an inn, where all were welcomed and feasted;
For with this simple people, who lived like brothers together,
All things were held in common, and what one had was
    another's.
Yet under Benedict's roof hospitality seemed more abundant:
For Evangeline stood among the guests of her father;
Bright was her face with smiles, and words of welcome and
    gladness
Fell from her beautiful lips, and blessed the cup as she gave it.

Under the open sky, in the odorous air of the orchard,
Bending with golden fruit, was spread the feast of betrothal.
There in the shade of the porch were the priest and the notary
    seated;
There good Benedict sat, and sturdy Basil the blacksmith.
Not far withdrawn from these, by the cider-press and the
    beehives,
Michael the fiddler was placed, with the gayest of hearts and
    of waistcoats.
Shadow and light from the leaves alternately played on his
    snow-white
Hair, as it waved in the wind; and the jolly face of the
    fiddler
Glowed like a living coal when the ashes are blown from the
    embers.
Gayly the old man sang to the vibrant sound of his fiddle,
Tous les Bourgeois de Chartres, and *Le Carillon de Dun-
    kerque,*
And anon with his wooden shoes beat time to the music.
Merrily, merrily whirled the wheels of the dizzying dances
Under the orchard-trees and down the path to the meadows;
Old folk and young together, and children mingled among
    them.

Fairest of all the maids was Evangeline, Benedict's daughter!
Noblest of all the youths was Gabriel, son of the blacksmith!

So passed the morning away. And lo! with a summons
　　sonorous
Sounded the bell from its tower, and over the meadows a
　　drum beat.
Thronged ere long was the church with men. Without, in
　　the churchyard,
Waited the women. They stood by the graves, and hung on
　　the headstones
Garlands of autumn-leaves and evergreens fresh from the
　　forest.
Then came the guard from the ships, and marching proudly
　　among them
Entered the sacred portal. With loud and dissonant clangor
Echoed the sound of their brazen drums from ceiling and
　　casement,—
Echoed a moment only, and slowly the ponderous portal
Closed, and in silence the crowd awaited the will of the
　　soldiers.
Then uprose their commander, and spake from the steps of
　　the altar,
Holding aloft in his hands, with its seals, the royal com-
　　mission.
"You are convened this day," he said, "by his Majesty's
　　orders.
Clement and kind has he been; but how you have answered
　　his kindness
Let your own hearts reply! To my natural make and my
　　temper
Painful the task is I do, which to you I know must be
　　grievous.
Yet must I bow and obey, and deliver the will of our
　　monarch;
Namely, that all your lands, and dwellings, and cattle of all
　　kinds
Forfeited be to the crown; and that you yourselves from this
　　province
Be transported to other lands. God grant you may dwell
　　there
Ever as faithful subjects, a happy and peaceable people!

Prisoners now I declare you; for such is his Majesty's
    pleasure!"
As, when the air is serene in the sultry solstice of summer,
Suddenly gathers a storm, and the deadly sling of the hail-
    stones
Beats down the farmer's corn in the field and shatters his
    windows,
Hiding the sun, and strewing the ground with thatch from the
    house-roofs,
Bellowing fly the herds, and seek to break their enclosures;
So on the hearts of the people descended the words of the
    speaker.
Silent a moment they stood in speechless wonder, and then
    rose
Louder and ever louder a wail of sorrow and anger,
And, by one impulse moved, they madly rushed to the door-
    way.
Vain was the hope of escape; and cries and fierce imprecations
Rang through the house of prayer; and high o'er the heads
    of the others
Rose, with his arms uplifted, the figure of Basil the black-
    smith,
As, on a stormy sea, a spar is tossed by the billows.
Flushed was his face and distorted with passion; and wildly
    he shouted:—
"Down with the tyrants of England! we never have sworn
    them allegiance!
Death to these foreign soldiers, who seize on our homes and
    our harvests!"
More he fain would have said, but the merciless hand of a
    soldier
Smote him upon the mouth, and dragged him down to the
    pavement.

In the midst of the strife and tumult of angry contention,
Lo! the door of the chancel opened and Father Felician
Entered, with serious mien, and ascended the steps of the
    altar.
Raising his reverend hand, with a gesture he awed into silence
All that clamorous throng; and thus he spake to his people;
Deep were his tones and solemn; in accents measured and
    mournful

Spake he, as, after the tocsin's alarum, distinctly the clock
strikes.
"What is this that ye do, my children? what madness has
seized you?
Forty years of my life have I labored among you, and taught
you,
Not in word alone, but in deed, to love one another!
Is this the fruit of my toils, of my vigils and prayers and
privations?
Have you so soon forgotten all lessons of love and forgive-
ness?
This is the house of the Prince of Peace, and would you
profane it
Thus with violent deeds and hearts overflowing with hatred?
Lo! where the crucified Christ from his cross is gazing upon
you!
See! in those sorrowful eyes what meekness and holy com-
passion!
Hark! how those lips still repeat the prayer, 'O Father, forgive
them!'
Let us repeat that prayer in the hour when the wicked assail
us,
Let us repeat it now, and say, 'O Father, forgive them!' "
Few were his words of rebuke, but deep in the hearts of his
people
Sank they, and sobs of contrition succeeded that passionate
outbreak;
And they repeated his prayer, and said, "O Father, forgive
them!"

Then came the evening service. The tapers gleamed from
the altar.
Fervent and deep was the voice of the priest, and the people
responded,
Not with their lips alone, but their hearts; and the Ave Maria
Sang they, and fell on their knees, and their souls, with
devotion translated,
Rose on the ardor of prayer, like Elijah ascending to heaven.

Meanwhile had spread in the village the tidings of ill, and
on all sides

Wandered, wailing, from house to house the women and children.

Long at her father's door Evangeline stood, with her right hand

Shielding her eyes from the level rays of the sun, that, descending,

Lighted the village street with mysterious splendor, and roofed each

Peasant's cottage with golden thatch, and emblazoned its windows.

Long within had been spread the snow-white cloth on the table;

There stood the wheaten loaf, and the honey fragrant with wild flowers;

There stood the tankard of ale, and the cheese fresh brought from the dairy;

And at the head of the board the great arm-chair of the farmer.

Thus did Evangeline wait at her father's door, as the sunset

Threw the long shadows of trees o'er the broad ambrosial meadows.

Ah! on her spirit within a deeper shadow had fallen,

And from the fields of her soul a fragrance celestial ascended,—

Charity, meekness, love, and hope, and forgiveness, and patience!

Then, all-forgetful of self, she wandered into the village,

Cheering with looks and words the disconsolate hearts of the women,

As o'er the darkening fields with lingering steps they departed,

Urged by their household cares, and the weary feet of their children.

Down sank the great red sun, and in golden, glimmering vapors

Veiled the light of his face, like the Prophet descending from Sinai.

Sweetly over the village the bell of the Angelus sounded.

Meanwhile, amid the gloom, by the church Evangeline lingered.

All was silent within; and in vain at the door and the windows

Stood she, and listened and looked, until, overcome by
    emotion
"Gabriel!" cried she aloud with tremulous voice; but no
    answer
Came from the graves of the dead, nor the gloomier grave
    of the living.
Slowly at length she returned to the tenantless house of her
    father.
Smouldered the fire on the hearth, on the board stood the
    supper untasted,
Empty and drear was each room, and haunted with phantoms
    of terror.
Sadly echoed her step on the stair and the floor of her
    chamber.
In the dead of the night she heard the whispering rain fall
Loud on the withered leaves of the sycamore-tree by the
    window,
Keenly the lightning flashed; and the voice of the echoing
    thunder
Told her that God was in heaven, and governed the world
    he created!
Then she remembered the tale she had heard of the justice
    of heaven;
Soothed was her troubled soul, and she peacefully slumbered
    till morning.

v.

Four times the sun had risen and set; and now on the fifth
    day
Cheerily called the cock to the sleeping maids of the farm-
    house.
Soon o'er the yellow fields, in silent and mournful procession,
Came from the neighboring hamlets and farms the Acadian
    women,
Driving in ponderous wains their household goods to the sea-
    shore,
Pausing and looking back to gaze once more on their dwell-
    ings,
Ere they were shut from sight by the winding road and the
    woodland.
Close at their sides their children ran, and urged on the oxen,

While in their little hands they clasped some fragments of
    playthings.

Thus to the Gaspereau's mouth they hurried and there on
    the sea-beach
Piled in confusion lay the household goods of the peasants.
All day long between the shore and the ships did the boats
    ply;
All day long the wains came laboring down from the village.
Late in the afternoon, when the sun was near to his setting,
Echoing far o'er the fields came the roll of drums from the
    church-yard.
Thither the women and children thronged. On a sudden the
    church-doors
Opened, and forth came the guard, and marching in gloomy
    procession
Followed the long-imprisoned, but patient, Acadian farmers.
Even as pilgrims, who journey afar from their homes and
    their country,
Sing as they go, and in singing forget they are weary and
    way-worn,
So with songs on their lips the Acadian peasants descended
Down from the church to the shore, amid their wives and
    their daughters.
Foremost the young men came; and, raising together their
    voices,
Sang they with tremulous lips a chant of the Catholic Mis-
    sions:—
"Sacred heart of the Saviour! O inexhaustible fountain!
Fill our hearts this day with strength and submission and
    patience!"
Then the old men, as they marched, and the women that
    stood by the way-side
Joined in the sacred psalm, and the birds in the sunshine
    above them
Mingled their notes therewith, like voices of spirits departed.

Halfway down to the shore Evangeline waited in silence,
Not overcome with grief, but strong in the hour of affliction,—
Calmly and sadly waited, until the procession approached her,
And she beheld the face of Gabriel pale with emotion.
Tears then filled her eyes, and, eagerly running to meet him,

Clasped she his hands, and laid her head on his shoulder, and
    whispered,—
"Gabriel! be of good cheer! for if we love one another,
Nothing, in truth, can harm us, whatever mischances may
    happen!"
Smiling she spake these words; then suddenly paused, for her
    father
Saw she slowly advancing. Alas! how changed was his aspect!
Gone was the glow from his cheek, and the fire from his eye,
    and his footstep
Heavier seemed with the weight of the weary heart in his
    bosom.
But with a smile and a sigh, she clasped his neck and em-
    braced him,
Speaking words of endearment where words of comfort availed
    not.
Thus to the Gaspereau's mouth moved on that mournful
    procession.

There disorder prevailed, and the tumult and stir of em-
    barking.
Busily plied the freighted boats; and in the confusion
Wives were torn from their husbands, and mothers, too late,
    saw their children
Left on the land, extending their arms, with wildest entreaties.
So unto separate ships were Basil and Gabriel carried,
While in despair on the shore Evangeline stood with her
    father.
Half the task was not done when the sun went down, and the
    twilight
Deepened and darkened around; and in haste the refluent
    ocean
Fled away from the shore, and left the line of the sand-beach
Covered with waifs of the tide, with kelp and the slippery
    sea-weed.
Farther back in the midst of the household goods and the
    wagons,
Like to a gipsy camp, or a leaguer after a battle,
All escape, cut off by the sea, and the sentinels near them,
Lay encamped for the night the houseless Acadian farmers.
Back to its nethermost caves retreated the bellowing ocean,
Dragging adown the beach the rattling pebbles, and leaving

Inland and far up the shore the stranded boats of the sailors.
Then, as the night descended, the herds returned from their
    pastures;
Sweet was the moist still air with the odor of milk from their
    udders;
Lowing they waited, and long, at the well-known bars of the
    farm-yard,—
Waited and looked in vain for the voice and the hand of the
    milk-maid.
Silence reigned in the streets; from the church no Angelus
    sounded,
Rose no smoke from the roofs, and gleamed no lights from
    the windows.

But on the shores meanwhile the evening fires had been
    kindled,
Built of the drift-wood thrown on the sands from wrecks in
    the tempest.
Round them shapes of gloom and sorrowful faces were gath-
    ered,
Voices of women were heard, and of men, and the crying of
    children.
Onward from fire to fire, as from hearth to hearth in his
    parish,
Wandered the faithful priest, consoling and blessing and
    cheering,
Like unto shipwrecked Paul on Melita's desolate sea-shore.
Thus he approached the place where Evangeline sat with her
    father,
And in the flickering light beheld the face of the old man,
Haggard and hollow and wan, and without either thought or
    emotion,
E'en as the face of a clock from which the hands have been
    taken.
Vainly Evangeline strove with words and caresses to cheer
    him,
Vainly offered him food; yet he moved not, he looked not, he
    spake not,
But, with a vacant stare, ever gazed at the flickering fire-light.
"*Benedicite!*" murmured the priest, in tones of compassion.
More he fain would have said, but his heart was full, and
    his accents

Faltered and paused on his lips, as the feet of a child on a
    threshold,
Hushed by the scene he beholds, and the awful presence of
    sorrow.
Silently, therefore, he laid his hand on the head of the
    maiden,
Raising his eyes, full of tears, to the silent stars that above
    them
Moved on their way, unperturbed by the wrongs and sorrows
    of mortals.
Then sat he down at her side, and they wept together in
    silence.

Suddenly rose from the south a light, as in autumn the
    blood-red
Moon climbs the crystal walls of heaven, and o'er the horizon
Titan-like stretches its hundred hands upon mountain and
    meadow,
Seizing the rocks and the rivers, and piling huge shadows
    together.
Broader and ever broader it gleamed on the roofs of the
    village,
Gleamed on the sky and the sea, and the ships that lay in
    the roadstead.
Columns of shining smoke uprose, and flashes of flame were
Thrust through their folds and withdrawn, like the quivering
    hands of a martyr.
Then as the wind seized the gleeds and the burning thatch,
    and, uplifting,
Whirled them aloft through the air, at once from a hundred
    housetops
Started the sheeted smoke with flashes of flame intermingled.

These things beheld in dismay the crowd on the shore and
    on shipboard.
Speechless at first they stood, then cried aloud in their
    anguish,
"We shall behold no more our homes in the village of Grand-
    Pré!"
Loud on a sudden the cocks began to crow in the farm-yards,
Thinking the day had dawned; and anon the lowing of cattle
Came on the evening breeze, by the barking of dogs inter-
    rupted.

Then rose a sound of dread, such as startles the sleeping
    encampments
Far in the western prairies or forests that skirt the Nebraska,
When the wild horses affrighted sweep by with the speed of
    the whirlwind,
Or the loud bellowing herds of buffaloes rush to the river.
Such was the sound that arose on the night, as the herds and
    the horses
Broke through their folds and fences, and madly rushed o'er
    the meadows.

  Overwhelmed with the sight, yet speechless, the priest and
    the maiden
Gazed on the scene of terror that reddened and widened be-
    fore them;
And as they turned at length to speak to their silent com-
    panion,
Lo! from his seat he had fallen, and stretched abroad on the
    seashore
Motionless lay his form, from which the soul had departed.
Slowly the priest uplifted the lifeless head, and the maiden
Knelt at her father's side, and wailed aloud in her terror.
Then in a swoon she sank, and lay with her head on his
    bosom.
Through the long night she lay in deep, oblivious slumber;
And when she woke from the trance, she beheld a multitude
    near her,
Faces of friends she beheld, that were mournfully gazing upon
    her,
Pallid with tearful eyes, and looks of saddest compassion.
Still the blaze of the burning village illumined the landscape,
Reddened the sky overhead, and gleamed on the faces around
    her,
And like the day of doom it seemed to her wavering senses.
Then a familiar voice she heard, as it said to the people,—
"Let us bury him here by the sea. When a happier season
Brings us again to our homes from the unknown land of our
    exile,
Then shall his sacred dust be piously laid in the church-yard."
Such were the words of the priest. And there in haste by the
    seaside,
Having the glare of the burning village for funeral torches,

But without bell or book, they buried the farmer of Grand-
Pré.
And as the voice of the priest repeated the service of sorrow,
Lo! with a mournful sound, like the voice of a vast congre-
gation,
Solemnly answered the sea, and mingled its roar with the
dirges.
'T was the returning tide, that afar from the waste of the
ocean,
With the first dawn of the day, came heaving and hurrying
landward.
Then recommenced once more the stir and noise of em-
barking;
And with the ebb of that tide the ships sailed out of the
harbor,
Leaving behind them the dead on the shore, and the village
in ruins.

PART THE SECOND.

I.

MANY a weary year had passed since the burning of Grand-
Pré,
When on the falling tide the freighted vessels departed,
Bearing a nation, with all its household gods, into exile,
Exile without an end, and without an example in story.
Far asunder, on separate coasts, the Acadians landed;
Scattered were they, like flakes of snow, when the wind from
the northeast
Strikes aslant through the fogs that darken the Banks of
Newfoundland.
Friendless, homeless, hopeless, they wandered from city to
city,
From the cold lakes of the North to sultry Southern sa-
vannas,—
From the bleak shores of the sea to the lands where the
Father of Waters
Seizes the hills in his hands, and drags them down to the
ocean,
Deep in their sands to bury the scattered bones of the mam-
moth.

Friends they sought and homes; and many, despairing, heart-
    broken,
Asked of the earth but a grave, and no longer a friend nor a
    fireside.
Written their history stands on tablets of stone in the church-
    yards.
Long among them was seen a maiden who waited and wan-
    dered,
Lowly and meek in spirit, and patiently suffering all things.
Fair was she and young; but, alas! before her extended,
Dreary and vast and silent, the desert of life, with its pathway
Marked by the graves of those who had sorrowed and suffered
    before her,
Passions long extinguished, and hopes long dead and aban-
    doned,
As the emigrant's way o'er the Western desert is marked by
Camp-fires long consumed, and bones that bleach in the
    sunshine.
Something there was in her life incomplete, imperfect, un-
    finished;
As if a morning of June, with all its music and sunshine,
Suddenly paused in the sky, and, fading, slowly descended
Into the east again, from whence it late had arisen.
Sometimes she lingered in towns, till, urged by the fever
    within her,
Urged by a restless longing, the hunger and thirst of the spirit,
She would commence again her endless search and endeavor;
Sometimes in church-yards strayed, and gazed on the crosses
    and tombstones,
Sat by some nameless grave, and thought that perhaps in its
    bosom
He was already at rest, and she longed to slumber beside him.
Sometimes a rumor, a hearsay, an inarticulate whisper,
Came with its airy hand to point and beckon her forward.
Sometimes she spake with those who had seen her beloved
    and known him,
But it was long ago, in some far-off place or forgotten.
"Gabriel Lajeunesse!" said they; "O, yes! we have seen him.
He was with Basil the blacksmith, and both have gone to the
    prairies;
Coureurs-des-Bois are they, and famous hunters and trappers."

"Gabriel Lajeunesse!" said others; "O, yes! we have seen him.
He is a *Voyageur* in the lowlands of Louisiana."
Then would they say,—"Dear child! why dream and wait for
    him longer?
Are there not other youths as fair as Gabriel? others
Who have hearts as tender and true, and spirits as loyal?
Here is Baptiste Leblanc, the notary's son, who has loved thee
Many a tedious year; come, give him thy hand and be happy!
Thou art too fair to be left to braid St. Catherine's tresses."
Then would Evangeline answer, serenely but sadly,—"I can-
    not!
Whither my heart has gone, there follows my hand, and not
    elsewhere.
For when the heart goes before, like a lamp, and illumines
    the pathway,
Many things are made clear, that else lie hidden in darkness."
And thereupon the priest, her friend and father-confessor,
Said, with a smile,—"O daughter! thy God thus speaketh
    within thee!
Talk not of wasted affection, affection never was wasted;
If it enrich not the heart of another, its waters, returning
Back to their springs, like the rain, shall fill them full of
    refreshment;
That which the fountain sends forth returns again to the
    fountain.
Patience; accomplish thy labor; accomplish thy work of affec-
    tion!
Sorrow and silence are strong, and patient endurance is god-
    like.
Therefore accomplish thy labor of love, till the heart is made
    godlike,
Purified, strengthened, perfected, and rendered more worthy
    of heaven!"
Cheered by the good man's words, Evangeline labored and
    waited.
Still in her heart she heard the funeral dirge of the ocean,
But with its sound there was mingled a voice that whispered,
    "Despair not!"
Thus did that poor soul wander in want and cheerless dis-
    comfort,
Bleeding, barefooted, over the shards and thorns of existence.
Let me essay, O Muse! to follow the wanderer's footsteps;—

Not through each devious path, each changeful year of
    existence;
But as a traveller follows a streamlet's course through the
    valley:
Far from its margin at times, and seeing the gleam of its
    water
Here and there, in some open space, and at intervals only;
Then drawing nearer its banks, through sylvan glooms that
    conceal it,
Though he behold it not, he can hear its continuous murmur;
Happy, at length, if he find the spot where it reaches an
    outlet.

II.

IT WAS the month of May. Far down the Beautiful River,
Past the Ohio shore and past the mouth of the Wabash,
Into the golden stream of the broad and swift Mississippi,
Floated a cumbrous boat, that was rowed by Acadian boat-
    men.
It was a band of exiles: a raft, as it were, from the ship-
    wrecked
Nation, scattered along the coast, now floating together,
Bound by the bonds of a common belief and a common
    misfortune;
Men and women and children, who, guided by hope or by
    hearsay,
Sought for their kith and their kin among the few-acred
    farmers
On the Acadian coast, and the prairies of fair Opelousas.
With them Evangeline went, and her guide, the Father
    Felician.
Onward o'er sunken sands, through a wilderness sombre with
    forests,
Day after day they glided adown the turbulent river;
Night after night, by their blazing fires, encamped on its
    borders.
Now through rushing chutes, among green islands, where
    plumelike
Cotton-trees nodded their shadowy crests, they swept with the
    current,
Then emerged into broad lagoons, where silvery sand-bars

Lay in the stream, and along the wimpling waves of their
    margin,
Shining with snow-white plumes, large flocks of pelicans
    waded.
Level the landscape grew, and along the shores of the river,
Shaded by China-trees, in the midst of luxuriant gardens,
Stood the houses of planters with negro-cabins and dove-cots.
They were approaching the region where reigns perpetual
    summer,
Where through the Golden Coast, and groves of orange and
    citron,
Sweeps with majestic curve the river away to the eastward.
They, too, swerved from their course, and, entering the Bayou
    of Plaquemine,
Soon were lost in a maze of sluggish and devious waters,
Which, like a network of steel, extended in every direction.
Over their heads the towering and tenebrous boughs of the
    cypress
Met in a dusky arch, and trailing mosses in mid-air,
Waved like banners that hang on the walls of ancient cathe-
    drals.
Deathlike the silence seemed, and unbroken, save by the
    herons
Home to their roosts in the cedar-trees returning at sunset,
Or by the owl, as he greeted the moon with demoniac laughter.
Lovely the moonlight was as it glanced and gleamed on the
    water,
Gleamed on the columns of cypress and cedar sustaining the
    arches,
Down through whose broken vaults it fell as through chinks
    in a ruin.
Dreamlike, and indistinct, and strange were all things around
    them;
And o'er their spirits there came a feeling of wonder and
    sadness,—
Strange forebodings of ill, unseen and that cannot be com-
    passed.
As, at the tramp of a horse's hoof on the turf of the prairies,
Far in advance are closed the leaves of the shrinking mimosa,
So, at the hoof-beats of fate, with sad forebodings of evil,
Shrinks and closes the heart, ere the stroke of doom has
    attained it.

But Evangeline's heart was sustained by a vision, that faintly
Floated before her eyes, and beckoned her on through the
    moonlight.
It was the thought of her brain that assumed the shape of a
    phantom.
Through those shadowy aisles had Gabriel wandered before
    her,
And every stroke of the oar now brought him nearer and
    nearer.

Then in his place, at the prow of the boat, rose one of the
    oarsmen,
And, as a signal sound, if others like them peradventure
Sailed on those gloomy and midnight streams, blew a blast
    on his bugle.
Wild through the dark colonnades and corridors leafy the
    blast rang,
Breaking the seal of silence, and giving tongues to the forest.
Soundless above them the banners of moss just stirred to the
    music
Multitudinous echoes awoke and died in the distance,
Over the watery floor, and beneath the reverberant branches;
But not a voice replied; no answer came from the darkness;
And when the echoes had ceased, like a sense of pain was the
    silence.
Then Evangeline slept; but the boatmen rowed through the
    midnight,
Silent at times, then singing familiar Canadian boat-songs,
Such as they sang of old on their own Acadian rivers.
And through the night were heard the mysterious sounds of
    the desert,
Far off, indistinct, as of wave or wind in the forest,
Mixed with the whoop of the crane and the roar of the grim
    alligator.

Thus ere another noon they emerged from those shades;
    and before them
Lay, in the golden sun, the lakes of the Atchafalaya.
Water-lilies in myriads rocked on the slight undulations
Made by the passing oars, and, resplendent in beauty, the
    lotus,
Lifted her golden crown above the heads of the boatmen.

Faint was the air with the odorous breath of magnolia
blossoms,
And with the heat of noon; and numberless sylvan islands,
Fragrant and thickly embowered with blossoming hedges of
roses,
Near to whose shores they glided along, invited to slumber.
Soon by the fairest of these their weary oars were suspended.
Under the boughs of Wachita willows, that grew by the
margin,
Safely their boat was moored; and scattered about on the
greensward,
Tired with their midnight toil, the weary travellers slumbered.
Over them vast and high extended the cope of a cedar.
Swinging from its great arms, the trumpet-flower and the
grape-vine
Hung their ladder of ropes aloft like the ladder of Jacob,
On whose pendulous stairs the angels ascending, descending,
Were the swift humming-birds, that flitted from blossom to
blossom.
Such was the vision Evangeline saw as she slumbered beneath
it.
Filled was her heart with love, and the dawn of an opening
heaven
Lighted her soul in sleep with the glory of regions celestial.

Nearer and ever nearer, among the numberless islands,
Darted a light swift boat, that sped away o'er the water,
Urged on its course by the sinewy arms of hunters and
trappers.
Northward its prow was turned, to the land of the bison and
beaver.
At the helm sat a youth, with countenance thoughtful and
careworn.
Dark and neglected locks overshadowed his brow, and a sad-
ness
Somewhat beyond his years on his face was legibly written.
Gabriel was it, who, weary with waiting, unhappy and restless
Sought in the Western wilds oblivion of self and of sorrow.
Swiftly they glided along, close under the lea of the island,
But by the opposite bank, and behind a screen of palmettos,
So that they saw not the boat, where it lay concealed in the
willows,

And undisturbed by the dash of their oars, and unseen, were
    the sleepers;
Angel of God was there none to awaken the slumbering
    maiden.
Swiftly they glided away, like the shade of a cloud on the
    prairie.
After the sound of their oars on the tholes had died in the
    distance,
As from a magic trance the sleepers awoke, and the maiden
Said with a sigh to the friendly priest,—"O, Father Felician!
Something says in my heart that near me Gabriel wanders.
Is it a foolish dream, an idle and vague superstition?
Or has an angel passed, and revealed the truth to my spirit?"
Then, with a blush, she added,—"Alas for my credulous fancy!
Unto ears like thine such words as these have no meaning."
But made answer the reverend man, and he smiled as he
    answered:—
"Daughter, thy words are not idle; nor are they to me with-
    out meaning.
Feeling is deep and still; and the word that floats on the
    surface
Is as the tossing buoy, that betrays where the anchor is
    hidden.
Therefore trust to thy heart, and to what the world calls
    illusions.
Gabriel truly is near thee; for not far away to the southward,
On the banks of the Têche, are the towns of St. Maur and
    St. Martin.
There the long-wandering bride shall be given again to her
    bridegroom,
There the long-absent pastor regain his flock and his sheep-
    fold.
Beautiful is the land, with its prairies and forests of fruit-
    trees;
Under the feet a garden of flowers, and the bluest of heavens
Bending above, and resting its dome on the walls of the forest.
They who dwell there have named it the Eden of Louisiana."

And with these words of cheer they arose and continued
    their journey.
Softly the evening came. The sun from the western horizon
Like a magician extended his golden wand o'er the landscape;

Twinkling vapors arose; and sky and water and forest
Seemed all on fire at the touch, and melted and mingled
    together.
Hanging between two skies, a cloud with edges of silver,
Floated the boat, with its dripping oars, on the motionless
    water.
Filled was Evangeline's heart with inexpressible sweetness.
Touched by the magic spell, the sacred fountain of feeling
Glowed with the light of love, as the skies and waters around
    her.
Then from a neighboring thicket the mocking-bird, wildest of
    singers,
Swinging aloft on a willow spray that hung o'er the water,
Shook from his little throat such floods of delirious music,
That the whole air and the woods and the waves seemed
    silent to listen.
Plaintive at first were the tones and sad; then soaring to
    madness
Seemed they to follow or guide the revel of frenzied Bac-
    chantes.
Single notes were then heard, in sorrowful, low lamentation;
Till, having gathered them all, he flung them abroad in
    derision,
As when, after a storm, a gust of wind through the tree-tops
Shakes down the rattling rain in a crystal shower on the
    branches.
With such a prelude as this, and hearts that throbbed with
    emotion,
Slowly they entered the Têche, where it flows through the
    green Opelousas,
And through the amber air, above the crest of the woodland,
Saw the column of smoke that arose from a neighboring
    dwelling;—
Sounds of a horn they heard, and the distant lowing of cattle.

III.

Near to the bank of the river, o'ershadowed by oaks, from
    whose branches
Garlands of Spanish moss and of mystic mistletoe flaunted,
Such as the Druids cut down with golden hatchets at Yule-
    tide,

Stood, secluded and still, the house of the herdsman. A
    garden
Girded it round about with a belt of luxuriant blossoms,
Filling the air with fragrance. The house itself was of timbers
Hewn from the cypress-tree, and carefully fitted together.
Large and low was the roof; and on slender columns sup-
    ported,
Rose-wreathed, vine-encircled, a broad and spacious veranda,
Haunt of the humming-bird and the bee, extended around it.
At each end of the house, amid the flowers of the garden,
Stationed the dove-cots were, as love's perpetual symbol,
Scenes of endless wooing, and endless contentions of rivals.
Silence reigned o'er the place. The line of shadow and sun-
    shine
Ran near the tops of the trees; but the house itself was in
    shadow,
And from its chimney-top, ascending and slowly expanding
Into the evening air, a thin blue column of smoke rose.
In the rear of the house, from the garden gate, ran a pathway
Through the great groves of oak to the skirts of the limitless
    prairie,
Into whose sea of flowers the sun was slowly descending.
Full in his track of light, like ships with shadowy canvas
Hanging loose from their spars in a motionless calm in the
    tropics,
Stood a cluster of trees, with tangled cordage of grape-vines.

   Just where the woodlands met the flowery surf of the
    prairie,
Mounted upon his horse, with Spanish saddle and stirrups,
Sat a herdsman, arrayed in gaiters and doublet of deerskin.
Broad and brown was the face that from under the Spanish
    sombrero
Gazed on the peaceful scene, with the lordly look of its
    master.
Round about him were numberless herds of kine, that were
    grazing
Quietly in the meadows, and breathing the vapory freshness
That uprose from the river, and spread itself over the land-
    scape.
Slowly lifting the horn that hung at his side, and expanding
Fully his broad, deep chest, he blew a blast, that resounded

Wildly and sweet and far, through the still damp air of the
    evening.
Suddenly out of the grass the long white horns of the cattle
Rose like flakes of foam on the adverse currents of ocean.
Silent a moment they gazed, then bellowing rushed o'er the
    prairie,
And the whole mass became a cloud, a shade in the distance.
Then, as the herdsman turned to the house, through the gate
    of the garden
Saw he the forms of the priest and the maiden advancing to
    meet him.
Suddenly down from his horse he sprang in amazement, and
    forward
Rushed with extended arms and exclamations of wonder;
When they beheld his face, they recognized Basil the black-
    smith.
Hearty his welcome was, as he led his guests to the garden.
There in an arbor of roses with endless question and answer
Gave they vent to their hearts, and renewed their friendly
    embraces,
Laughing and weeping by turns, or sitting silent and thought-
    ful.
Thoughtful, for Gabriel came not; and now dark doubts and
    misgivings
Stole o'er the maiden's heart; and Basil, somewhat embar-
    rassed,
Broke the silence and said,—"If you came by the Atchafalaya,
How have you nowhere encountered my Gabriel's boat on the
    bayous?"
Over Evangeline's face at the words of Basil a shade passed.
Tears came into her eyes, and she said, with a tremulous
    accent,—
"Gone? is Gabriel gone?" and, concealing her face on his
    shoulder,
All her o'erburdened heart gave way, and she wept and
    lamented.
Then the good Basil said,—and his voice grew blithe as he
    said it,—
"Be of good cheer, my child; it is only to-day he departed.
Foolish boy! he has left me alone with my herds and my
    horses.
Moody and restless grown, and tired and troubled, his spirit

Could no longer endure the calm of this quiet existence.
Thinking ever of thee, uncertain and sorrowful ever,
Ever silent, or speaking only of thee and his troubles,
He at length had become so tedious to men and to maidens,
Tedious even to me, that at length I bethought me, and sent him
Unto the town of Adayes to trade for mules with the Spaniards.
Thence he will follow the Indian trails to the Ozark Mountains,
Hunting for furs in the forests, on rivers trapping the beaver.
Therefore be of good cheer; we will follow the fugitive lover;
He is not far on his way, and the Fates and the streams are against him.
Up and away to-morrow, and through the red dew of the morning
We will follow him fast, and bring him back to his prison."

Then glad voices were heard, and up from the banks of the river,
Borne aloft on his comrades' arms, came Michael the fiddler.
Long under Basil's roof had he lived like a god on Olympus,
Having no other care than dispensing music to mortals.
Far renowned was he for his silver locks and his fiddle.
"Long live Michael," they cried, "our brave Acadian minstrel!"
As they bore him aloft in triumphal procession; and straightway
Father Felician advanced with Evangeline, greeting the old man
Kindly and oft, and recalling the past, while Basil, enraptured,
Hailed with hilarious joy his old companions and gossips,
Laughing loud and long, and embracing mothers and daughters.
Much they marvelled to see the wealth of the ci-devant blacksmith,
All his domains and his herds, and his patriarchal demeanor;
Much they marvelled to hear his tales of the soil and the climate,
And of the prairies, whose numberless herds were his who would take them;

Each one thought in his heart, that he, too, would go and do
    likewise.
Thus they ascended the steps, and, crossing the airy veranda,
Entered the hall of the house, where already the supper of
    Basil
Waited his late return; and they rested and feasted together.

Over the joyous feast the sudden darkness descended.
All was silent without, and, illuming the landscape with silver,
Fair rose the dewy moon and the myriad stars; but within
    doors,
Brighter than these, shone the faces of friends in the glimmer-
    ing lamp-light.
Then from his station aloft, at the head of the table, the
    herdsman
Poured forth his heart and his wine together in endless
    profusion.
Lighting his pipe, that was filled with sweet Natchitoches
    tobacco,
Thus he spake to his guests, who listened, and smiled as they
    listened:—
"Welcome once more, my friends, who so long have been
    friendless and homeless,
Welcome once more to a home, that is better perchance than
    the old one!
Here no hungry winter congeals our blood like the rivers;
Here no stony ground provokes the wrath of the farmer.
Smoothly the ploughshare runs through the soil as a keel
    through the water.
All the year round the orange-groves are in blossom; and
    grass grows
More in a single night than a whole Canadian summer.
Here, too, numberless herds run wild and unclaimed in the
    prairies;
Here, too, lands may be had for the asking, and forests of
    timber
With a few blows of the axe are hewn and framed into houses.
After your houses are built, and your fields are yellow with
    harvests,
No King George of England shall drive you away from your
    homesteads,

Burning your dwellings and barns, and stealing your farms
and your cattle."
Speaking these words, he blew a wrathful cloud from his
nostrils,
And his huge, brawny hand came thundering down on the
table,
So that the guests all started; and Father Felician, astounded,
Suddenly paused, with a pinch of snuff halfway to his nostrils.
But the brave Basil resumed, and his words were milder and
gayer:—
"Only beware of the fever, my friends, beware of the fever!
For it is not like that of our cold Acadian climate,
Cured by wearing a spider hung around one's neck in a nut-
shell!"
Then there were voices heard at the door, and footsteps
approaching
Sounded upon the stairs and the floor of the breezy veranda.
It was the neighboring Creoles and small Acadian planters,
Who had been summoned all to the house of Basil the herds-
man.
Merry the meeting was of ancient comrades and neighbors:
Friend clasped friend in his arms; and they who before were
as strangers,
Meeting in exile, became straightway as friends to each other,
Drawn by the gentle bond of a common country together.
But in the neighboring hall a strain of music, proceeding
From the accordant strings of Michael's melodious fiddle,
Broke up all further speech. Away, like children delighted,
All things forgotten beside, they gave themselves to the
maddening
Whirl of the dizzy dance, as it swept and swayed to the music,
Dreamlike, with beaming eyes and the rush of fluttering
garments.

Meanwhile, apart, at the head of the hall, the priest and
the herdsman
Sat, conversing together of past and present and future;
While Evangeline stood like one entranced, for within her
Olden memories rose, and loud in the midst of the music
Heard she the sound of the sea, and an irrepressible sadness
Came o'er her heart, and unseen she stole forth into the
garden.

Beautiful was the night. Behind the black wall of the forest,
Tipping its summit with silver, arose the moon. On the river
Fell here and there through the branches a tremulous gleam
    of the moonlight,
Like the sweet thoughts of love on a darkened and devious
    spirit.
Nearer and round about her, the manifold flowers of the
    garden
Poured out their souls in odors, that were their prayers and
    confessions
Unto the night, as it went its way, like a silent Carthusian.
Fuller of fragrance than they, and as heavy with shadows and
    night-dews,
Hung the heart of the maiden. The calm of the magical
    moonlight
Seemed to inundate her soul with indefinable longings,
As, through the garden gate, beneath the brown shade of the
    oak-trees,
Passed she along the path to the edge of the measureless
    prairie.
Silent it lay, with a silvery haze upon it, and fire-flies
Gleaming and floating away in mingled and infinite numbers.
Over her head the stars, the thoughts of God in the heavens,
Shone on the eyes of man, who had ceased to marvel and
    worship,
Save when a blazing comet was seen on the walls of that
    temple,
As if a hand had appeared and written upon them, "Uphar-
    sin."
And the soul of the maiden, between the stars and the fire-
    flies,
Wandered alone, and she cried,—"O Gabriel! O my beloved!
Art thou so near unto me, and yet I cannot behold thee?
Art thou so near unto me, and yet thy voice does not reach
    me?
Ah! how often thy feet have trod this path to the prairie!
Ah! how often thine eyes have looked on the woodlands
    around me!
Ah! how often beneath this oak, returning from labor,
Thou hast lain down to rest, and to dream of me in thy
    slumbers.

When shall these eyes behold, these arms be folded about
    thee?"
Loud and sudden and near the note of a whippoorwill sounded
Like a flute in the woods; and anon, through the neighboring
    thickets,
Farther and farther away it floated and dropped into silence.
"Patience!" whispered the oaks from oracular caverns of
    darkness;
And, from the moonlit meadow, a sigh responded, "To-
    morrow!"

Bright rose the sun next day; and all the flowers of the
    garden
Bathed his shining feet with their tears, and anointed his
    tresses
With the delicious balm that they bore in their vases of
    crystal.
"Farewell!" said the priest, as he stood at the shadowy
    threshold;
"See that you bring us the Prodigal Son from his fasting and
    famine,
And, too, the Foolish Virgin, who slept when the bridegroom
    was coming."
"Farewell!" answered the maiden, and, smiling, with Basil
    descended
Down to the river's brink, where the boatmen already were
    waiting.
Thus beginning their journey with morning, and sunshine, and
    gladness,
Swiftly they followed the flight of him who was speeding
    before them,
Blown by the blast of fate like a dead leaf over the desert.
Not that day, nor the next, nor yet the day that succeeded,
Found they trace of his course, in lake or forest or river,
Nor after many days, had they found him; but vague and
    uncertain
Rumors alone were their guides through a wild and desolate
    country;
Till, at the little inn of the Spanish town of Adayes,
Weary and worn, they alighted, and learned from the gar-
    rulous landlord,

That on the day before, with horses and guides and companions,
Gabriel left the village, and took the road of the prairies.

IV.

Far in the West there lies a desert land, where the mountains
Lift, through perpetual snows, their lofty and luminous summits.
Down from their jagged, deep ravines, where the gorge, like a gateway,
Opens a passage rude to the wheels of the emigrant's wagon,
Westward the Oregon flows and the Walleway and Owyhee.
Eastward, with devious course, among the Windriver Mountains,
Through the Sweet-water Valley precipitate leaps the Nebraska;
And to the South, from Fontaine-qui-bout and the Spanish sierras,
Fretted with sands and rocks, and swept by the wind of the desert,
Numberless torrents, with ceaseless sound, descend to the ocean,
Like the great chords of a harp, in loud and solemn vibrations.
Spreading between these streams are the wondrous, beautiful prairies,
Billowy bays of grass ever rolling in shadow and sunshine,
Bright with luxuriant clusters of roses and purple amorphas.
Over them wander the buffalo herds, and the elk and the roebuck;
Over them wander the wolves, and herds of riderless horses;
Fires that blast and blight, and winds that are weary with travel;
Over them wander the scattered tribes of Ishmael's children,
Staining the desert with blood; and above their terrible war-trails
Circles and sails aloft, on pinions majestic, the vulture,
Like the implacable soul of a chieftain slaughtered in battle,
By invisible stairs ascending and scaling the heavens.
Here and there rise smokes from the camps of these savage marauders;

Here and there rise groves from the margins of swift-running
    rivers;
And the grim, taciturn bear, the anchorite monk of the
    desert,
Climbs down their dark ravines to dig for roots by the
    brook-side;
And over all is the sky, the clear and crystalline heaven,
Like the protecting hand of God inverted above them.

Into this wonderful land, at the base of the Ozark Moun-
    tains,
Gabriel far had entered, with hunters and trappers behind
    him.
Day after day, with their Indian guides, the maiden and Basil
Followed his flying steps, and thought each day to o'ertake
    him.
Sometimes they saw, or thought they saw, the smoke of his
    camp-fire
Rise in the morning air from the distant plain, but at night-
    fall,
When they had reached the place, they found only embers
    and ashes.
And, though their hearts were sad at times and their bodies
    were weary,
Hope still guided them on, as the magic Fata Morgana
Showed them her lakes of light, that retreated and vanished
    before them.

Once, as they sat by their evening fire, there silently entered
Into the little camp an Indian woman, whose features
Wore deep traces of sorrow, and patience as great as her
    sorrow.
She was a Shawnee woman returning home to her people,
From the far-off hunting-grounds of the cruel Camanches,
Where her Canadian husband, a Coureur-des-Bois, had been
    murdered.
Touched were their hearts at her story, and warmest and
    friendliest welcome
Gave they, with words of cheer, and she sat and feasted
    among them
On the buffalo-meat and the venison cooked on the embers.

But when their meal was done, and Basil and all his companions,
Worn with the long day's march and the chase of the deer and the bison,
Stretched themselves on the ground, and slept where the quivering firelight
Flashed on their swarthy cheeks, and their forms wrapped up in their blankets,
Then at the door of Evangeline's tent she sat and repeated
Slowly, with soft, low voice, and the charm of her Indian accent,
All the tale of her love, with its pleasures, and pains, and reverses.
Much Evangeline wept at the tale, and to know that another
Hapless heart like her own had loved and had been disappointed.
Moved to the depths of her soul by pity and woman's compassion,
Yet in her sorrow pleased that one who had suffered was near her,
She in turn related her love and all its disasters.
Mute with wonder the Shawnee sat, and when she had ended
Still was mute; but at length, as if a mysterious horror
Passed through her brain, she spake, and repeated the tale of the Mowis;
Mowis, the bridegroom of snow, who won and wedded a maiden,
But, when the morning came, arose and passed from the wigwam,
Fading and melting away and dissolving into the sunshine,
Till she beheld him no more, though she followed him far into the forest.
Then, in those sweet, low tones that seemed like a weird incantation,
Told she the tale of the fair Lilinau, who was wooed by a phantom,
That, through the pines o'er her father's lodge, in the hush of the twilight,
Breathed like the evening wind, and whispered love to the maiden,
Till she followed his green and waving plume through the forest,

And never more returned, nor was seen again by her people.
Silent with wonder and strange surprise, Evangeline listened
To the soft flow of her magical words, till the region around
    her
Seemed like enchanted ground, and her swarthy guest the
    enchantress.
Slowly over the tops of the Ozark Mountains the moon rose,
Lighting the little tent, and with a mysterious splendor
Touching the sombre leaves, and embracing and filling the
    woodland.
With a delicious sound the brook rushed by, and the branches
Swayed and sighed overhead in scarcely audible whispers.
Filled with the thoughts of love was Evangeline's heart, but
    a secret,
Subtle sense crept in of pain and indefinite terror,
As the cold, poisonous snake creeps into the nest of the
    swallow.
It was no earthly fear. A breath from the region of spirits
Seemed to float in the air of night; and she felt for a moment
That, like the Indian maid, she, too, was pursuing a phantom.
And with this thought she slept, and the fear and the phan-
    tom had vanished.

  Early upon the morrow the march was resumed; and the
    Shawnee
Said, as they journeyed along,—"On the western slope of these
    mountains
Dwells in his little village the Black Robe chief of the Mis-
    sion.
Much he teaches the people, and tells them of Mary and
    Jesus;
Loud laugh their hearts with joy, and weep with pain, as
    they hear him."
Then, with a sudden and secret emotion, Evangeline an-
    swered,—
"Let us go to the Mission, for there good tidings await us!"
Thither they turned their steeds; and behind a spur of the
    mountains,
Just as the sun went down, they heard a murmur of voices,
And in a meadow green and broad, by the bank of a river,
Saw the tents of the Christians, the tents of the Jesuit
    Mission.

Under a towering oak, that stood in the midst of the village,
Knelt the Black Robe chief with his children. A crucifix fastened
High on the trunk of the tree, and overshadowed by grape-vines,
Looked with its agonized face on the multitude kneeling be-neath it.
This was their rural chapel. Aloft, through the intricate arches
Of its aerial roof, arose the chant of their vespers,
Mingling its notes with the soft susurrus and sighs of the branches.
Silent, with heads uncovered, the travellers, nearer approach-ing,
Knelt on the swarded floor, and joined in the evening devo-tions.
But when the service was done, and the benediction had fallen
Forth from the hands of the priest like seed from the hands of the sower,
Slowly the reverend man advanced to the strangers, and bade them
Welcome; and when they replied, he smiled with benignant expression,
Hearing the homelike sounds of his mother-tongue in the forest,
And with words of kindness conducted them into his wig-wam.
There upon mats and skins they reposed, and on cakes of the maize-ear
Feasted, and slaked their thirst from the water-gourd of the teacher.
Soon was their story told; and the priest with solemnity answered:—
"Not six suns have risen and set since Gabriel, seated
On this mat by my side, where now the maiden reposes,
Told me this same sad tale; then arose and continued his journey!"
Soft was the voice of the priest, and he spake with an accent of kindness;
But on Evangeline's heart fell his words as in winter the snow-flakes
Fall into some lone nest from which the birds have departed.

"Far to the north he has gone," continued the priest; "but in autumn,
When the chase is done, will return again to the Mission."
Then Evangeline said, and her voice was meek and submissive,—
"Let me remain with thee, for my soul is sad and afflicted."
So seemed it wise and well unto all; and betimes on the morrow,
Mounting his Mexican steed, with his Indian guides and companions,
Homeward Basil returned, and Evangeline stayed at the Mission.

Slowly, slowly, slowly the days succeeded each other,—
Days and weeks and months; and the fields of maize that were springing
Green from the ground when a stranger she came, now waving above her,
Lifted their slender shafts, with leaves interlacing, and forming
Cloisters for mendicant crows and granaries pillaged by squirrels.
Then in the golden weather the maize was husked, and the maidens
Blushed at each blood-red ear, for that betokened a lover,
But at the crooked laughed, and called it a thief in the cornfield.
Even the blood-red ear to Evangeline brought not her lover.
"Patience!" the priest would say; "have faith, and thy prayer will be answered!
Look at this delicate plant that lifts its head from the meadow,
See how its leaves all point to the north, as true as the magnet;
It is the compass-flower, that the finger of God has suspended
Here on its fragile stalk, to direct the traveller's journey
Over the sea-like, pathless, limitless waste of the desert.
Such in the soul of man is faith. The blossoms of passion,
Gay and luxuriant flowers, are brighter and fuller of fragrance.
But they beguile us, and lead us astray, and their odor is deadly.
Only this humble plant can guide us here, and hereafter

Crown us with asphodel flowers, that are wet with the dews
    of nepenthe."

  So came the autumn, and passed, and the winter,—yet
    Gabriel came not;
Blossomed the opening spring, and the notes of the robin
    and bluebird
Sounded sweet upon wold and in wood, yet Gabriel came not.
But on the breath of the summer winds a rumor was wafted
Sweeter than song of bird, or hue or odor of blossom.
Far to the north and east, it said, in the Michigan forests,
Gabriel had his lodge by the banks of the Saginaw River.
And, with returning guides, that sought the lakes of St. Law-
    rence,
Saying a sad farewell, Evangeline went from the Mission.
When over weary ways, by long and perilous marches,
She had attained at length the depths of the Michigan forests,
Found she the hunter's lodge deserted and fallen to ruin!

  Thus did the long sad years glide on, and in seasons and
    places
Divers and distant far was seen the wandering maiden;—
Now in the tents of grace of the meek Moravian Missions,
Now in the noisy camps and the battle-fields of the army,
Now in secluded hamlets, in towns and populous cities.
Like a phantom she came, and passed away unremembered.
Fair was she and young, when in hope began the long jour-
    ney;
Faded was she and old, when in disappointment it ended.
Each succeeding year stole something away from her beauty,
Leaving behind it, broader and deeper, the gloom and the
    shadow.
Then there appeared and spread faint streaks of gray o'er her
    forehead,
Dawn of another life, that broke o'er her earthly horizon,
As in the eastern sky the first faint streaks of the morning.

v.

In THAT delightful land which is washed by the Delaware's
    waters,
Guarding in sylvan shades the name of Penn the apostle,

Stands on the banks of its beautiful stream the city he
    founded.
There all the air is balm, and the peach is the emblem of
    beauty,
And the streets still reëcho the names of the trees of the
    forest,
As if they fain would appease the Dryads whose haunts they
    molested.
There from the troubled sea had Evangeline landed, an exile,
Finding among the children of Penn a home and a country.
There old René Leblanc had died; and when he departed,
Saw at his side only one of all his hundred descendants.
Something at least there was in the friendly streets of the
    city,
Something that spake to her heart, and made her no longer
    a stranger;
And her ear was pleased with the Thee and Thou of the
    Quakers,
For it recalled the past, the old Acadian country,
Where all men were equal, and all were brothers and sisters·
So, when the fruitless search, the disappointed endeavor,
Ended, to recommence no more upon earth, uncomplaining,
Thither, as leaves to the light, were turned her thoughts and
    her footsteps.
As from a mountain's top the rainy mists of the morning
Roll away, and afar we behold the landscape below us,
Sun-illumined, with shining rivers and cities and hamlets,
So fell the mists from her mind, and she saw the world far
    below her,
Dark no longer, but all illumined with love; and the pathway
Which she had climbed so far, lying smooth and fair in the
    distance.
Gabriel was not forgotten. Within her heart was his image,
Clothed in the beauty of love and youth, as last she beheld
    him,
Only more beautiful made by his deathlike silence and ab-
    sence.
Into her thoughts of him time entered not, for it was not.
Over him years had no power; he was not changed, but
    transfigured;
He had become to her heart as one who is dead, and not
    absent;

Patience and abnegation of self, and devotion to others,
This was the lesson a life of trial and sorrow had taught her.
So was her love diffused, but, like to some odorous spices,
Suffered no waste nor loss, though filling the air with aroma.
Other hope had she none, nor wish in life, but to follow
Meekly, with reverent steps, the sacred feet of her Saviour.
Thus many years she lived as a Sister of Mercy, frequenting
Lonely and wretched roofs in the crowded lanes of the city,
Where distress and want concealed themselves from the sun-
    light,
Where disease and sorrow in garrets languished neglected.
Night after night, when the world was asleep, as the watch-
    man repeated
Loud, through the gusty streets, that all was well in the city,
High at some lonely window he saw the light of her taper.
Day after day, in the gray of the dawn, as slow through the
    suburbs
Plodded the German farmer, with flowers and fruits for the
    market,
Met he that meek, pale face, returning home from its watch-
    ings.

    Then it came to pass that a pestilence fell on the city,
Presaged by wondrous signs, and mostly by flocks of wild
    pigeons,
Darkening the sun in their flight, with naught in their craws
    but an acorn.
And, as the tides of the sea arise in the month of September,
Flooding some silver stream, till it spreads to a lake in the
    meadow,
So death flooded life, and, o'erflowing its natural margin,
Spread to a brackish lake, the silver stream of existence.
Wealth had no power to bribe, nor beauty to charm, the
    oppressor;
But all perished alike beneath the scourge of his anger;—
Only, alas! the poor, who had neither friends nor attendants,
Crept away to die in the almshouse, home of the homeless.
Then in the suburbs it stood, in the midst of meadows and
    woodlands;—
Now the city surrounds it; but still, with its gateway and
    wicket
Meek, in the midst of splendor, its humble walls seem to echo

Softly the words of the Lord:—"The poor ye always have
    with you."
Thither, by night and by day, came the Sister of Mercy.
    The dying
Looked up into her face, and thought, indeed, to behold there
Gleams of celestial light encircle her forehead with splendor,
Such as the artist paints o'er the brows of saints and apostles,
Or such as hangs by night o'er a city seen at a distance.
Unto their eyes it seemed the lamps of the city celestial,
Into whose shining gates ere long their spirits would enter.

   Thus, on a Sabbath morn, through the streets, deserted and
    silent,
Wending her quiet way, she entered the door of the alms-
    house.
Sweet on the summer air was the odor of flowers in the
    garden;
And she paused on her way to gather the fairest among them,
That the dying once more might rejoice in their fragrance
    and beauty.
Then, as she mounted the stairs to the corridors, cooled by
    the east wind,
Distant and soft on her ear fell the chimes from the belfry
    of Christ Church,
While, intermingled with these, across the meadows were
    wafted
Sounds of psalms, that were sung by the Swedes in their
    Church at Wicaco.
Soft as descending wings fell the calm of the hour on her
    spirit;
Something within her said,—"At length thy trials are ended";
And, with light in her looks, she entered the chambers of
    sickness.
Noiselessly moved about the assiduous, careful attendants,
Moistening the feverish lip, and the aching brow, and in
    silence
Closing the sightless eyes of the dead, and concealing their
    faces,
Where on their pallets they lay, like drifts of snow by the
    road-side.
Many a languid head, upraised as Evangeline entered,

Turned on its pillow of pain to gaze while she passed, for her
    presence
Fell on their hearts like a ray of the sun on the walls of a
    prison.
And, as she looked around, she saw how Death, the consoler,
Laying his hand upon many a heart, had healed it forever.
Many familiar forms had disappeared in the night-time;
Vacant their places were, or filled already by strangers.

    Suddenly, as if arrested by fear or a feeling of wonder,
Still she stood, with her colorless lips apart, while a shudder
Ran through her frame, and, forgotten, the flowerets dropped
    from her fingers,
And from her eyes and cheeks the light and bloom of the
    morning.
Then there escaped from her lips a cry of such terrible
    anguish,
That the dying heard it, and started up from their pillows.
On the pallet before her was stretched the form of an old man.
Long, and thin, and gray were the locks that shaded his
    temples;
But, as he lay in the morning light, his face for a moment
Seemed to assume once more the forms of its earlier man-
    hood;
So are wont to be changed the faces of those who are dying.
Hot and red on his lips still burned the flush of the fever,
As if life, like the Hebrew, with blood had besprinkled its
    portals,
That the Angel of Death might see the sign, and pass over.
Motionless, senseless, dying he lay, and his spirit exhausted
Seemed to be sinking down through infinite depths in the
    darkness,
Darkness of slumber and death, for ever sinking and sinking.
Then through those realms of shade in multiplied reverbera-
    tions,
Heard he that cry of pain, and through the hush that suc-
    ceeded
Whispered a gentle voice, in accents tender and saint-like,
"Gabriel! O my beloved!" and died away into silence.
Then he beheld, in a dream, once more the home of his
    childhood;
Green Acadian meadows, with sylvan rivers among them,

Village, and mountain, and woodlands; and, walking under
    their shadow
As in the days of her youth, Evangeline rose in his vision.
Tears came into his eyes; and as slowly he lifted his eyelids,
Vanished the vision away, but Evangeline knelt by his bed-
    side.
Vainly he strove to whisper her name, for the accents un-
    uttered
Died on his lips, and their motion revealed what his tongue
    would have spoken.
Vainly he strove to rise; and Evangeline, kneeling beside him,
Kissed his dying lips, and laid his head on her bosom.
Sweet was the light of his eyes; but it suddenly sank into
    darkness,
As when a lamp is blown out by a gust of wind at a casement.

    All was ended now, the hope, and the fear, and the sorrow,
All the aching of heart, the restless, unsatisfied longing,
All the dull, deep pain, and constant anguish of patience!
And, as she pressed once more the lifeless head to her bosom,
Meekly she bowed her own, and murmured, "Father, I thank
    thee!"

STILL stands the forest primeval; but far away from its
    shadow,
Side by side, in their nameless graves, the lovers are sleeping.
Under the humble walls of the little Catholic church-yard,
In the heart of the city, they lie, unknown and unnoticed.
Daily the tides of life go ebbing and flowing beside them,
Thousands of throbbing hearts, where theirs are at rest and
    forever,
Thousands of aching brains, where theirs no longer are busy,
Thousands of toiling hands, where theirs have ceased from
    their labors,
Thousands of weary feet, where theirs have completed their
    journey!

    Still stands the forest primeval; but under the shade of its
    branches
Dwells another race, with other customs and language.
Only along the shore of the mournful and misty Atlantic
Linger a few Acadian peasants, whose fathers from exile
Wandered back to their native land to die in its bosom.

In the fisherman's cot the wheel and the loom are still busy;
Maidens still wear their Norman caps and their kirtles of
    homespun,
And by the evening fire repeat Evangeline's story,
While from its rocky caverns the deep-voiced neighboring ocean
Speaks, and in accents disconsolate answers the wail of the
    forest.

THE SONG OF HIAWATHA, 1855.

SHOULD you ask me, whence these stories?
Whence these legends and traditions,
With the odors of the forest,
With the dew and damp of meadows,
With the curling smoke of wigwams,
With the rushing of great rivers,
With their frequent repetitions,
And their wild reverberations,
As of thunder in the mountains?
I should answer, I should tell you,
"From the forests and the prairies,
From the great lakes of the Northland,
From the land of the Ojibways,
From the land of the Dacotahs,
From the mountains, moors, and fenlands,
Where the heron, the Shuh-shuh-gah,
Feeds among the reeds and rushes.
I repeat them as I heard them
From the lips of Nawadaha,
The musician, the sweet singer."
    Should you ask where Nawadaha
Found these songs, so wild and wayward,
Found these legends and traditions,
I should answer, I should tell you,
"In the bird's-nests of the forest,
In the lodges of the beaver,
In the hoof-prints of the bison,
In the eyry of the eagle!
    "All the wild-fowl sang them to him,
In the moorlands and the fen-lands,
In the melancholy marshes;

Chetowaik, the plover, sang them,
Mahng, the loon, the wild goose, Wawa,
The blue heron, the Shuh-shuh-gah,
And the grouse, the Mushkodasa!"
    If still further you should ask me,
Saying, "Who was Nawadaha?
Tell us of this Nawadaha,"
I should answer your inquiries
Straightway in such words as follow
    "In the Vale of Tawasentha,
In the green and silent valley,
By the pleasant water-courses,
Dwelt the singer Nawadaha.
Round about the Indian village
Spread the meadows and the corn-fields,
And beyond them stood the forest,
Stood the groves of singing pine-trees.
Green in Summer, white in Winter,
Ever sighing, ever singing.
    "And the pleasant water-courses,
You could trace them through the valley,
By the rushing in the Spring-time,
By the alders in the Summer,
By the white fog in the Autumn,
By the black line in the Winter;
And beside them dwelt the singer,
In the Vale of Tawasentha,
In the green and silent valley.
    "There he sang of Hiawatha,
Sang the Song of Hiawatha,
Sang his wondrous birth and being,
How he prayed and how he fasted,
How he lived, and toiled, and suffered,
That the tribes of men might prosper,
That he might advance his people!"
    Ye who love the haunts of Nature,
Love the sunshine of the meadow,
Love the shadow of the forest,
Love the wind among the branches,
And the rain-shower and the snow-storm,
And the rushing of great rivers
Through their palisades of pine-trees,

And the thunder in the mountains,
Whose innumerable echoes
Flap like eagles in their eyries;—
Listen to these wild traditions,
To this Song of Hiawatha!
    Ye who love a nation's legends,
Love the ballads of a people,
That like voices from afar off
Call to us to pause and listen,
Speak in tones so plain and childlike,
Scarcely can the ear distinguish
Whether they are sung or spoken;—
Listen to this Indian Legend,
To this Song of Hiawatha!
    Ye whose hearts are fresh and simple,
Who have faith in God and Nature,
Who believe, that in all ages
Every human heart is human,
That in even savage bosoms
There are longings, yearnings, strivings
For the good they comprehend not,
That the feeble hands and helpless,
Groping blindly in the darkness,
Touch God's right hand in that darkness
And are lifted up and strengthened;—
Listen to this simple story,
To this Song of Hiawatha!
    Ye, who sometimes, in your rambles,
Through the green lanes of the country,
Where the tangled barberry-bushes
Hang their tufts of crimson berries
Over stone walls gray with mosses,
Pause by some neglected graveyard,
For a while to muse, and ponder
On a half-effaced inscription,
Written with little skill of song-craft,
Homely phrases, but each letter
Full of hope and yet of heart-break,
Full of all the tender pathos
Of the Here and the Hereafter;—
Stay and read this rude inscription,
Read this Song of Hiawatha!

I.

THE PEACE-PIPE.

On the Mountains of the Prairie,
On the great Red Pipe-stone Quarry
Gitche Manito, the mighty,
He the Master of Light, descending,
On the red crags of the quarry
Stood erect, and called the nations,
Called the tribes of men together.

From his footprints flowed a river,
Leaped into the light of morning,
O'er the precipice plunging downward
Gleamed like Ishkoodah, the comet.
And the Spirit, stooping earthward,
With his finger on the meadow
Traced a winding pathway for it,
Saying to it, "Run in this way!"

From the red stone of the quarry
With his hand he broke a fragment,
Moulded it into a pipe-head,
Shaped and fashioned it with figures.
From the margin of the river
Took a long reed for a pipe-stem,
With its dark green leaves upon it;
Filled the pipe with bark of willow,
With the bark of the red willow;
Breathed upon the neighboring forest,
Made its great boughs chafe together,
Till in flame they burst and kindled;
And erect upon the mountains,
Gitche Manito, the mighty,
Smoked the calumet, the Peace-Pipe,
As a signal to the nations.

And the smoke rose slowly, slowly,
Through the tranquil air of morning,
First a single line of darkness,
Then a denser, bluer vapor,
Then a snow-white cloud unfolding,
Like the tree-tops of the forest.
Ever rising, rising, rising,

Till it touched the top of heaven,
Till it broke against the heaven,
And rolled outward all around it.
From the Vale of Tawasentha,
From the Valley of Wyoming,
From the groves of Tuscaloosa,
From the far-off Rocky Mountains,
From the Northern lakes and rivers,
All the tribes beheld the signal,
Saw the distant smoke ascending,
The Pukwana of the Peace-Pipe.
And the Prophets of the nations
Said: "Behold it, the Pukwana!
By this signal from afar off,
Bending like a wand of willow,
Waving like a hand that beckons,
Gitche Manito, the mighty,
Calls the tribes of men together,
Calls the warriors to his council!"
Down the rivers, o'er the prairies,
Came the warriors of the nations,
Came the Delawares and Mohawks,
Came the Choctaws and Camanches,
Came the Shoshonies and Blackfeet,
Came the Pawnees and Omawhaws,
Came the Mandans and Dacotahs,
Came the Hurons and Ojibways,
All the warriors drawn together
By the signal of the Peace-Pipe,
To the Mountains of the Prairie,
To the great Red Pipe-stone Quarry.
And they stood there on the meadow,
With their weapons and their war gear,
Painted like the leaves of Autumn,
Painted like the sky of morning,
Wildly glaring at each other;
In their faces stern defiance,
In their hearts the feuds of ages,
The hereditary hatred,
The ancestral thirst of vengeance.
Gitche Manito, the mighty,
The creator of the nations,

Looked upon them with compassion,
With paternal love and pity;
Looked upon their wrath and wrangling
But as quarrels among children,
But as feuds and fights of children!
    Over them he stretched his right hand,
To subdue their stubborn natures,
To allay their thirst and fever,
By the shadow of his right hand;
Spake to them with voice majestic
As the sound of far-off waters,
Falling into deep abysses,
Warning, chiding, spake in this wise:—
    "O my children! my poor children!
Listen to the words of wisdom,
Listen to the words of warning,
From the lips of the Great Spirit,
From the Master of Life, who made you.
    "I have given you lands to hunt in,
I have given you streams to fish in,
I have given you bear and bison,
I have given you roe and reindeer,
I have given you brant and beaver,
Filled the marshes full of wild-fowl,
Filled the rivers full of fishes;
Why then are you not contented?
Why then will you hunt each other?
    "I am weary of your quarrels,
Weary of your wars and bloodshed,
Weary of your prayers for vengeance,
Of your wranglings and dissensions;
All your strength is in your union,
All your danger is in discord;
Therefore be at peace henceforward,
And as brothers live together.
    "I will send a Prophet to you,
A Deliverer of the nations,
Who shall guide you and shall teach you,
Who shall toil and suffer with you.
If you listen to his counsels,
You will multiply and prosper;
If his warnings pass unheeded,

You will fade away and perish!
    "Bathe now in the stream before you,
Wash the war-paint from your faces,
Wash the blood-stains from your fingers,
Bury your war-clubs and your weapons,
Break the red stone from this quarry,
Mould and make it into Peace-Pipes,
Take the reeds that grow beside you,
Deck them with your brightest feathers,
Smoke the calumet together,
And as brothers live henceforward!"
    Then upon the ground the warriors
Threw their cloaks and shirts of deerskin,
Threw their weapons and their war-gear,
Leaped into the rushing river,
Washed the war-paint from their faces.
Clear above them flowed the water,
Clear and limpid from the footprints
Of the Master of Life descending;
Dark below them flowed the water,
Soiled and stained with streaks of crimson,
As if blood were mingled with it!
    From the river came the warriors,
Clean and washed from all their war-paint;
On the banks their clubs they buried,
Buried all their warlike weapons.
Gitche Manito, the mighty,
The Great Spirit, the creator,
Smiled upon his helpless children!
    And in silence all the warriors
Broke the red stone of the quarry,
Smoothed and formed it into Peace-Pipes,
Broke the long reeds by the river,
Decked them with their brightest feathers,
And departed each one homeward,
While the Master of Life, ascending,
Through the opening of cloud-curtains,
Through the doorways of the heaven,
Vanished from before their faces,
In the smoke that rolled around him,
The Pukwana of the Peace-Pipe!

II.

THE FOUR WINDS.

"Honor be to Mudjekeewis!"
Cried the warriors, cried the old men,
When he came in triumph homeward
With the sacred Belt of Wampum,
From the regions of the North-Wind,
From the kingdom of Wabasso,
From the land of the White Rabbit.
    He had stolen the Belt of Wampum
From the neck of Mishe-Mokwa,
From the Great Bear of the mountains,
From the terror of the nations,
As he lay asleep and cumbrous
On the summit of the mountains,
Like a rock with mosses on it,
Spotted brown and gray with mosses.
    Silently he stole upon him,
Till the red nails of the monster
Almost touched him, almost scared him,
Till the hot breath of his nostrils
Warmed the hands of Mudjekeewis,
As he drew the Belt of Wampum
Over the round ears, that heard not,
Over the small eyes, that saw not,
Over the long nose and nostrils,
The black muffle of the nostrils,
Out of which the heavy breathing
Warmed the hands of Mudjekeewis.
    Then he swung aloft his war-club,
Shouted loud and long his war-cry,
Smote the mighty Mishe-Mokwa
In the middle of the forehead,
Right between the eyes he smote him.
    With the heavy blow bewildered,
Rose the Great Bear of the mountains;
But his knees beneath him trembled,
And he whimpered like a woman,
As he reeled and staggered forward,
As he sat upon his haunches;

And the mighty Mudjekeewis,
Standing fearlessly before him,
Taunted him in loud derision,
Spake disdainfully in this wise:—

　"Hark you, Bear! you are a coward,
And no Brave, as you pretended;
Else you would not cry and whimper
Like a miserable woman!
Bear! you know our tribes are hostile,
Long have been at war together;
Now you find that we are strongest,
You go sneaking in the forest,
You go hiding in the mountains!
Had you conquered me in battle
Not a groan would I have uttered;
But you, Bear! sit here and whimper
And disgrace your tribe by crying,
Like a wretched Shaugodaya,
Like a cowardly old woman!"

　Then again he raised his war-club,
Smote again the Mishe-Mokwa
In the middle of his forehead,
Broke his skull, as ice is broken
When one goes to fish in Winter.
Thus was slain the Mishe-Mokwa,
He the Great Bear of the mountains,
He the terror of the nations.

　"Honor be to Mudjekeewis!"
With a shout exclaimed the people.
"Honor be to Mudjekeewis!
Henceforth he shall be the West-Wind,
And hereafter and forever
Shall he hold supreme dominion
Over all the winds of heaven.
Call him no more Mudjekeewis,
Call him Kabeyun, the West-Wind!"

　Thus was Mudjekeewis chosen
Father of the Winds of Heaven.
For himself he kept the West-Wind,
Gave the others to his children;
Unto Wabun gave the East-Wind,
Gave the South to Shawondasee,

And the North-Wind, wild and cruel,
To the fierce Kabibonokka.
    Young and beautiful was Wabun;
He it was who brought the morning,
He it was whose silver arrows
Chased the dark o'er hill and valley;
He it was whose cheeks were painted
With the brightest streaks of crimson,
And whose voice awoke the village,
Called the deer, and called the hunter.
    Lonely in the sky was Wabun;
Though the birds sang gayly to him,
Though the wild-flowers of the meadow
Filled the air with odors for him,
Though the forests and the rivers
Sang and shouted at his coming,
Still his heart was sad within him,
For he was alone in heaven.
    But one morning, gazing earthward,
While the village still was sleeping,
And the fog lay on the river,
Like a ghost, that goes at sunrise,
He beheld a maiden walking
All alone upon a meadow,
Gathering water-flags and rushes
By a river in the meadow.
    Every morning, gazing earthward,
Still the first thing he beheld there
Was her blue eyes looking at him,
Two blue lakes among the rushes.
And he loved the lonely maiden,
Who thus waited for his coming;
For they both were solitary,
She on earth and he in heaven.
    And he wooed her with caresses,
Wooed her with his smile of sunshine,
With his flattering words he wooed her,
With his sighing and his singing,
Gentlest whispers in the branches,
Softest music, sweetest odors,
Till he drew her to his bosom,
Folded in his robes of crimson,

Till into a star he changed her,
Trembling still upon his bosom;
And forever in the heavens
They are seen together walking,
Wabun and the Wabun-Annung,
Wabun and the Star of Morning.

But the fierce Kabibonokka
Had his dwelling among icebergs,
In the everlasting snow-drifts,
In the kingdom of Wabasso,
In the land of the White Rabbit.
He it was whose hand in Autumn
Painted all the trees with scarlet,
Stained the leaves with red and yellow;
He it was who sent the snow-flakes,
Sifting, hissing through the forest,
Froze the ponds, the lakes, the rivers,
Drove the loon and sea-gull southward,
Drove the cormorant and curlew
To their nests of sedge and sea-tang
In the realms of Shawondasee.

Once the fierce Kabibonokka
Issued from his lodge of snow-drifts,
From his home among the icebergs,
And his hair, with snow besprinkled
Streamed behind him like a river,
Like a black and wintry river,
As he howled and hurried southward,
Over frozen lakes and moorlands.

There among the reeds and rushes
Found the Shingebis, the diver,
Trailing strings of fish behind him,
O'er the frozen fens and moorlands,
Lingering still among the moorlands,
Though his tribe had long departed
To the land of Shawondasee.

Cried the fierce Kabibonokka,
"Who is this that dares to brave me?
Dares to stay in my dominions,
When the Wawa has departed,
When the wild-goose has gone southward,
And the heron, the Shuh-shuh-gah,

Long ago departed southward?
I will go into his wigwam,
I will put his smouldering fire out!"
    And at night Kabibonokka
To the lodge came wild and wailing,
Heaped the snow in drifts about it,
Shouted down into the smoke-flue,
Shook the lodge-poles in his fury,
Flapped the curtain of the door-way.
Shingebis, the diver, feared not,
Shingebis, the diver, cared not;
Four great logs had he for fire-wood,
One for each moon of the winter,
And for food the fishes served him.
By his blazing fire he sat there,
Warm and merry, eating, laughing,
Singing, "O Kabibonokka,
You are but my fellow-mortal!"

    Then Kabibonokka entered,
And though Shingebis, the diver,
Felt his presence by the coldness,
Felt his icy breath upon him,
Still he did not cease his singing,
Still he did not leave his laughing,
Only turned the log a little,
Only made the fire burn brighter,
Made the sparks fly up the smoke-flue.

    From Kabibonokka's forehead,
From his snow-besprinkled tresses,
Drops of sweat fell fast and heavy,
Making dints upon the ashes,
As along the eaves of lodges,
As from drooping boughs of hemlock,
Drips the melting snow in spring-time,
Making hollows in the snow-drifts.

    Till at last he rose defeated.
Could not bear the heat and laughter,
Could not bear the merry singing,
But rushed headlong through the door-way,
Stamped upon the crusted snow-drifts,
Stamped upon the lakes and rivers,
Made the snow upon them harder,

Made the ice upon them thicker,
Challenged Shingebis, the diver,
To come forth and wrestle with him,
To come forth and wrestle naked
On the frozen fens and moorlands.
Forth went Shingebis, the diver,
Wrestled all night with the North-Wind,
Wrestled naked on the moorlands
With the fierce Kabibonokka,
Till his panting breath grew fainter,
Till his frozen grasp grew feebler,
Till he reeled and staggered backward,
And retreated, baffled, beaten,
To the kingdom of Wabasso,
To the land of the White Rabbit,
Hearing still the gusty laughter,
Hearing Shingebis, the diver,
Singing, "O Kabibonokka,
You are but my fellow-mortal!"
    Shawondasee, fat and lazy,
Had his dwelling far to southward,
In the drowsy, dreamy sunshine,
In the never-ending Summer.
He it was who sent the wood-birds,
Sent the robin, the Opechee,
Sent the blue-bird, the Owaissa,
Sent the Shawshaw, sent the swallow,
Sent the wild-goose, Wawa, northward,
Sent the melons and tobacco,
And the grapes in purple clusters.
    From his pipe the smoke ascending
Filled the sky with haze and vapor,
Filled the air with dreamy softness,
Gave a twinkle to the water,
Touched the rugged hills with smoothness,
Brought the tender Indian Summer
To the melancholy north-land,
In the dreary Moon of Snow-shoes.
    Listless, careless Shawondasee!
In his life he had one shadow,
In his heart one sorrow had he.
Once, as he was gazing northward,

Far away upon a prairie
He beheld a maiden standing,
Saw a tall and slender maiden
All alone upon a prairie;
Brightest green were all her garments,
And her hair was like the sunshine.
Day by day he gazed upon her,
Day by day he sighed with passion,
Day by day his heart within him
Grew more hot with love and longing
For the maid with yellow tresses.
But he was too fat and lazy
To bestir himself and woo her;
Yes, too indolent and easy
To pursue her and persuade her.
So he only gazed upon her,
Only sat and sighed with passion
For the maiden of the prairie.
Till one morning, looking northward,
He beheld her yellow tresses
Changed and covered o'er with whiteness,
Covered as with whitest snow-flakes,
"Ah! my brother from the North-land,
From the kingdom of Wabasso,
From the land of the White Rabbit!
You have stolen the maiden from me,
You have laid your hand upon her,
You have wooed and won my maiden,
With your stories of the North-land!"
Thus the wretched Shawondasee
Breathed into the air his sorrow;
And the South-Wind o'er the prairie
Wandered warm with sighs of passion,
With the sighs of Shawondasee,
Till the air seemed full of snow-flakes,
Full of thistle-down the prairie,
And the maid with hair like sunshine
Vanished from his sight forever;
Never more did Shawondasee
See the maid with yellow tresses!
Poor, deluded Shawondasee!
'T was no woman that you gazed at,

'T was no maiden that you sighed for,
'T was the prairie dandelion
That through all the dreamy Summer
You had gazed at with such longing,
You had sighed for with such passion,
And had puffed away forever,
Blown into the air with sighing.
Ah! deluded Shawondasee!

Thus the Four Winds were divided;
Thus the sons of Mudjekeewis
Had their stations in the heavens;
At the corners of the heavens;
For himself the West-Wind only
Kept the mighty Mudjekeewis.

III.

HIAWATHA'S CHILDHOOD.

DOWNWARD through the evening twilight,
In the days that are forgotten,
In the unremembered ages,
From the full moon fell Nokomis,
Fell the beautiful Nokomis,
She a wife, but not a mother.

She was sporting with her women,
Swinging in a swing of grape-vines,
When her rival, the rejected,
Full of jealousy and hatred,
Cut the leafy swing asunder,
Cut in twain the twisted grape-vines,
And Nokomis fell affrighted
Downward through the evening twilight,
On the Muskoday, the meadow,
On the prairie full of blossoms.
"See! a star falls!" said the people;
"From the sky a star is falling!"

There among the ferns and mosses,
There among the prairie lilies,
On the Muskoday, the meadow,
In the moonlight and the starlight,
Fair Nokomis bore a daughter.
And she called her name Wenonah,
As the first-born of her daughters.

And the daughter of Nokomis
Grew up like the prairie lilies,
Grew a tall and slender maiden,
With the beauty of the moonlight,
With the beauty of the starlight.

And Nokomis warned her often,
Saying oft, and oft repeating,
"O, beware of Mudjekeewis,
Of the West-Wind, Mudjekeewis;
Listen not to what he tells you;
Lie not down upon the meadow,
Stoop not down among the lilies,
Lest the West-Wind come and harm you!"

But she heeded not the warning,
Heeded not those words of wisdom,
And the West-Wind came at evening,
Walking lightly o'er the prairie,
Whispering to the leaves and blossoms,
Bending low the flowers and grasses,
Found the beautiful Wenonah,
Lying there among the lilies,
Wooed her with his words of sweetness,
Wooed her with his soft caresses,
Till she bore a son in sorrow,
Bore a son of love and sorrow.

Thus was born my Hiawatha,
Thus was born the child of wonder;
But the daughter of Nokomis,
Hiawatha's gentle mother,
In her anguish died deserted
By the West-Wind, false and faithless,
By the heartless Mudjekeewis.

For her daughter, long and loudly
Wailed and wept the sad Nokomis;
"O that I were dead!" she murmured,
"O that I were dead, as thou art!
No more work, and no more weeping,
Wahonowin! Wahonowin!"

By the shores of Gitche Gumee,
By the shining Big-Sea-Water,
Stood the wigwam of Nokomis,
Daughter of the Moon, Nokomis.

Dark behind it rose the forest,
Rose the black and gloomy pine-trees,
Rose the firs with cones upon them;
Bright before it beat the water,
Beat the clear and sunny water,
Beat the shining Big-Sea-Water.

There the wrinkled, old Nokomis
Nursed the little Hiawatha,
Rocked him in his linden cradle,
Bedded soft in moss and rushes,
Safely bound with reindeer sinews;
Stilled his fretful wail by saying,
"Hush! the Naked Bear will get thee!"
Lulled him into Slumber, singing,
"Ewa-yea! my little owlet!
Who is this, that lights the wigwam?
With his great eyes lights the wigwam?
Ewa-yea! my little owlet!"

Many things Nokomis taught him
Of the stars that shine in heaven;
Showed him Ishkoodah, the comet,
Ishkoodah, with fiery tresses;
Showed the Death-Dance of the spirits,
Warriors with their plumes and war-clubs,
Flaring far away to northward
In the frosty nights of Winter;
Showed the broad, white road in heaven,
Pathway of the ghosts, the shadows,
Running straight across the heavens,
Crowded with the ghosts, the shadows.

At the door on summer evenings
Sat the little Hiawatha;
Heard the whispering of the pine-trees,
Heard the lapping of the water,
Sounds of music, words of wonder;
"Minne-wawa!" said the pine-trees,
"Mudway-aushka!" said the water.

Saw the fire-fly, Wah-wah-taysee,
Flitting through the dusk of evening,
With the twinkle of its candle
Lighting up the brakes and bushes,
And he sang the song of children,

Sang the song Nokomis taught him:
"Wah-wah-taysee, little fire-fly,
Little, flitting, white-fire insect,
Little, dancing, white-fire creature,
Light me with your little candle;
Ere upon my bed I lay me,
Ere in sleep I close my eyelids!"

Saw the moon rise from the water
Rippling, rounding from the water,
Saw the flecks and shadows on it,
Whispered, "What is that, Nokomis?"
And the good Nokomis answered:
"Once a warrior, very angry,
Seized his grandmother, and threw her
Up into the sky at midnight;
Right against the moon he threw her;
'T is her body that you see there."

Saw the rainbow in the heaven,
In the eastern sky, the rainbow,
Whispered, "What is that, Nokomis?"
And the good Nokomis answered:
" 'T is the heaven of flowers you see there;
All the wild-flowers of the forest,
All the lilies of the prairie,
When on earth they fade and perish,
Blossom in that heaven above us."

When he heard the owls at midnight,
Hooting, laughing in the forest,
"What is that?" he cried in terror;
"What is that?" he said, "Nokomis?"
And the good Nokomis answered:
"That is but the owl and owlet,
Talking in their native language,
Talking, scolding at each other."

Then the little Hiawatha
Learned of every bird its language,
Learned their names and all their secrets,
How they built their nests in Summer,
Where they hid themselves in Winter,
Talked with them whene'er he met them,
Called them "Hiawatha's Chickens."

Of all beasts he learned the language,

Learned their names and all their secrets,
How the beavers built their lodges,
Where the squirrels hid their acorns,
How the reindeer ran so swiftly,
Why the rabbit was so timid,
Talked with them whene'er he met them,
Called them "Hiawatha's Brothers."

Then Iagoo, the great boaster,
He the marvellous story-teller,
He the traveller and the talker,
He the friend of old Nokomis,
Made a bow for Hiawatha;
From a branch of ash he made it,
From an oak-bough made the arrows
Tipped with flint, and winged with feathers,
And the cord he made of deer-skin.

Then he said to Hiawatha:
"Go, my son, into the forest,
Where the red deer herd together,
Kill for us a famous roebuck,
Kill for us a deer with antlers!"

Forth into the forest straightway
All alone walked Hiawatha
Proudly, with his bow and arrows;
And the birds sang round him, o'er him,
"Do not shoot us, Hiawatha!"
Sang the robin, the Opechee,
Sang the blue-bird, the Owaissa,
"Do not shoot us, Hiawatha!"

Up the oak-tree, close beside him,
Sprang the squirrel, Adjidaumo,
In and out among the branches,
Coughed and chattered from the oak-tree,
Laughed, and said between his laughing,
"Do not shoot me, Hiawatha!"

And the rabbit from his pathway
Leaped aside, and at a distance
Sat erect upon his haunches,
Half in fear and half in frolic,
Saying to the little hunter,
"Do not shoot me, Hiawatha!"

But he heeded not, nor heard them,

For his thoughts were with the red deer;
On their tracks his eyes were fastened,
Leading downward to the river,
To the ford across the river,
And as one in slumber walked he.

Hidden in the alder-bushes,
There he waited till the deer came,
Till he saw two antlers lifted,
Saw two eyes look from the thicket,
Saw two nostrils point to windward,
And a deer came down the pathway,
Flecked with leafy light and shadow.
And his heart within him fluttered,
Trembled like the leaves above him,
Like the birch-leaf palpitated,
As the deer came down the pathway.

Then, upon one knee uprising,
Hiawatha aimed an arrow;
Scarce a twig moved with his motion,
Scarce a leaf was stirred or rustled,
But the wary roebuck started,
Stamped with all his hoofs together,
Listened with one foot uplifted,
Leaped as if to meet the arrow,
Ah! the singing, fatal arrow;
Like a wasp it buzzed and stung him!

Dead he lay there in the forest,
By the ford across the river;
Beat his timid heart no longer,
But the heart of Hiawatha
Throbbed and shouted and exulted,
As he bore the red deer homeward,
And Iagoo and Nokomis
Hailed his coming with applauses.

From the red deer's hide Nokomis
Made a cloak for Hiawatha,
From the red deer's flesh Nokomis
Made a banquet in his honor.
All the village came and feasted,
All the guests praised Hiawatha,
Called him Strong-Heart, Soan-ge-taha!
Called him Loon-Heart, Mahn-go-taysee!

IV.

HIAWATHA AND MUDJEKEEWIS.

OUT of childhood into manhood
Now had grown my Hiawatha,
Skilled in all the craft of hunters,
Learned in all the lore of old men,
In all youthful sports and pastimes,
In all manly arts and labors.

Swift of foot was Hiawatha;
He could shoot an arrow from him,
And run forward with such fleetness,
That the arrow fell behind him!
Strong of arm was Hiawatha;
He could shoot ten arrows upward,
Shoot them with such strength and swiftness,
That the tenth had left the bow-string
Ere the first to earth had fallen!

He had mittens, Minjekahwun,
Magic mittens made of deer-skin;
When upon his hands he wore them,
He could smite the rocks asunder,
He could grind them into powder.
He had moccasins enchanted,
Magic moccasins of deer-skin;
When he bound them round his ankles,
When upon his feet he tied them,
At each stride a mile he measured!

Much he questioned old Nokomis
Of his father Mudjekeewis;
Learned from her the fatal secret
Of the beauty of his mother,
Of the falsehood of his father;
And his heart was hot within him,
Like a living coal his heart was.

Then he said to old Nokomis,
"I will go to Mudjekeewis,
See how fares it with my father,
At the doorways of the West-Wind,
At the portals of the Sunset!"

From his lodge went Hiawatha,

Dressed for travel, armed for hunting;
Dressed in deer-skin shirt and leggings,
Richly wrought with quills and wampum;
On his head his eagle-feathers,
Round his waist his belt of wampum
In his hand his bow of ash-wood,
Strung with sinews of the reindeer;
In his quiver oaken arrows,
Tipped with jasper, winged with feathers;
With his mittens, Minjekahwun,
With his moccasins enchanted.
   Warning said the old Nokomis,
"Go not forth, O Hiawatha!
To the kingdom of the West-Wind,
To the realms of Mudjekeewis,
Lest he harm you with his magic,
Lest he kill you with his cunning!"
   But the fearless Hiawatha
Heeded not her woman's warning;
Forth he strode into the forest,
At each stride a mile he measured;
Lurid seemed the sky above him,
Lurid seemed the earth beneath him,
Hot and close the air around him,
Filled with smoke and fiery vapors,
As of burning woods and prairies,
For his heart was hot within him,
Like a living coal his heart was.
   So he journeyed westward, westward,
Left the fleetest deer behind him,
Left the antelope and bison;
Crossed the rushing Esconawbaw,
Crossed the mighty Mississippi,
Passed the Mountains of the Prairie,
Passed the land of Crows and Foxes,
Passed the dwellings of the Blackfeet,
Came unto the Rocky Mountains,
To the kingdom of the West-Wind,
Where upon the gusty summits
Sat the ancient Mudjekeewis,
Ruler of the winds of heaven.
   Filled with awe was Hiawatha

At the aspect of his father.
On the air about him wildly
Tossed and streamed his cloudy tresses,
Gleamed like drifting snow his tresses,
Glared like Ishkoodah, the comet,
Like the star with fiery tresses.

Filled with joy was Mudjekeewis
When he looked on Hiawatha,
Saw his youth rise up before him
In the face of Hiawatha,
Saw the beauty of Wenonah
From the grave rise up before him.

"Welcome!" said he, "Hiawatha,
To the kingdom of the West-Wind!
Long have I been waiting for you!
Youth is lovely, age is lonely,
Youth is fiery, age is frosty;
You bring back the days departed,
You bring back my youth of passion,
And the beautiful Wenonah!"

Many days they talked together,
Questioned, listened, waited, answered;
Much the mighty Mudjekeewis
Boasted of his ancient prowess,
Of his perilous adventures,
His indomitable courage,
His invulnerable body.

Patiently sat Hiawatha,
Listening to his father's boasting;
With a smile he sat and listened,
Uttered neither threat nor menace,
Neither word nor look betrayed him,
But his heart was hot within him,
Like a living coal his heart was.

Then he said, "O Mudjekeewis,
Is there nothing that can harm you?
Nothing that you are afraid of?"
And the mighty Mudjekeewis,
Grand and gracious in his boasting,
Answered, saying, "There is nothing
Nothing but the black rock yonder,
Nothing but the fatal Wawbeek!"

And he looked at Hiawatha
With a wise look and benignant,
With a countenance paternal,
Looked with pride upon the beauty
Of his tall and graceful figure,
Saying, "O my Hiawatha!
Is there anything can harm you?
Anything you are afraid of?"

But the wary Hiawatha
Paused awhile, as if uncertain,
Held his peace, as if resolving,
And then answered, "There is nothing,
Nothing but the bulrush yonder,
Nothing but the great Apukwa!"

And as Mudjekeewis, rising,
Stretched his hand to pluck the bulrush,
Hiawatha cried in terror,
Cried in well-dissembled terror,
"Kago! kago! do not touch it!"
"Ah, kaween!" said Mudjekeewis,
"No indeed, I will not touch it!"

Then they talked of other matters
First of Hiawatha's brothers,
First of Wabun, of the East-Wind,
Of the South-Wind, Shawondasee,
Of the North, Kabibonokka;
Then of Hiawatha's mother,
Of the beautiful Wenonah,
Of her birth upon the meadow,
Of her death, as old Nokomis
Had remembered and related.

And he cried, "O Mudjekeewis,
It was you who killed Wenonah,
Took her young life and her beauty,
Broke the Lily of the Prairie,
Trampled it beneath your footsteps.
You confess it! you confess it!"
And the mighty Mudjekeewis
Tossed upon the wind his tresses,
Bowed his hoary head in anguish,
With a silent nod assented.

Then up started Hiawatha,

And with threatening look and gesture
Laid his hand upon the black rock,
On the fatal Wawbeek laid it,
With his mittens, Minjekahwun,
Rent the jutting crag asunder,
Smote and crushed it into fragments,
Hurled them madly at his father,
The remorseful Mudjekeewis,
For his heart was hot within him,
Like a living coal his heart was.

But the ruler of the West-Wind
Blew the fragments backward from him,
With the breathing of his nostrils,
With the tempest of his anger,
Blew them back at his assailant;
Seized the bulrush, the Apukwa,
Dragged it with its roots and fibres
From the margin of the meadow,
From its ooze, the giant bulrush;
Long and loud laughed Hiawatha!

Then began the deadly conflict,
Hand to hand among the mountains;
From his eyry screamed the eagle,
The Keneu, the great war-eagle;
Sat upon the crags around them,
Wheeling flapped his wings above them.

Like a tall tree in the tempest
Bent and lashed the giant bulrush;
And in masses huge and heavy
Crashing fell the fatal Wawbeek;
Till the earth shook with the tumult
And confusion of the battle,
And the air was full of shoutings,
And the thunder of the mountains,
Starting, answered, "Baim-wawa!"

Back retreated Mudjekeewis,
Rushing westward o'er the mountains,
Stumbling westward down the mountains,
Three whole days retreated fighting,
Still pursued by Hiawatha
To the doorways of the West-Wind,
To the portals of the Sunset,

To the earth's remotest border,
Where into the empty spaces
Sinks the sun, as a flamingo
Drops into her nest at nightfall,
In the melancholy marshes.

"Hold!" at length cried Mudjekeewis,
"Hold, my son, my Hiawatha!
'T is impossible to kill me,
For you cannot kill the immortal
I have put you to this trial,
But to know and prove your courage;
Now receive the prize of valor!

"Go back to your home and people,
Live among them, toil among them,
Cleanse the earth from all that harms it,
Clear the fishing-grounds and rivers,
Slay all monsters and magicians,
All the Wendigoes, the giants,
All the serpents, the Kenabeeks,
As I slew the Mishe-Mokwa,
Slew the Great Bear of the mountains.

"And at last when Death draws near you,
When the awful eyes of Pauguk
Glare upon you in the darkness,
I will share my kingdom with you,
Ruler shall you be thenceforward
Of the Northwest-Wind, Keewaydin
Of the home-wind, the Keewaydin."

Thus was fought that famous battle
In the dreadful days of Shah-shah,
In the days long since departed,
In the kingdom of the West-Wind.
Still the hunter sees its traces
Scattered far o'er hill and valley;
Sees the giant bulrush growing
By the ponds and water-courses,
Sees the masses of the Wawbeek
Lying still in every valley.

Homeward now went Hiawatha;
Pleasant was the landscape round him,
Pleasant was the air above him,
For the bitterness of anger

Had departed wholly from him,
From his brain the thought of vengeance,
From his heart the burning fever.
    Only once his pace he slackened,
Only once he paused or halted,
Paused to purchase heads of arrows
Of the ancient Arrow-maker,
In the land of the Dacotahs,
Where the Falls of Minnehaha
Flash and gleam among the oak-trees,
Laugh and leap into the valley.
    There the ancient Arrow-maker
Made his arrow-heads of sandstone,
Arrow-heads of chalcedony,
Arrow-heads of flint and jasper,
Smoothed and sharpened at the edges,
Hard and polished, keen and costly.
    With him dwelt his dark-eyed daughter,
Wayward as the Minnehaha,
With her moods of shade and sunshine,
Eyes that smiled and frowned alternate,
Feet as rapid as the river,
Tresses flowing like the water,
And as musical a laughter;
And he named her from the river,
From the water-fall he named her,
Minnehaha, Laughing Water.
    Was it then for heads of arrows,
Arrow-heads of chalcedony,
Arrow-heads of flint and jasper,
That my Hiawatha halted
In the land of the Dacotahs?
    Was it not to see the maiden,
See the face of Laughing Water
Peeping from behind the curtain,
Hear the rustling of her garments
From behind the waving curtain,
As one sees the Minnehaha
Gleaming, glancing through the branches,
As one hears the Laughing Water
From behind its screen of branches?
    Who shall say what thoughts and visions

Fill the fiery brains of young men?
Who shall say what dreams of beauty
Filled the heart of Hiawatha?
All he told to old Nokomis,
When he reached the lodge at sunset,
Was the meeting with his father,
Was his fight with Mudjekeewis;
Not a word he said of arrows,
Not a word of Laughing Water!

V.

HIAWATHA'S FASTING.

You shall hear how Hiawatha
Prayed and fasted in the forest,
Not for greater skill in hunting,
Not for greater craft in fishing,
Not for triumphs in the battle,
And renown among the warriors,
But for profit of the people,
For advantage of the nations.

First he built a lodge for fasting,
Built a wigwam in the forest,
By the shining Big-Sea-Water,
In the blithe and pleasant Spring-time,
In the Moon of Leaves he built it,
And, with dreams and visions many,
Seven whole days and nights he fasted.

On the first day of his fasting
Through the leafy woods he wandered;
Saw the deer start from the thicket,
Saw the rabbit in his burrow,
Heard the pheasant, Bena, drumming,
Heard the squirrel, Adjidaumo,
Rattling in his hoard of acorns,
Saw the pigeon, the Omeme,
Building nests among the pine-trees,
And in flocks the wild goose, Wawa,
Flying to the fen-lands northward,
Whirring, wailing far above him.
"Master of Life!" he cried, desponding,

"Must our lives depend on these things?"
  On the next day of his fasting
By the river's brink he wandered,
Through the Muskoday, the meadow,
Saw the wild rice, Mahnomonee,
Saw the blueberry, Meenahga,
And the strawberry, Odahmin,
And the gooseberry, Shahbomin,
And the grape-vine, the Bemahgut,
Trailing o'er the alder-branches,
Filling all the air with fragrance!
"Master of Life!" he cried, desponding,
"Must our lives depend on these things?"
  On the third day of his fasting
By the lake he sat and pondered,
By the still, transparent water;
Saw the sturgeon, Nahma, leaping,
Scattering drops like beads of wampum,
Saw the yellow perch, the Sahwa,
Like a sunbeam in the water,
Saw the pike, the Maskenozha,
And the herring, Okahahwis,
And the Shawgashee, the craw-fish!
"Master of Life!" he cried, desponding,
"Must our lives depend on these things?"
  On the fourth day of his fasting
In his lodge he lay exhausted;
From his couch of leaves and branches
Gazing with half-open eyelids,
Full of shadowy dreams and visions,
On the dizzy, swimming landscape,
On the gleaming of the water,
On the splendor of the sunset.
  And he saw a youth approaching,
Dressed in garments green and yellow,
Coming through the purple twilight,
Through the splendor of the sunset;
Plumes of green bent o'er his forehead,
And his hair was soft and golden.
  Standing at the open doorway,
Long he looked at Hiawatha,
Looked with pity and compassion

On his wasted form and features,
And, in accents like the sighing
Of the South-Wind in the tree-tops,
Said he, "O my Hiawatha!
All your prayers are heard in heaven,
For you pray not like the others,
Not for greater skill in hunting,
Not for greater craft in fishing,
Not for triumph in the battle,
Nor renown among the warriors,
But for profit of the people,
For advantage of the nations.
    "From the Master of Life descending,
I, the friend of man, Mondamin,
Come to warn you and instruct you,
How by struggle and by labor
You shall gain what you have prayed for.
Rise up from your bed of branches,
Rise, O youth, and wrestle with me!"
    Faint with famine, Hiawatha
Started from his bed of branches.
From the twilight of his wigwam
Forth into the flush of sunset
Came, and wrestled with Mondamin;
At his touch he felt new courage
Throbbing in his brain and bosom,
Felt new life and hope and vigor
Run through every nerve and fibre.
    So they wrestled there together
In the glory of the sunset.
And the more they strove and struggled,
Stronger still grew Hiawatha;
Till the darkness fell around them,
And the heron, the Shuh-shuh-gah,
From her nest among the pine-trees,
Gave a cry of lamentation,
Gave a scream of pain and famine.
    "'T is enough!" then said Mondamin,
Smiling upon Hiawatha,
"But to-morrow, when the sun sets,
I will come again to try you."
And he vanished, and was seen not;

Whether sinking as the rain sinks,
Whether rising as the mists rise,
Hiawatha saw not, knew not,
Only saw that he had vanished,
Leaving him alone and fainting,
With the misty lake below him,
And the reeling stars above him.

On the morrow and the next day,
When the sun through heaven descending,
Like a red and burning cinder,
From the hearth of the Great Spirit,
Fell into the western waters,
Came Mondamin for the trial,
For the strife with Hiawatha;
Came as silent as the dew comes,
From the empty air appearing,
Into empty air returning,
Taking shape when earth it touches,
But invisible to all men
In its coming and its going.

Thrice they wrestled there together
In the glory of the sunset,
Till the darkness fell around them,
Till the heron, the Shuh-shuh-gah,
From her nest among the pine-trees,
Uttered her loud cry of famine,
And Mondamin paused to listen.

Tall and beautiful he stood there,
In his garments green and yellow;
To and fro his plumes above him
Waved and nodded with his breathing,
And the sweat of the encounter
Stood like drops of dew upon him.

And he cried, "O Hiawatha!
Bravely have you wrestled with me,
Thrice have wrestled stoutly with me,
And the Master of Life, who sees us,
He will give to you the triumph!"

Then he smiled, and said: "To-morrow
Is the last day of your conflict,
Is the last day of your fasting.
You will conquer and o'ercome me;

Make a bed for me to lie in,
Where the rain may fall upon me,
Where the sun may come and warm me;
Strip these garments, green and yellow,
Strip this nodding plumage from me,
Lay me in the earth, and make it
Soft and loose and light above me.

"Let no hand disturb my slumber,
Let no weed nor worm molest me,
Let not Kahgahgee, the raven,
Come to haunt me and molest me,
Only come yourself to watch me,
Till I wake, and start, and quicken,
Till I leap into the sunshine."

And thus saying, he departed;
Peacefully slept Hiawatha,
But he heard the Wawonaissa,
Heard the whippoorwill complaining,
Perched upon his lonely wigwam;
Heard the rushing Sebowisha,
Heard the rivulet rippling near him,
Talking to the darksome forest;
Heard the sighing of the branches,
As they lifted and subsided
At the passing of the night-wind,
Heard them, as one hears in slumber
Far-off murmurs, dreamy whispers:
Peacefully slept Hiawatha.

On the morrow came Nokomis,
On the seventh day of his fasting,
Came with food for Hiawatha,
Came imploring and bewailing,
Lest his hunger should o'ercome him,
Lest his fasting should be fatal.

But he tasted not, and touched not,
Only said to her, "Nokomis,
Wait until the sun is setting,
Till the darkness falls around us,
Till the heron, the Shuh-shuh-gah,
Crying from the desolate marshes,
Tells us that the day is ended."

Homeward weeping went Nokomis,

Sorrowing for her Hiawatha,
Fearing lest his strength should fail **him,**
Lest his fasting should be fatal.
He meanwhile sat weary waiting
For the coming of Mondamin,
Till the shadows, pointing eastward,
Lengthened over field and forest,
Till the sun dropped from the heaven,
Floating on the waters westward,
As a red leaf in the Autumn
Falls and floats upon the water,
Falls and sinks into its bosom.

And behold! the young Mondamin,
With his soft and shining tresses,
With his garments green and yellow,
With his long and glossy plumage,
Stood and beckoned at the doorway.
And as one in slumber walking,
Pale and haggard, but undaunted,
From the wigwam Hiawatha
Came and wrestled with Mondamin.

Round about him spun the landscape,
Sky and forest reeled together,
And his strong heart leaped within him,
As the sturgeon leaps and struggles
In a net to break its meshes.
Like a ring of fire around him
Blazed and flared the red horizon,
And a hundred suns seemed looking
At the combat of the wrestlers.

Suddenly upon the greensward
All alone stood Hiawatha,
Panting with his wild exertion,
Palpitating with the struggle;
And before him, breathless, lifeless,
Lay the youth, with hair dishevelled,
Plumage torn, and garments tattered,
Dead he lay there in the sunset.

And victorious Hiawatha
Made the grave as he commanded,
Stripped the garments from Mondamin,
Stripped his tattered plumage from him,

Laid him in the earth, and made it
Soft and loose and light above him;
And the heron, the Shuh-shuh-gah,
From the melancholy moorlands,
Gave a cry of lamentation,
Gave a cry of pain and anguish!
    Homeward then went Hiawatha
To the lodge of old Nokomis,
And the seven days of his fasting
Were accomplished and completed,
But the place was not forgotten
Where he wrestled with Mondamin;
Nor forgotten nor neglected
Was the grave where lay Mondamin,
Sleeping in the rain and sunshine,
Where his scattered plumes and garments
Faded in the rain and sunshine.
    Day by day did Hiawatha
Go to wait and watch beside it;
Kept the dark mould soft above it,
Kept it clean from weeds and insects,
Drove away, with scoffs and shoutings,
Kahgahgee, the king of ravens.
    Till at length a small green feather
From the earth shot slowly upward,
Then another and another,
And before the Summer ended
Stood the maize in all its beauty,
With its shining robes about it,
And its long, soft, yellow tresses;
And in rapture Hiawatha
Cried aloud, "It is Mondamin!
Yes, the friend of man, Mondamin!"
    Then he called to old Nokomis
And Iagoo, the great boaster,
Showed them where the maize was growing,
Told them of his wondrous vision
Of his wrestling and his triumph,
Of this new gift to the nations,
Which should be their food forever.
    And still later, when the Autumn
Changed the long, green leaves to yellow,

And the soft and juicy kernels
Grew like wampum hard and yellow,
Then the ripened ears he gathered,
Stripped the withered husks from off them,
As he once had stripped the wrestler,
Gave the first Feast of Mondamin,
And made known unto the people
This new gift of the Great Spirit.

VI.

HIAWATHA'S FRIENDS.

Two good friends had Hiawatha,
Singled out from all the others,
Bound to him in closest union,
And to whom he gave the right hand
Of his heart, in joy and sorrow:
Chibiabos, the musician,
And the very strong man, Kwasind.

Straight between them ran the pathway,
Never grew the grass upon it;
Singing birds, that utter falsehoods,
Story-tellers, mischief-makers,
Found no eager ear to listen,
Could not breed ill-will between them,
For they kept each other's counsel,
Spake with naked hearts together,
Pondering much and much contriving
How the tribes of men might prosper.

Most beloved by Hiawatha
Was the gentle Chibiabos,
He the best of all musicians,
He the sweetest of all singers.
Beautiful and childlike was he,
Brave as man is, soft as woman,
Pliant as a wand of willow,
Stately as a deer with antlers.

When he sang, the village listened;
All the warriors gathered round him,
All the women came to hear him;
Now he stirred their souls to passion,
Now he melted them to pity.

From the hollow reeds he fashioned
Flutes so musical and mellow,
That the brook, the Sebowisha,
Ceased to murmur in the woodland,
That the wood-birds ceased from singing,
And the squirrel, Adjidaumo,
Ceased his chatter in the oak-tree,
And the rabbit, the Wabasso,
Sat upright to look and listen.
 Yes, the brook, the Sebowisha,
Pausing, said, "O Chibiabos,
Teach my waves to flow in music,
Softly as your words in singing!"
 Yes, the blue-bird, the Owaissa,
Envious, said, "O Chibiabos,
Teach me tones as wild and wayward,
Teach me songs as full of frenzy!"
 Yes, the robin, the Opechee,
Joyous, said, "O Chibiabos,
Teach me tones as sweet and tender,
Teach me songs as full of gladness!"
 And the whippoorwill, Wawonaissa,
Sobbing, said, "O Chibiabos,
Teach me tones as melancholy,
Teach me songs as full of sadness!"
 All the many sounds of nature
Borrowed sweetness from his singing;
All the hearts of men were softened
By the pathos of his music;
For he sang of peace and freedom,
Sang of beauty, love, and longing;
Sang of death, and life undying
In the Islands of the Blessed,
In the kingdom of Ponemah,
In the land of the Hereafter.
 Very dear to Hiawatha
Was the gentle Chibiabos,
He the best of all musicians,
He the sweetest of all singers;
For his gentleness he loved him,
And the magic of his singing.
 Dear, too, unto Hiawatha

Was the very strong man, Kwasind,
He the strongest of all mortals,
He the mightiest among many;
For his very strength he loved him,
For his strength allied to goodness.
    Idle in his youth was Kwasind,
Very listless, dull, and dreamy,
Never played with other children,
Never fished and never hunted,
Not like other children was he;
But they saw that much he fasted,
Much his Manito entreated,
Much besought his Guardian Spirit.
    "Lazy Kwasind!" said his mother,
"In my work you never help me!
In the summer you are roaming
Idly in the fields and forests;
In the Winter you are cowering
O'er the firebrands in the wigwam!
In the coldest days of Winter
I must break the ice for fishing;
With my nets you never help me!
At the door my nets are hanging,
Dripping, freezing with the water;
Go and wring them, Yenadizze!
Go and dry them in the sunshine!"
    Slowly, from the ashes, Kwasind
Rose, but made no angry answer;
From the lodge went forth in silence,
Took the nets, that hung together,
Dripping, freezing at the doorway;
Like a wisp of straw he wrung them,
Like a wisp of straw he broke them,
Could not wring them without breaking,
Such the strength was in his fingers.
    "Lazy Kwasind!" said his father,
"In the hunt you never help me;
Every bow you touch is broken,
Snapped asunder every arrow;
Yet come with me to the forest,
You shall bring the hunting homeward."
    Down a narrow pass they wandered,

Where a brooklet led them onward,
Where the trail of deer and bison
Marked the soft mud on the margin,
Till they found all further passage
Shut against them, barred securely
By the trunks of trees uprooted,
Lying lengthwise, lying crosswise,
And forbidding further passage.

"We must go back," said the old man,
"O'er these logs we cannot clamber;
Not a woodchuck could get through them,
Not a squirrel clamber o'er them!"
And straightway his pipe he lighted,
And sat down to smoke and ponder.
But before his pipe was finished,
Lo! the path was cleared before him;
All the trunks had Kwasind lifted,
To the right hand, to the left hand,
Shot the pine-trees swift as arrows,
Hurled the cedars light as lances.

"Lazy Kwasind!" said the young men,
As they sported in the meadow;
"Why stand idly looking at us,
Leaning on the rock behind you?
Come and wrestle with the others,
Let us pitch the quoit together!"

Lazy Kwasind made no answer,
To their challenge made no answer,
Only rose, and, slowly turning,
Seized the huge rock in his fingers,
Tore it from its deep foundation,
Poised it in the air a moment,
Pitched it sheer into the river,
Sheer into the swift Pauwating,
Where it still is seen in Summer.

Once as down that foaming river,
Down the rapids of Pauwating,
Kwasind sailed with his companions,
In the stream he saw a beaver,
Saw Ahmeek, the King of Beavers,
Struggling with the rushing currents,
Rising, sinking in the water.

Without speaking, without pausing,
Kwasind leaped into the river,
Plunged beneath the bubbling surface,
Through the whirlpools chased the beaver,
Followed him among the islands,
Stayed so long beneath the water,
That his terrified companions
Cried, "Alas! good-by to Kwasind!
We shall never more see Kwasind!"
But he reappeared triumphant,
And upon his shining shoulders
Brought the beaver, dead and dripping,
Brought the King of all the Beavers

And these two, as I have told you
Were the friends of Hiawatha,
Chibiabos, the musician,
And the very strong man, Kwasind.
Long they lived in peace together,
Spake with naked hearts together,
Pondering much and much contriving
How the tribes of men might prosper.

VII.

HIAWATHA'S SAILING.

"Give me of your bark, O Birch-Tree!
Of your yellow bark, O Birch-Tree!
Growing by the rushing river,
Tall and stately in the valley!
I a light canoe will build me,
Build a swift Cheemaun for sailing,
That shall float upon the river,
Like a yellow leaf in Autumn,
Like a yellow water-lily!

"Lay aside your cloak, O Birch-Tree!
Lay aside your white-skin wrapper,
For the summer-time is coming,
And the sun is warm in heaven,
And you need no white-skin wrapper!"

Thus aloud cried Hiawatha
In the solitary forest,

By the rushing Taquamenaw,
When the birds were singing gayly,
In the Moon of Leaves were singing,
And the sun, from sleep awaking,
Started up and said, "Behold me!
Geezis, the great Sun, behold me!"
     And the tree with all its branches
Rustled in the breeze of morning,
Saying, with a sigh of patience,
"Take my cloak, O Hiawatha!"
     With his knife the tree he girdled;
Just beneath its lowest branches,
Just above the roots, he cut it,
Till the sap came oozing outward;
Down the trunk, from top to bottom,
Sheer he cleft the bark asunder,
With a wooden wedge he raised it,
Stripped it from the trunk unbroken.
     "Give me of your boughs, O Cedar!
Of your strong and pliant branches,
My canoe to make more steady,
Make more strong and firm beneath me!"
     Through the summit of the Cedar
Went a sound, a cry of horror,
Went a murmur of resistance;
But it whispered, bending downward,
"Take my boughs, O Hiawatha!"
     Down he hewed the boughs of cedar,
Shaped them straightway to a framework,
Like two bows he formed and shaped them,
Like two bended bows together.
     "Give me of your roots, O Tamarack!
Of your fibrous roots, O Larch-Tree!
My canoe to bind together,
So to bind the ends together
That the water may not enter,
That the river may not wet me!"
     And the Larch, with all its fibres,
Shivered in the air of morning,
Touched his forehead with its tassels,
Said, with one long sigh of sorrow,
"Take them all, O Hiawatha!"

From the earth he tore the fibres,
Tore the tough roots of the Larch-Tree,
Closely sewed the bark together,
Bound it closely to the framework.
　"Give me of your balm, O Fir-Tree!
Of your balsam and your resin,
So to close the seams together
That the water may not enter,
That the river may not wet me!"
　And the Fir-Tree, tall and sombre,
Sobbed through all its robes of darkness,
Rattled like a shore with pebbles,
Answered wailing, answered weeping,
"Take my balm, O Hiawatha!"
　And he took the tears of balsam,
Took the resin of the Fir-Tree,
Smeared therewith each seam and fissure,
Made each crevice safe from water.
　"Give me of your quills, O Hedgehog!
All your quills, O Kagh, the Hedgehog!
I will make a necklace of them,
Make a girdle for my beauty,
And two stars to deck her bosom!"
　From a hollow tree the Hedgehog,
With his sleepy eyes looked at him,
Shot his shining quills, like arrows,
Saying, with a drowsy murmur,
Through the tangle of his whiskers,
"Take my quills, O Hiawatha!"
　From the ground the quills he gathered,
All the little shining arrows,
Stained them red and blue and yellow,
With the juice of roots and berries;
Into his canoe he wrought them,
Round its waist a shining girdle,
Round its bows a gleaming necklace,
On its breast two stars resplendent.
　Thus the Birch-Canoe was builded
In the valley, by the river,
In the bosom of the forest;
And the forest's life was in it,

All its mystery and its magic,
All the lightness of the birch-tree,
All the toughness of the cedar,
All the larch's supple sinews;
And it floated on the river
Like a yellow leaf in Autumn,
Like a yellow water-lily.

Paddles none had Hiawatha,
Paddles none he had or needed,
For his thoughts as paddles served him,
And his wishes served to guide him;
Swift or slow at will he glided,
Veered to right or left at pleasure.

Then he called aloud to Kwasind,
To his friend, the strong man, Kwasind,
Saying, "Help me clear this river
Of its sunken logs and sand-bars."

Straight into the river Kwasind
Plunged as if he were an otter,
Dived as if he were a beaver,
Stood up to his waist in water,
To his arm-pits in the river,
Swam and shouted in the river,
Tugged at sunken logs and branches,
With his hands he scooped the sand-bars,
With his feet the ooze and tangle.

And thus sailed my Hiawatha
Down the rushing Taquamenaw,
Sailed through all its bends and windings,
Sailed through all its deeps and shallows,
While his friend, the strong man, Kwasind
Swam the deeps, the shallows waded.

Up and down the river went they,
In and out among its islands,
Cleared its bed of root and sand-bar,
Dragged the dead trees from its channel,
Made its passage safe and certain,
Made a pathway for the people,
From its springs among the mountains,
To the waters of Pauwating,
To the bay of Taquamenaw.

VIII.

HIAWATHA'S FISHING.

FORTH upon the Gitche Gumee,
On the shining Big-Sea-Water,
With his fishing-line of cedar,
Of the twisted bark of cedar,
Forth to catch the sturgeon Nahma,
Mishe-Nahma, King of Fishes,
In his birch-canoe exulting,
All alone went Hiawatha.

Through the clear, transparent water
He could see the fishes swimming
Far down in the depths below him;
See the yellow perch, the Sahwa,
Like a sunbeam in the water,
See the Shawgashee, the craw-fish,
Like a spider on the bottom,
On the white and sandy bottom.

At the stern sat Hiawatha,
With his fishing-line of cedar;
In his plumes the breeze of morning
Played as in the hemlock branches;
On the bows, with tail erected,
Sat the squirrel, Adjidaumo;
In his fur the breeze of morning
Played as in the prairie grasses.

On the white sand of the bottom
Lay the monster Mishe-Nahma,
Lay the sturgeon, King of Fishes;
Through his gills he breathed the water,
With his fins he fanned and winnowed,
With his tail he swept the sand-floor.

There he lay in all his armor;
On each side a shield to guard him,
Plates of bone upon his forehead,
Down his sides and back and shoulders
Plates of bone with spines projecting!
Painted was he with his war-paints,
Stripes of yellow, red, and azure,
Spots of brown and spots of sable;

And he lay there on the bottom,
Fanning with his fins of purple,
As above him Hiawatha
In his birch-canoe came sailing,
With his fishing-line of cedar.
  "Take my bait!" cried Hiawatha,
Down into the depths beneath him,
"Take my bait, O Sturgeon, Nahma!
Come up from below the water,
Let us see which is the stronger!"
And he dropped his line of cedar
Through the clear, transparent water,
Waited vainly for an answer,
Long sat waiting for an answer,
And repeating loud and louder,
"Take my bait, O King of Fishes!"
  Quiet lay the sturgeon, Nahma,
Fanning slowly in the water,
Looking up at Hiawatha,
Listening to his call and clamor,
His unnecessary tumult,
Till he wearied of the shouting;
And he said to the Kenozha,
To the pike, the Maskenozha,
"Take the bait of this rude fellow,
Break the line of Hiawatha!"
  In his fingers Hiawatha
Felt the loose line jerk and tighten;
As he drew it in, he tugged so
That the birch-canoe stood endwise,
Like a birch log in the water,
With the squirrel, Adjidaumo,
Perched and frisking on the summit.
  Full of scorn was Hiawatha
When he saw the fish rise upward,
Saw the pike, the Maskenozha,
Coming nearer, nearer to him,
And he shouted through the water,
"Esa! esa! shame upon you!
You are but the pike, Kenozha,
You are not the fish I wanted,
You are not the King of Fishes!"

Reeling downward to the bottom
Sank the pike in great confusion,
And the mighty sturgeon, Nahma,
Said to Ugudwash, the sun-fish,
To the bream, with scales of crimson,
"Take the bait of this great boaster,
Break the line of Hiawatha!"
Slowly upward, wavering, gleaming,
Rose the Ugudwash, the sun-fish,
Seized the line of Hiawatha,
Swung with all his weight upon it,
Made a whirlpool in the water,
Whirled the birch-canoe in circles,
Round and round in gurgling eddies,
Till the circles in the water
Reached the far-off sandy beaches,
Till the water-flags and rushes
Nodded on the distant margins.
But when Hiawatha saw him
Slowly rising through the water,
Lifting up his disk refulgent,
Loud he shouted in derision,
"Esa! esa! shame upon you!
You are Ugudwash, the sun-fish,
You are not the fish I wanted,
You are not the King of Fishes!"
Slowly downward, wavering, gleaming,
Sank the Ugudwash, the sun-fish,
And again the sturgeon, Nahma,
Heard the shout of Hiawatha,
Heard his challenge of defiance,
The unnecessary tumult,
Ringing far across the water.
From the white sand of the bottom
Up he rose with angry gesture,
Quivering in each nerve and fibre,
Clashing all his plates of armor,
Gleaming bright with all his war-paint;
In his wrath he darted upward,
Flashing leaped into the sunshine,
Opened his great jaws, and swallowed
Both canoe and Hiawatha.

Down into that darksome cavern
Plunged the headlong Hiawatha,
As a log on some black river
Shoots and plunges down the rapids,
Found himself in utter darkness,
Groped about in helpless wonder,
Till he felt a great heart beating,
Throbbing in that utter darkness.

And he smote it in his anger,
With his fist, the heart of Nahma,
Felt the mighty King of Fishes
Shudder through each nerve and fibre,
Heard the water gurgle round him
As he leaped and staggered through it,
Sick at heart, and faint and weary.

Crosswise then did Hiawatha
Drag his birch-canoe for safety.
Lest from out the jaws of Nahma,
In the turmoil and confusion,
Forth he might be hurled and perish
And the squirrel, Adjidaumo,
Frisked and chattered very gayly,
Toiled and tugged with Hiawatha
Till the labor was completed.

Then said Hiawatha to him,
"O my little friend, the squirrel,
Bravely have you toiled to help me;
Take the thanks of Hiawatha,
And the name which now he gives you;
For hereafter and forever
Boys shall call you Adjidaumo,
Tail-in-air the boys shall call you!"

And again the sturgeon, Nahma,
Gasped and quivered in the water,
Then was still, and drifted landward
Till he grated on the pebbles,
Till the listening Hiawatha
Heard him grate upon the margin,
Felt him strand upon the pebbles,
Knew that Nahma, King of Fishes,
Lay there dead upon the margin.

Then he heard a clang and flapping,

As of many wings assembling,
Heard a screaming and confusion,
As of birds of prey contending,
Saw a gleam of light above him,
Shining through the ribs of Nahma,
Saw the glittering eyes of sea-gulls,
Of Kayoshk, the sea-gulls, peering,
Gazing at him through the opening,
Heard them saying to each other,
" 'T is our brother, Hiawatha!"
    And he shouted from below them,
Cried exulting from the caverns:
"O ye sea-gulls! O my brothers!
I have slain the sturgeon, Nahma;
Make the rifts a little larger,
With your claws the openings widen,
Set me free from this dark prison,
And henceforward and forever
Men shall speak of your achievements,
Calling you Kayoshk, the sea-gulls,
Yes, Kayoshk, the Noble Scratchers!"
    And the wild and clamorous sea-gulls
Toiled with beak and claws together,
Made the rifts and openings wider
In the mighty ribs of Nahma,
And from peril and from prison,
From the body of the sturgeon,
From the peril of the water,
They released my Hiawatha.
    He was standing near his wigwam
On the margin of the water,
And he called to old Nokomis,
Called and beckoned to Nokomis,
Pointed to the sturgeon, Nahma,
Lying lifeless on the pebbles,
With the sea-gulls feeding on him.
    "I have slain the Mishe-Nahma,
Slain the King of Fishes!" said he;
"Look! the sea-gulls feed upon him,
Yes, my friend Kayoshk, the sea-gulls
Drive them not away, Nokomis,
They have saved me from great peril

In the body of the sturgeon;
Wait until their meal is ended,
Till their craws are full with feasting,
Till they homeward fly, at sunset,
To their nests among the marshes;
Then bring all your pots and kettles,
And make oil for us in Winter."

And she waited till the sun set,
Till the pallid moon, the night-sun,
Rose above the tranquil water,
Till Kayoshk, the sated sea-gulls,
From their banquet rose with clamor,
And across the fiery sunset
Winged their way to far-off islands,
To their nests among the rushes.

To his sleep went Hiawatha,
And Nokomis to her labor,
Toiling patient in the moonlight,
Till the sun and moon changed places,
Till the sky was red with sunrise,
And Kayoshk, the hungry sea-gulls,
Came back from the reedy islands,
Clamorous for their morning banquet.

Three whole days and nights alternate
Old Nokomis and the sea-gulls
Stripped the oily flesh of Nahma,
Till the waves washed through the rib-bones,
Till the sea-gulls came no longer,
And upon the sands lay nothing
But the skeleton of Nahma.

IX.

HIAWATHA AND THE PEARL-FEATHER.

ON the shores of Gitche Gumee,
Of the shining Big-Sea-Water,
Stood Nokomis, the old woman,
Pointing with her finger westward,
O'er the water pointing westward,
To the purple clouds of sunset.

Fiercely the red sun descending

Burned his way along the heavens,
Set the sky on fire behind him,
As war-parties, when retreating,
Burn the prairies on their war-trail;
And the moon, the Night-Sun, eastward,
Suddenly starting from his ambush,
Followed fast those bloody footprints,
Followed in that fiery war-trail,
With its glare upon its features.

And Nokomis, the old woman,
Pointing with her finger westward,
Spake these words to Hiawatha:
"Yonder dwells the great Pearl-Feather,
Megissogwon, the Magician,
Manito of Wealth and Wampum,
Guarded by his fiery serpents,
Guarded by the black pitch-water.
You can see his fiery serpents,
The Kenabeek, the great serpents,
Coiling, playing in the water;
You can see the black pitch-water
Stretching far away beyond them,
To the purple clouds of sunset!

"He it was who slew my father,
By his wicked wiles and cunning,
When he from the moon descended,
When he came on earth to seek me.
He, the mightiest of Magicians,
Sends the fever from the marshes,
Sends the pestilential vapors,
Sends the poisonous exhalations,
Sends the white fog from the fen-lands,
Sends disease and death among us!

"Take your bow, O Hiawatha,
Take your arrows, jasper-headed,
Take your war-club, Puggawaugua,
And your mittens, Minjekahwun,
And your birch-canoe for sailing,
And the oil of Mishe-Nahma,
So to smear its sides, that swiftly
You may pass the black pitch-water;
Slay this merciless magician,

Save the people from the fever
That he breathes across the fen-lands,
And avenge my father's murder!".
   Straightway then my Hiawatha
Armed himself with all his war-gear,
Launched his birch-canoe for sailing;
With his palm its sides he patted,
Said with glee, "Cheemaun, my darling,
O my Birch-Canoe! leap forward,
Where you see the fiery serpents,
Where you see the black pitch-water!"
   Forward leaped Cheemaun exulting,
And the noble Hiawatha
Sang his war-song wild and woful,
And above him the war-eagle,
The Keneu, the great war-eagle,
Master of all fowls with feathers,
Screamed and hurtled through the heavens.
   Soon he reached the fiery serpents,
The Kenabeek, the great serpents,
Lying huge upon the water,
Sparkling, rippling in the water,
Lying coiled across the passage,
With their blazing crests uplifted,
Breathing fiery fogs and vapors,
So that none could pass beyond them.
   But the fearless Hiawatha
Cried aloud, and spake in this wise:
"Let me pass my way, Kenabeek,
Let me go upon my journey!"
And they answered, hissing fiercely,
With their fiery breath made answer:
"Back, go back! O Shaugodaya!
Back to old Nokomis, Faint-heart!"
   Then the angry Hiawatha
Raised his mighty bow of ash-tree,
Seized his arrows, jasper-headed,
Shot them fast among the serpents;
Every twanging of the bow-string
Was a war-cry and a death-cry,
Every whizzing of an arrow
Was a death-song of Kenabeek.

Weltering in the bloody water,
Dead lay all the fiery serpents,
And among them Hiawatha
Harmless sailed, and cried exulting:
"Onward, O Cheemaun, my darling!
Onward to the black pitch-water!"
    Then he took the oil of Nahma,
And the bows and sides anointed,
Smeared them well with oil, that swiftly
He might pass the black pitch-water.
    All night long he sailed upon it,
Sailed upon that sluggish water,
Covered with its mould of ages,
Black with rotting water-rushes,
Rank with flags and leaves of lilies,
Stagnant, lifeless, dreary, dismal,
Lighted by the shimmering moonlight,
And by will-o'-the-wisps illumined,
Fires by ghosts of dead men kindled,
In their weary night-encampments.
    All the air was white with moonlight,
All the water black with shadow,
And around him the Suggema,
The mosquitos, sang their war-song,
And the fire-flies, Wah-wah-taysee,
Waved their torches to mislead him;
And the bull-frog, the Dahinda,
Thrust his head into the moonlight,
Fixed his yellow eyes upon him,
Sobbed and sank beneath the surface;
And anon a thousand whistles,
Answered over all the fen-lands,
And the heron, the Shuh-shuh-gah,
Far off on the reedy margin,
Heralded the hero's coming.
    Westward thus fared Hiawatha,
Toward the realm of Megissogwon,
Toward the land of the Pearl-Feather,
Till the level moon stared at him,
In his face stared pale and haggard,
Till the sun was hot behind him,
Till it burned upon his shoulders,

And before him on the upland
He could see the Shining Wigwam
Of the Manito of Wampum,
Of the mightiest of Magicians.
   Then once more Cheemaun he patted,
To his birch-canoe said, "Onward!"
And it stirred in all its fibres,
And with one great bound of triumph
Leaped across the water-lilies,
Leaped through tangled flags and rushes,
And upon the beach beyond them
Dry-shod landed Hiawatha.
   Straight he took his bow of ash-tree,
On the sand one end he rested,
With his knee he pressed the middle,
Stretched the faithful bow-string tighter,
Took an arrow, jasper-headed,
Shot it at the Shining Wigwam,
Sent it singing as a herald,
As a bearer of his message,
Of his challenge loud and lofty:
"Come forth from your lodge, Pearl-Feather!
Hiawatha waits your coming!"
   Straightway from the Shining Wigwam
Came the mighty Megissogwon,
Tall of stature, broad of shoulder,
Dark and terrible in aspect,
Clad from head to foot in wampum,
Armed with all his warlike weapons,
Painted like the sky of morning,
Streaked with crimson, blue, and yellow,
Crested with great eagle-feathers,
Streaming upward, streaming outward.
   "Well I know you, Hiawatha!"
Cried he in a voice of thunder,
In a tone of loud derision.
"Hasten back, O Shaugodaya!
Hasten back among the women,
Back to old Nokomis, Faint-heart!
I will slay you as you stand there,
As of old I slew her father!"
   But my Hiawatha answered,

Nothing daunted, fearing nothing:
"Big words do not smite like war-clubs,
Boastful breath is not a bow-string,
Taunts are not so sharp as arrows,
Deeds are better things than words are,
Actions mightier than boastings!"
    Then began the greatest battle
That the sun had ever looked on,
That the war-birds ever witnessed.
All a Summer's day it lasted,
From the sunrise to the sunset;
For the shafts of Hiawatha
Harmless hit the shirt of wampum,
Harmless fell the blows he dealt it
With his mittens, Minjekahwun,
Harmless fell the heavy war-club;
It could dash the rocks asunder,
But it could not break the meshes
Of that magic shirt of wampum.
    Till at sunset Hiawatha,
Leaning on his bow of ash-tree,
Wounded, weary, and desponding,
With his mighty war-club broken,
With his mittens torn and tattered,
And three useless arrows only,
Paused to rest beneath a pine-tree,
From whose branches trailed the mosses,
And whose trunk was coated over
With the Dead-man's Moccasin-leather,
With the fungus white and yellow.
    Suddenly from the boughs above him
Sang the Mama, the woodpecker:
"Aim your arrows, Hiawatha,
At the head of Megissogwon,
Strike the tuft of hair upon it,
At their roots the long black tresses;
There alone can he be wounded!"
    Winged with feathers, tipped with jasper,
Swift flew Hiawatha's arrow,
Just as Megissogwon, stooping,
Raised a heavy stone to throw it.

Full upon the crown it struck him,
At the roots of his long tresses,
And he reeled and staggered forward,
Plunging like a wounded bison,
Yes, like Pezhekee, the bison,
When the snow is on the prairie.

Swifter flew the second arrow,
In the pathway of the other,
Piercing deeper than the other,
Wounding sorer than the other;
And the knees of Megissogwon
Shook like windy reeds beneath him,
Bent and trembled like the rushes.

But the third and latest arrow
Swiftest flew, and wounded sorest,
And the mighty Megissogwon
Saw the fiery eyes of Pauguk,
Saw the eyes of Death glare at him,
Heard his voice call in the darkness;
At the feet of Hiawatha
Lifeless lay the great Pearl-Feather,
Lay the mightiest of Magicians.

Then the grateful Hiawatha
Called the Mama, the woodpecker,
From his perch among the branches
Of the melancholy pine-tree,
And, in honor of his service,
Stained with blood the tuft of feathers
On the little head of Mama;
Even to this day he wears it,
Wears the tuft of crimson feathers,
As a symbol of his service.

Then he stripped the shirt of wampum
From the back of Megissogwon,
As a trophy of the battle,
As a signal of his conquest.
On the shore he left the body,
Half on land and half in water,
In the sand his feet were buried,
And his face was in the water.
And above him wheeled and clamored

The Keneu, the great war-eagle,
Sailing round in narrower circles,
Hovering nearer, nearer, nearer.

From the wigwam Hiawatha
Bore the wealth of Megissogwon,
All his wealth of skins and wampum.
Furs of bison and of beaver,
Furs of sable and of ermine,
Wampum belts and strings and pouches,
Quivers wrought with beads of wampum,
Filled with arrows, silver-headed.

Homeward then he sailed exulting,
Homeward through the black pitch-water,
Homeward through the weltering serpents,
With the trophies of the battle,
With a shout and song of triumph.

On the shore stood old Nokomis,
On the shore stood Chibiabos,
And the very strong man, Kwasind,
Waiting for the hero's coming,
Listening to his song of triumph.
And the people of the village
Welcomed him with songs and dances,
Made a joyous feast, and shouted:
"Honor be to Hiawatha!
He has slain the great Pearl-Feather,
Slain the mightiest of Magicians,
Him, who sent the fiery fever,
Sent the white fog from the fen-lands,
Sent disease and death among us!"

Ever dear to Hiawatha
Was the memory of Mama!
And in token of his friendship,
As a mark of his remembrance,
He adorned and decked his pipe-stem
With the crimson tuft of feathers,
With the blood-red crest of Mama.
But the wealth of Megissogwon,
All the trophies of the battle,
He divided with his people,
Shared it equally among them.

X.

HIAWATHA'S WOOING.

"As unto the bow the cord is,
So unto the man is woman:
Though she bends him, she obeys him,
Though she draws him, yet she follows,
Useless each without the other!"
    Thus the youthful Hiawatha
Said within himself and pondered,
Much perplexed by various feelings
Listless, longing, hoping, fearing,
Dreaming still of Minnehaha,
Of the lovely Laughing Water,
In the land of the Dacotahs.
    "Wed a maiden of your people,"
Warning said the old Nokomis;
"Go not eastward, go not westward,
For a stranger, whom we know not!
Like a fire upon the hearth-stone
Is a neighbor's homely daughter,
Like the starlight or the moonlight
Is the handsomest of strangers!"
    Thus dissuading spake Nokomis,
And my Hiawatha answered
Only this: "Dear old Nokomis,
Very pleasant is the firelight,
But I like the starlight better,
Better do I like the moonlight!"
    Gravely then said old Nokomis:
"Bring not here an idle maiden,
Bring not here a useless woman,
Hands unskilful, feet unwilling;
Bring a wife with nimble fingers,
Heart and hand that move together,
Feet that run on willing errands!"
    Smiling answered Hiawatha:
"In the land of the Dacotahs
Lives the Arrow-maker's daughter,
Minnehaha, Laughing Water,
Handsomest of all the women.

I will bring her to your wigwam,
She shall run upon your errands,
Be your starlight, moonlight, firelight,
Be the sunlight of my people!"
    Still dissuading said Nokomis:
"Bring not to my lodge a stranger
From the land of the Dacotahs!
Very fierce are the Dacotahs,
Often is there war between us,
There are feuds yet unforgotten,
Wounds that ache and still may open!"
    Laughing answered Hiawatha:
"For that reason, if no other,
Would I wed the fair Dacotah,
That our tribes might be united,
That old feuds might be forgotten,
And old wounds be healed forever!"
    Thus departed Hiawatha
To the land of the Dacotahs,
To the land of handsome women;
Striding over moor and meadow,
Through interminable forests,
Through uninterrupted silence.
    With his moccasins of magic,
At each stride a mile he measured;
Yet the way seemed long before him,
And his heart outran his footsteps;
And he journeyed without resting,
Till he heard the cataract's laughter,
Heard the Falls of Minnehaha
Calling to him through the silence.
"Pleasant is the sound!" he murmured,
"Pleasant is the voice that calls me!"
    On the outskirts of the forest,
'Twixt the shadow and the sunshine,
Herds of fallow deer were feeding,
But they saw not Hiawatha;
To his bow he whispered, "Fail not!"
To his arrow whispered, "Swerve not!"
Sent it singing on its errand,
To the red heart of the roebuck;
Threw the deer across his shoulder

And sped forward without pausing.
  At the doorway of his wigwam
Sat the ancient Arrow-maker,
In the land of the Dacotahs,
Making arrow-heads of jasper,
Arrow-heads of chalcedony.
At his side, in all her beauty,
Sat the lovely Minnehaha,
Sat his daughter, Laughing Water,
Plaiting mats of flags and rushes;
Of the past the old man's thoughts **were,**
And the maiden's of the future.
  He was thinking, as he sat there,
Of the days when with such arrows
He had struck the deer and bison,
On the Muskoday, the meadow;
Shot the wild goose, flying southward,
On the wing, the clamorous Wawa;
Thinking of the great war-parties,
How they came to buy his arrows,
Could not fight without his arrows.
Ah, no more such noble warriors
Could be found on earth as they **were;**
Now the men were all like women,
Only used their tongues for weapons.
  She was thinking of a hunter,
From another tribe and country,
Young and tall and very handsome,
Who one morning, in the Spring-time,
Came to buy her father's arrows,
Sat and rested in the wigwam,
Lingered long about the doorway,
Looking back as he departed.
She had heard her father praise **him,**
Praise his courage and his wisdom;
Would he come again for arrows
To the Falls of Minnehaha?
On the mat her hands lay idle,
And her eyes were very dreamy.
  Through their thoughts they heard **a footstep,**
Heard a rustling in the branches,
And with glowing cheek and forehead,

With the deer upon his shoulders,
Suddenly from out the woodlands
Hiawatha stood before them.

Straight the ancient Arrow-maker
Looked up gravely from his labor,
Laid aside the unfinished arrow,
Bade him enter at the doorway,
Saying, as he rose to meet him,
"Hiawatha, you are welcome!"

At the feet of Laughing Water
Hiawatha laid his burden,
Threw the red deer from his shoulders;
And the maiden looked up at him,
Looked up from her mat of rushes,
Said with gentle look and accent,
"You are welcome, Hiawatha!"

Very spacious was the wigwam,
Made of deer-skin dressed and whitened,
With the Gods of the Dacotahs
Drawn and painted on its curtains,
And so tall the doorway, hardly
Hiawatha stooped to enter,
Hardly touched his eagle-feathers
As he entered at the doorway.

Then uprose the Laughing Water,
From the ground fair Minnehaha
Laid aside her mat unfinished,
Brought forth food and set before them,
Water brought them from the brooklet,
Gave them food in earthen vessels,
Gave them drink in bowls of bass-wood,
Listened while the guest was speaking,
Listened while her father answered,
But not once her lips she opened,
Not a single word she uttered.

Yes, as in a dream she listened
To the words of Hiawatha,
As he talked of old Nokomis,
Who had nursed him in his childhood,
As he told of his companions.
Chibiabos, the musician,
And the very strong man, Kwasind,

And of happiness and plenty
In the land of the Ojibways,
In the pleasant land and peaceful.
"After many years of warfare.
Many years of strife and bloodshed,
There is peace between the Ojibways
And the tribe of the Dacotahs."
Thus continued Hiawatha,
And then added, speaking slowly,
"That this peace may last forever,
And our hands be clasped more closely,
And our hearts be more united,
Give me as my wife this maiden,
Minnehaha, Laughing Water,
Loveliest of Dacotah women!"

And the ancient Arrow-maker
Paused a moment ere he answered,
Smoked a little while in silence,
Looked at Hiawatha proudly,
Fondly looked at Laughing Water,
And made answer very gravely:
"Yes, if Minnehaha wishes;
Let your heart speak, Minnehaha!"

And the lovely Laughing Water
Seemed more lovely, as she stood there,
Neither willing nor reluctant,
As she went to Hiawatha,
Softly took the seat beside him,
While she said, and blushed to say it,
"I will follow you, my husband!"

This was Hiawatha's wooing!
Thus it was he won the daughter
Of the ancient Arrow-maker,
In the land of the Dacotahs!

From the wigwam he departed,
Leading with him Laughing Water;
Hand in hand they went together,
Through the woodland and the meadow,
Left the old man standing lonely
At the doorway of his wigwam,
Heard the Falls of Minnehaha
Calling to them from the distance,

Crying to them from afar off,
"Fare thee well, O Minnehaha!"
   And the ancient Arrow-maker
Turned again unto his labor,
Sat down by his sunny doorway,
Murmuring to himself, and saying,
"Thus it is our daughters leave us,
Those we love, and those who love us!
Just when they have learned to help us,
When we are old and lean upon them,
Comes a youth with flaunting feathers,
With his flute of reeds, a stranger
Wanders piping through the village,
Beckons to the fairest maiden,
And she follows where he leads her,
Leaving all things for the stranger!"
   Pleasant was the journey homeward,
Through interminable forests,
Over meadow, over mountain,
Over river, hill, and hollow,
Short it seemed to Hiawatha,
Though they journeyed very slowly,
Though his pace he checked and slackened
To the steps of Laughing Water.
   Over wide and rushing rivers
In his arms he bore the maiden;
Light he thought her as a feather,
As the plume upon his head-gear;
Cleared the tangled pathway for her,
Bent aside the swaying branches,
Made at night a lodge of branches,
And a bed with boughs of hemlock,
And a fire before the doorway
With the dry cones of the pine-tree.
   All the travelling winds went with them,
O'er the meadow, through the forest;
All the stars of night looked at them,
Watched with sleepless eyes their slumber;
From his ambush in the oak-tree
Peeped the squirrel, Adjidaumo,
Watched with eager eyes the lovers;
And the rabbit, the Wabasso,

Scampered from the path before them,
Peering, peeping from his burrow,
Sat erect upon his haunches,
Watched with curious eyes the lovers.
    Pleasant was the journey homeward!
All the birds sang loud and sweetly
Songs of happiness and heart's-ease;
Sang the blue-bird, the Owaissa,
"Happy are you, Hiawatha,
Having such a wife to love you!"
Sang the robin, the Opechee,
"Happy are you, Laughing Water,
Having such a noble husband!"
    From the sky the sun benignant
Looked upon them through the branches,
Saying to them, "O my children,
Love is sunshine, hate is shadow,
Life is checkered shade and sunshine,
Rule by love, O Hiawatha!"
    From the sky the moon looked at them,
Filled the lodge with mystic splendors,
Whispered to them, "O my children,
Day is restless, night is quiet,
Man imperious, woman feeble;
Half is mine, although I follow;
Rule by patience, Laughing Water!"
    Thus it was they journeyed homeward;
Thus it was that Hiawatha
To the lodge of old Nokomis
Brought the moonlight, starlight, firelight,
Brought the sunshine of his people,
Minnehaha, Laughing Water,
Handsomest of all the women
In the land of the Dacotahs,
In the land of handsome women.

XI.

HIAWATHA'S WEDDING-FEAST.

You shall hear how Pau-Puk-Keewis
How the handsome Yenadizze
Danced at Hiawatha's wedding;
How the gentle Chibiabos,

He the sweetest of musicians
Sang his songs of love and longing;
How Iagoo, the great boaster,
He the marvellous story-teller,
Told his tales of strange adventure,
That the feast might be more joyous,
That the time might pass more gayly,
And the guests be more contented.

Sumptuous was the feast Nokomis
Made at Hiawatha's wedding;
All the bowls were made of bass-wood,
White and polished very smoothly,
All the spoons of horn of bison,
Black and polished very smoothly.

She had sent through all the village
Messengers with wands of willow,
As a sign of invitation,
As a token of the feasting;
And the wedding guests assembled,
Clad in all their richest raiment,
Robes of fur and belts of wampum,
Splendid with their paint and plumage,
Beautiful with beads and tassels.

First they ate the sturgeon, Nahma,
And the pike, the Maskenozha,
Caught and cooked by old Nokomis;
Then on pemican they feasted,
Pemican and buffalo marrow,
Haunch of deer and hump of bison,
Yellow cakes of the Mondamin,
And the wild rice of the river.

But the gracious Hiawatha,
And the lovely Laughing Water,
And the careful old Nokomis,
Tasted not the food before them,
Only waited on the others,
Only served their guests in silence.

And when all the guests had finished,
Old Nokomis, brisk and busy,
From an ample pouch of otter,
Filled the red stone pipes for smoking
With tobacco from the South-land,

Mixed with bark of the red willow,
And with herbs and leaves of fragrance.
  Then she said, "O Pau-Puk-Keewis,
Dance for us your merry dances,
Dance the Beggar's Dance to please us,
That the feast may be more joyous,
That the time may pass more gayly,
And our guests be more contented!"
  Then the handsome Pau-Puk-Keewis,
He the idle Yenadizze,
He the merry mischief-maker,
Whom the people called the Storm-Fool,
Rose among the guests assembled.
  Skilled was he in sports and pastimes,
In the merry dance of snow-shoes,
In the play of quoits and ball-play;
Skilled was he in games of hazard,
In all games of skill and hazard,
Pugasaing, the Bowl and Counters,
Kuntassoo, the Game of Plum-stones.
  Though the warriors called him Faint-heart,
Called him coward, Shaugodaya,
Idler, gambler, Yenadizze,
Little heeded he their jesting,
Little cared he for their insults,
For the women and the maidens
Loved the handsome Pau-Puk-Keewis.
  He was dressed in shirt of doe-skin,
White and soft, and fringed with ermine,
All inwrought with beads of wampum;
He was dressed in deer-skin leggins,
Fringed with hedgehog quills and ermine,
And in moccasins of buck-skin,
Thick with quills and beads embroidered.
On his head were plumes of swan's down,
On his heels were tails of foxes,
In one hand a fan of feathers,
And a pipe was in the other.
  Barred with streaks of red and yellow,
Streaks of blue and bright vermilion,
Shone the face of Pau-Puk-Keewis.
From his forehead fell his tresses,

Smooth, and parted like a woman's,
Shining bright with oil, and plaited,
Hung with braids of scented grasses,
As among the guests assembled,
To the sound of flutes and singing,
To the sound of drums and voices,
Rose the handsome Pau-Puk-Keewis,
And began his mystic dances.

First he danced a solemn measure,
Very slow in step and gesture,
In and out among the pine-trees,
Through the shadows and the sunshine,
Treading softly like a panther.
Then more swiftly and still swifter,
Whirling, spinning round in circles,
Leaping o'er the guests assembled,
Eddying round and round the wigwam,
Till the leaves went whirling with him,
Till the dust and wind together
Swept in eddies round about him.

Then along the sandy margin
Of the lake, the Big-Sea-Water,
On he sped with frenzied gestures,
Stamped upon the sand, and tossed it
Wildly in the air around him;
Till the wind became a whirlwind,
Till the sand was blown and sifted
Like great snowdrifts o'er the landscape,
Heaping all the shores with Sand Dunes,
Sand Hills of the Nagow Wudjoo!

Thus the merry Pau-Puk-Keewis
Danced his Beggar's Dance to please them,
And, returning, sat down laughing
There among the guests assembled,
Sat and fanned himself serenely
With his fan of turkey-feathers.

Then they said to Chibiabos,
To the friend of Hiawatha,
To the sweetest of all singers,
To the best of all musicians,
"Sing to us, O Chibiabos!
Songs of love and songs of longing,

That the feast may be more joyous,
That the time may pass more gayly,
And our guests be more contented!"
    And the gentle Chibiabos
Sang in accents sweet and tender,
Sang in tones of deep emotion,
Songs of love and songs of longing;
Looking still at Hiawatha,
Looking at fair Laughing Water,
Sang he softly, sang in this wise:
    "Onaway! Awake, beloved!
Thou the wild-flower of the forest!
Thou the wild-bird of the prairie!
Thou with eyes so soft and fawn-like!
    "If thou only lookest at me,
I am happy, I am happy,
As the lilies of the prairie,
When they feel the dew upon them!
    "Sweet thy breath is as the fragrance
Of the wild-flowers in the morning,
As their fragrance is at evening,
In the Moon when leaves are falling.
    "Does not all the blood within me
Leap to meet thee, leap to meet thee,
As the springs to meet the sunshine,
In the Moon when nights are brightest?
    "Onaway! my heart sings to thee,
Sings with joy when thou art near me,
As the sighing, singing branches
In the pleasant Moon of Strawberries!
    "When thou art not pleased, beloved,
Then my heart is sad and darkened,
As the shining river darkens,
When the clouds drop shadows on it!
    "When thou smilest, my beloved,
Then my troubled heart is brightened,
As in sunshine gleam the ripples
That the cold wind makes in rivers.
    "Smiles the earth, and smile the waters,
Smile the cloudless skies above us,
But I lose the way of smiling
When thou art no longer near me!

"I myself, myself! behold me!
Blood of my beating heart, behold me!
O awake, awake, beloved!
Onaway! awake, beloved!"
Thus the gentle Chibiabos
Sang his song of love and longing;
And Iagoo, the great boaster,
He the marvellous story-teller,
He the friend of old Nokomis,
Jealous of the sweet musician,
Jealous of the applause they gave him,
Saw in all the eyes around him,
Saw in all their looks and gestures,
That the wedding guests assembled
Longed to hear his pleasant stories,
His immeasurable falsehoods.

Very boastful was Iagoo;
Never heard he an adventure
But himself had met a greater;
Never any deed of daring
But himself had done a bolder;
Never any marvellous story
But himself could tell a stranger.

Would you listen to his boasting,
Would you only give him credence,
No one ever shot an arrow
Half so far and high as he had;
Ever caught so many fishes,
Ever killed so many reindeer,
Ever trapped so many beaver!

None could run so fast as he could,
None could dive so deep as he could,
None could swim so far as he could;
None had made so many journeys,
None had seen so many wonders,
As this wonderful Iagoo,
As this marvellous story-teller!

Thus his name became a by-word
And a jest among the people;
And whene'er a boastful hunter
Praised his own address too highly,
Or a warrior, home returning,

Talked too much of his achievements,
All his hearers cried, "Iagoo!
Here's Iagoo come among us!"
    He it was who carved the cradle
Of the little Hiawatha,
Carved its framework out of linden,
Bound it strong with reindeer sinews
He it was who taught him later
How to make his bows and arrows,
How to make the bows of ash-tree,
And the arrows of the oak-tree.
So among the guests assembled
At my Hiawatha's wedding
Sat Iagoo, old and ugly,
Sat the marvellous story-teller.
    And they said, "O good Iagoo,
Tell us now a tale of wonder,
Tell us of some strange adventure,
That the feast may be more joyous,
That the time may pass more gayly,
And our guests be more contented!"
    And Iagoo answered straightway,
"You shall hear a tale of wonder,
You shall hear the strange adventures
Of Osseo, the Magician,
From the Evening Star descended."

XII.

THE SON OF THE EVENING STAR.

CAN it be the sun descending
O'er the level plain of water?
Or the Red Swan floating, flying,
Wounded by the magic arrow,
Staining all the waves with crimson,
With the crimson of its life-blood,
Filling all the air with splendor,
With the splendor of its plumage?
    Yes; it is the sun descending,
Sinking down into the water;
All the sky is stained with purple,

All the water flushed with crimson!
No; it is the Red Swan floating,
Diving down beneath the water;
To the sky its wings are lifted,
With its blood the waves are reddened!
    Over it the Star of Evening
Melts and trembles through the purple,
Hangs suspended in the twilight.
No; it is a bead of wampum
On the robes of the Great Spirit,
As he passes through the twilight,
Walks in silence through the heavens!
    This with joy beheld Iagoo
And he said in haste: "Behold it!
See the sacred Star of Evening!
You shall hear a tale of wonder,
Hear the story of Osseo,
Son of the Evening Star, Osseo!
    "Once, in days no more remembered,
Ages nearer the beginning,
When the heavens were closer to us,
And the Gods were more familiar,
In the North-land lived a hunter,
With ten young and comely daughters,
Tall and lithe as wands of willow;
Only Oweenee, the youngest,
She the wilful and the wayward,
She the silent, dreamy maiden,
Was the fairest of the sisters.
    "All these women married warriors,
Married brave and haughty husbands;
Only Oweenee, the youngest,
Laughed and flouted all her lovers,
All her young and handsome suitors,
And then married old Osseo,
Old Osseo, poor and ugly,
Broken with age and weak with coughing,
Always coughing like a squirrel.
    "Ah, but beautiful within him
Was the spirit of Osseo,
From the Evening Star descended,
Star of Evening, Star of Woman,

Star of tenderness and passion!
All its fire was in his bosom,
All its beauty in his spirit,
All its mystery in his being,
All its splendor in his language!
   "And her lovers, the rejected,
Handsome men with belts of wampum,
Handsome men with paint and feathers,
Pointed at her in derision,
Followed her with jest and laughter.
But she said: 'I care not for you,
Care not for your belts of wampum,
Care not for your paint and feathers,
Care not for your jests and laughter;
I am happy with Osseo!'
   "Once, to some great feast invited,
Through the damp and dusk of evening
Walked together the ten sisters,
Walked together with their husbands;
Slowly followed old Osseo,
With fair Oweenee beside him;
All the others chatted gayly,
These two only walked in silence.
   "At the western sky Osseo
Gazed intent, as if imploring,
Often stopped and gazed imploring
At the trembling Star of Evening,
At the tender Star of Woman;
And they heard him murmur softly,
'Ah, showain nemeshin, Nosa!
Pity, pity me, my father!'
   "'Listen!' said the eldest sister,
'He is praying to his father!
What a pity that the old man
Does not stumble in the pathway,
Does not break his neck by falling!'
And they laughed till all the forest
Rang with their unseemly laughter.
   "On their pathway through the woodlands
Lay an oak, by storms uprooted,
Lay the great trunk of an oak-tree,
Buried half in leaves and mosses,

Mouldering, crumbling, huge, and hollow.
And Osseo, when he saw it,
Gave a shout, a cry of anguish,
Leaped into its yawning cavern,
At one end went in an old man,
Wasted, wrinkled, old, and ugly;
From the other came a young man,
Tall and straight and strong and handsome.

"Thus Osseo was transfigured,
Thus restored to youth and beauty;
But, alas for good Osseo,
And for Oweenee, the faithful!
Strangely, too, was she transfigured.
Changed into a weak old woman,
With a staff she tottered onward,
Wasted, wrinkled, old, and ugly!
And the sisters and their husbands
Laughed until the echoing forest
Rang with their unseemly laughter.

"But Osseo turned not from her,
Walked with slower step beside her,
Took her hand, as brown and withered
As an oak-leaf is in Winter,
Called her sweetheart, Nenemoosha,
Soothed her with soft words of kindness,
Till they reached the lodge of feasting,
Till they sat down in the wigwam,
Sacred to the Star of Evening,
To the tender Star of Woman.

"Wrapt in visions, lost in dreaming,
At the banquet sat Osseo;
All were merry, all were happy,
All were joyous but Osseo.
Neither food nor drink he tasted,
Neither did he speak nor listen,
But as one bewildered sat he,
Looking dreamily and sadly,
First at Oweenee, then upward
At the gleaming sky above them.

"Then a voice was heard, a whisper,
Coming from the starry distance,
Coming from the empty vastness,

Low, and musical, and tender;
And the voice said: 'O Osseo!
O my son, my best beloved!
Broken are the spells that bound you,
All the charms of the magicians,
All the magic powers of evil;
Come to me; ascend, Osseo!
　" 'Taste the food that stands before you:
It is blessed and enchanted,
It has magic virtues in it,
It will change you to a spirit.
All your bowls and all your kettles
Shall be wood and clay no longer;
But the bowls be changed to wampum,
And the kettles shall be silver;
They shall shine like shells of scarlet,
Like the fire shall gleam and glimmer.
　" 'And the women shall no longer
Bear the dreary doom of labor,
But be changed to birds, and glisten
With the beauty of the starlight,
Painted with the dusky splendors
Of the skies and clouds of evening!'
　"What Osseo heard as whispers,
What as words he comprehended,
Was but music to the others,
Music as of birds afar off,
Of the whippoorwill afar off,
Of the lonely Wawonaissa
Singing in the darksome forest.
　"Then the lodge began to tremble,
Straight began to shake and tremble,
And they felt it rising, rising,
Slowly through the air ascending,
From the darkness of the tree-tops
Forth into the dewy starlight,
Till it passed the topmost branches;
And behold! the wooden dishes
All were changed to shells of scarlet!
And behold! the earthen kettles
All were changed to bowls of silver!
And the roof-poles of the wigwam

Were as glittering rods of silver,
And the roof of bark upon them
As the shining shards of beetles.
    "Then Osseo gazed around him,
And he saw the nine fair sisters,
All the sisters and their husbands,
Changed to birds of various plumage.
Some were jays and some were magpies,
Others thrushes, others blackbirds;
And they hopped, and sang, and twittered,
Perked and fluttered all their feathers,
Strutted in their shining plumage,
And their tails like fans unfolded.
    "Only Oweenee, the youngest,
Was not changed, but sat in silence,
Wasted, wrinkled, old, and ugly,
Looking sadly at the others;
Till Osseo, gazing upward,
Gave another cry of anguish,
Such a cry as he had uttered
By the oak-tree in the forest.
    "Then returned her youth and beauty,
And her soiled and tattered garments
Were transformed to robes of ermine,
And her staff became a feather,
Yes, a shining silver feather!
    "And again the wigwam trembled,
Swayed and rushed through airy currents,
Through transparent cloud and vapor,
And amid celestial splendors
On the Evening Star alighted,
As a snow-flake falls on snow-flake.
As a leaf drops on a river,
As the thistle-down on water.
    "Forth with cheerful words of welcome
Came the father of Osseo,
He with radiant locks of silver,
He with eyes serene and tender.
And he said: 'My son, Osseo,
Hang the cage of birds you bring there,
Hang the cage with rods of silver,
And the birds with glistening feathers.

At the doorway of my wigwam.'
"At the door he hung the bird-cage,
And they entered in and gladly
Listened to Osseo's father,
Ruler of the Star of Evening,
As he said: 'O my Osseo!
I have had compassion on you,
Given you back your youth and beauty,
Into birds of various plumage
Changed your sisters and their husbands;
Changed them thus because they mocked you
In the figure of the old man,
In that aspect sad and wrinkled,
Could not see your heart of passion,
Could not see your youth immortal;
Only Oweenee, the faithful,
Saw your naked heart and loved you.
" 'In the lodge that glimmers yonder
In the little star that twinkles
Through the vapors, on the left hand,
Lives the envious Evil Spirit,
The Wabeno, the magician,
Who transformed you to an old man,
Take heed lest his beams fall on you,
For the rays he darts around him
Are the power of his enchantment,
Are the arrows that he uses.'
"Many years, in peace and quiet,
On the peaceful Star of Evening
Dwelt Osseo with his father;
Many years, in song and flutter,
At the doorway of the wigwam,
Hung the cage with rods of silver,
And fair Oweenee, the faithful,
Bore a son unto Osseo,
With the beauty of his mother,
With the courage of his father.
"And the boy grew up and prospered,
And Osseo, to delight him,
Made him little bows and arrows,
Opened the great cage of silver,
And let loose his aunts and uncles,

All those birds with glossy feathers,
For his little son to shoot at.
    "Round and round they wheeled and darted,
Filled the Evening Star with music,
With their songs of joy and freedom;
Filled the Evening Star with splendor,
With the fluttering of their plumage;
Till the boy, the little hunter,
Bent his bow and shot an arrow,
Shot a swift and fatal arrow,
And a bird, with shining feathers,
At his feet fell wounded sorely.
    "But, O wondrous transformation!
'T was no bird he saw before him,
'T was a beautiful young woman,
With the arrow in her bosom!
    "When her blood fell on the planet,
On the sacred Star of Evening,
Broken was the spell of magic,
Powerless was the strange enchantment,
And the youth, the fearless bowman,
Suddenly felt himself descending,
Held by unseen hands, but sinking
Downward through the empty spaces,
Downward through the clouds and vapors,
Till he rested on an island,
On an island green and grassy,
Yonder in the Big-Sea-Water.
    "After him he saw descending
All the birds with shining feathers,
Fluttering, falling, wafted downward,
Like the painted leaves of Autumn;
And the lodge with poles of silver,
With its roof like wings of beetles,
Like the shining shards of beetles,
By the winds of heaven uplifted,
Slowly sank upon the island,
Bringing back the good Osseo,
Bringing Oweenee, the faithful.
    "Then the birds, again transfigured,
Reassumed the shape of mortals,
Took their shape, but not their stature;

They remained as Little People,
Like the pygmies, the Puk-Wudjies,
And on pleasant nights of Summer,
When the Evening Star was shining,
Hand in hand they danced together
On the island's craggy headlands,
On the sand-beach low and level.
   "Still their glittering lodge is seen there,
On the tranquil Summer evenings,
And upon the shore the fisher
Sometimes hears their happy voices,
Sees them dancing in the starlight!"
   When the story was completed,
When the wondrous tale was ended,
Looking round upon his listeners,
Solemnly Iagoo added:
"There are great men, I have known such,
Whom their people understand not,
Whom they even make a jest of,
Scoff and jeer at in derision.
From the story of Osseo
Let us learn the fate of jesters!"
   All the wedding guests delighted,
Listened to the marvellous story,
Listened laughing and applauding,
And they whispered to each other,
"Does he mean himself, I wonder?
And are we the aunts and uncles?"
   Then again sang Chibiabos,
Sang a song of love and longing,
In those accents sweet and tender,
In those tones of pensive sadness,
Sang a maiden's lamentation
For her lover, her Algonquin.
   "When I think of my beloved,
Ah me! think of my beloved,
When my heart is thinking of him,
O my sweetheart, my Algonquin!
   "Ah me! when I parted from him,
Round my neck he hung the wampum,
As a pledge, the snow-white wampum,
O my sweetheart, my Algonquin!

"I will go with you, he whispered,
Ah me! to your native country;
Let me go with you, he whispered,
O my sweetheart, my Algonquin!
    "Far away, away, I answered,
Very far away, I answered,
Ah me! is my native country,
O my sweetheart, my Algonquin!
    "When I looked back to behold him,
Where we parted, to behold him,
After me he still was gazing,
O my sweetheart, my Algonquin!
    "By the tree he still was standing,
By the fallen tree was standing,
That had dropped into the water,
O my sweetheart, my Algonquin!
    "When I think of my beloved,
Ah me! think of my beloved,
When my heart is thinking of him,
O my sweetheart, my Algonquin!"
    Such was Hiawatha's Wedding,
Such the dance of Pau-Puk-Keewis,
Such the story of Iagoo,
Such the songs of Chibiabos;
Thus the wedding banquet ended,
And the wedding guests departed,
Leaving Hiawatha happy
With the night and Minnehaha.

XIII.

BLESSING THE CORN-FIELDS.

SING, O Song of Hiawatha,
Of the happy days that followed,
In the land of the Ojibways,
In the pleasant land and peaceful!
Sing the mysteries of Mondamin,
Sing the Blessing of the Corn-fields!
    Buried was the bloody hatchet,
Buried was the dreadful war-club,
Buried were all warlike weapons,
And the war-cry was forgotten.

There was peace among the nations;
Unmolested roved the hunters,
Built the birch-canoe for sailing,
Caught the fish in lake and river,
Shot the deer and trapped the beaver;
Unmolested worked the women,
Made their sugar from the maple,
Gathered wild rice in the meadows,
Dressed the skins of deer and beaver.
　　All around the happy village
Stood the maize-fields, green and shining,
Waved the green plumes of Mondamin,
Waved his soft and sunny tresses,
Filling all the land with plenty.
'T was the women who in Spring-time
Planted the broad fields and fruitful,
Buried in the earth Mondamin;
'T was the women who in Autumn
Stripped the yellow husks of harvest,
Stripped the garments from Mondamin,
Even as Hiawatha taught them.
　　Once, when all the maize was planted,
Hiawatha, wise and thoughtful,
Spake and said to Minnehaha,
To his wife, the Laughing Water:
"You shall bless to-night the corn-fields,
Draw a magic circle round them,
To protect them from destruction,
Blast of mildew, blight of insect,
Wagemin, the thief of corn-fields,
Paimosaid, who steals the maize-ear!
　　"In the night, when all is silence,
In the night, when all is darkness,
When the Spirit of Sleep, Nepahwin,
Shuts the doors of all the wigwams,
So that not an ear can hear you,
So that not an eye can see you,
Rise up from your bed in silence,
Lay aside your garments wholly,
Walk around the fields you planted,
Round the borders of the corn-fields,
Covered by your tresses only,

Robed with darkness as a garment.
    "Thus the fields shall be more fruitful,
And the passing of your footsteps
Draw a magic circle round them,
So that neither blight nor mildew,
Neither burrowing worm nor insect,
Shall pass o'er the magic circle;
Not the dragon-fly, Kwo-ne-she,
Nor the spider, Subbekashe,
Nor the grasshopper, Pah-puk-keena,
Nor the mighty caterpillar,
Way-muk-kwana, with the bear-skin,
King of all the caterpillars!"
    On the tree-tops near the corn-fields
Sat the hungry crows and ravens,
Kahgahgee, the King of Ravens,
With his band of black marauders.
And they laughed at Hiawatha,
Till the tree-tops shook with laughter,
With their melancholy laughter
At the words of Hiawatha.
"Hear him!" said they; "hear the Wise Man!
Hear the plots of Hiawatha!"
    When the noiseless night descended
Broad and dark o'er field and forest,
When the mournful Wawonaissa,
Sorrowing sang among the hemlocks,
And the Spirit of Sleep, Nepahwin,
Shut the doors of all the wigwams,
From her bed rose Laughing Water,
Laid aside her garments wholly,
And with darkness clothed and guarded,
Unashamed and unaffrighted,
Walked securely round the corn-fields,
Drew the sacred, magic circle
Of her footprints round the corn-fields.
    No one but the Midnight only
Saw her beauty in the darkness,
No one but the Wawonaissa
Heard the panting of her bosom;
Guskewau, the darkness, wrapped her
Closely in his sacred mantle,

So that none might see her beauty,
So that none might boast, "I saw her!"
  On the morrow, as the day dawned,
Kahgahgee, the King of Ravens,
Gathered all his black marauders,
Crows and blackbirds, jays and ravens,
Clamorous on the dusky tree-tops,
And descended, fast and fearless,
On the fields of Hiawatha,
On the grave of the Mondamin.
  "We will drag Mondamin," said they,
"From the grave where he is buried,
Spite of all the magic circles
Laughing Water draws around it,
Spite of all the sacred footprints
Minnehaha stamps upon it!"
  But the wary Hiawatha,
Ever thoughtful, careful, watchful,
Had o'erheard the scornful laughter
When they mocked him from the tree-tops.
"Kaw!" he said, "my friends the ravens!
Kahgahgee, my King of Ravens!
I will teach you all a lesson
That shall not be soon forgotten!"
  He had risen before the daybreak,
He had spread o'er all the corn-fields
Snares to catch the black marauders,
And was lying now in ambush
In the neighboring grove of pine-trees,
Waiting for the crows and blackbirds,
Waiting for the jays and ravens.
  Soon they came with caw and clamor,
Rush of wings and cry of voices,
To their work of devastation,
Settling down upon the corn-fields,
Delving deep with beak and talon
For the body of Mondamin,
And with all their craft and cunning,
All their skill in wiles of warfare,
They perceived no danger near them,
Till their claws became entangled,
Till they found themselves imprisoned

In the snares of Hiawatha.

From his place of ambush came he,
Striding terrible among them,
And so awful was his aspect
That the bravest quailed with terror.
Without mercy he destroyed them
Right and left, by tens and twenties,
And their wretched, lifeless bodies
Hung aloft on poles for scarecrows
Round the consecrated corn-fields,
As a signal of his vengeance,
As a warning to marauders.

Only Kahgahgee, the leader,
Kahgahgee, the King of Ravens,
He alone was spared among them
As a hostage for his people.
With his prisoner-string he bound him,
Led him captive to his wigwam,
Tied him fast with cords of elm-bark
To the ridge-pole of his wigwam.

"Kahgahgee, my raven!" said he,
"You the leader of the robbers,
You the plotter of this mischief,
The contriver of this outrage,
I will keep you, I will hold you,
As a hostage for your people,
As a pledge of good behavior!"

And he left him, grim and sulky,
Sitting in the morning sunshine
On the summit of the wigwam,
Croaking fiercely his displeasure,
Flapping his great sable pinions,
Vainly struggling for his freedom,
Vainly calling on his people!

Summer passed, and Shawondasee
Breathed his sighs o'er all the landscape,
From the South-land sent his ardors,
Wafted kisses warm and tender;
And the maize-field grew and ripened,
Till it stood in all the splendor
Of its garments green and yellow,
Of its tassels and its plumage,

And the maize-ears full and shining
Gleamed from bursting sheaths of verdure.
   Then Nokomis, the old woman,
Spake, and said to Minnehaha:
" 'T is the Moon when leaves are falling;
All the wild-rice has been gathered,
And the maize is ripe and ready;
Let us gather in the harvest,
Let us wrestle with Mondamin,
Strip him of his plumes and tassels,
Of his garments green and yellow!"
   And the merry Laughing Water
Went rejoicing from the wigwam,
With Nokomis, old and wrinkled,
And they called the women round them,
Called the young men and the maidens,
To the harvest of the corn-fields,
To the husking of the maize-ear.
   On the border of the forest,
Underneath the fragrant pine-trees,
Sat the old men and the warriors
Smoking in the pleasant shadow.
In uninterrupted silence
Looked they at the gamesome labor
Of the young men and the women;
Listened to their noisy talking,
To their laughter and their singing,
Heard them chattering like the magpies,
Heard them laughing like the bluejays,
Heard them singing like the robins.
   And whene'er some lucky maiden
Found a red ear in the husking,
Found a maize-ear red as blood is,
"Nushka!" cried they all together,
"Nushka! you shall have a sweetheart,
You shall have a handsome husband!"
"Ugh!" the old men all responded
From their seats beneath the pine-trees.
   And whene'er a youth or maiden
Found a crooked ear in husking,
Found a maize-ear in the husking,
Blighted, mildewed, or misshapen,

Then they laughed and sang together,
Crept and limped about the corn-fields,
Mimicked in their gait and gestures
Some old man, bent almost double,
Singing singly or together:
"Wagemin, the thief of corn-fields!
Paimosaid, who steals the maize-ear!"
     Till the corn-fields rang with laughter,
Till from Hiawatha's wigwam
Kahgahgee, the King of Ravens,
Screamed and quivered in his anger,
And from all the neighboring tree-tops
Cawed and croaked the black marauders.
"Ugh!" the old men all responded,
From their seats beneath the pine-trees!

XIV.

PICTURE-WRITING.

In those days said Hiawatha,
"Lo! how all things fade and perish!
From the memory of the old men
Pass away the great traditions,
The achievements of the warriors,
The adventures of the hunters,
All the wisdom of the Medas,
All the craft of the Wabenos,
All the marvellous dreams and visions
Of the Jossakeeds, the Prophets!
     "Great men die and are forgotten,
Wise men speak; their words of wisdom
Perish in the ears that hear them,
Do not reach the generations
That, as yet unborn, are waiting
In the great, mysterious darkness
Of the speechless days that shall be!
     "On the grave-posts of our fathers
Are no signs, no figures painted;
Who are in those graves we know not,
Only know they are our fathers.
Of what kith they are and kindred,

From what old, ancestral Totem,
Be it Eagle, Bear, or Beaver,
They descended, this we know not,
Only know they are our fathers.

"Face to face we speak together,
But we cannot speak when absent,
Cannot send our voices from us
To the friends that dwell afar off;
Cannot send a secret message,
But the bearer learns our secret,
May pervert it, may betray it,
May reveal it unto others."

Thus said Hiawatha, walking
In the solitary forest,
Pondering, musing in the forest,
On the welfare of his people.

From his pouch he took his colors,
Took his paints of different colors,
On the smooth bark of a birch-tree
Painted many shapes and figures
Wonderful and mystic figures,
And each figure had a meaning,
Each some word or thought suggested.

Gitche Manito the Mighty,
He, the Master of Life, was painted
As an egg, with points projecting
To the four winds of the heavens.
Everywhere is the Great Spirit,
Was the meaning of this symbol.

Gitche Manito the Mighty,
He the dreadful Spirit of Evil,
As a serpent was depicted,
As Kenabeek, the great serpent.
Very crafty, very cunning,
Is the creeping Spirit of Evil,
Was the meaning of this symbol.

Life and Death he drew as circles,
Life was white, but Death was darkened;
Sun and moon and stars he painted,
Man and beast, and fish and reptile,
Forests, mountains, lakes, and rivers.

For the earth he drew a straight line,

For the sky a bow above it;
White the space between for day-time,
Filled with little stars for night-time:
On the left a point for sunrise,
On the right a point for sunset,
On the top a point for noon-tide,
And for rain and cloudy weather
Waving lines descending from it.

Footprints pointing towards a **wigwam**
Were a sign of invitation,
Were a sign of guests assembling;
Bloody hands with palms uplifted
Were a symbol of destruction,
Were a hostile sign and symbol.

All these things did Hiawatha
Show unto his wondering people,
And interpreted their meaning,
And he said: "Behold, your grave-posts
Have no mark, no sign, nor symbol.
Go and paint them all with figures;
Each one with its household symbol,
With its own ancestral Totem;
So that those who follow after
May distinguish them and know them."

And they painted on the grave-posts
Of the graves yet unforgotten,
Each his own ancestral Totem,
Each the symbol of his household;
Figures of the Bear and Reindeer,
Of the Turtle, Crane, and Beaver,
Each inverted as a token
That the owner was departed,
That the chief who bore the symbol
Lay beneath in dust and ashes.

And the Jossakeeds, the Prophets,
The Wabenos, the Magicians,
And the Medicine-men, the Medas,
Painted upon bark and deer-skin
Figures for the songs they chanted,
For each song a separate symbol,
Figures mystical and awful,
Figures strange and brightly colored;

And each figure had its meaning,
Each some magic song suggested.
  The Great Spirit, the Creator,
Flashing light through all the heaven;
The Great Serpent, the Kenabeek,
With a bloody crest erected,
Creeping, looking into heaven;
In the sky the sun, that listens,
And the moon eclipsed and dying;
Cwl and eagle, crane and hen-hawk,
And the cormorant, bird of magic;
Headless men, that walk the heavens,
Bodies lying pierced with arrows,
Bloody hands of death uplifted,
Flags on graves, and great war-captains
Grasping both the earth and heaven!
  Such as these the shapes they painted
On the birch-bark and the deer-skin;
Songs of war and songs of hunting,
Songs of medicine and of magic,
All were written in these figures,
For each figure had its meaning,
Each its separate song recorded.
  Nor forgotten was the Love-Song,
The most subtle of all medicines,
The most potent spell of magic,
Dangerous more than war or hunting,
Thus the Love-Song was recorded,
Symbol and interpretation.
  First a human figure standing,
Painted in the brightest scarlet;
'T is the lover, the musician,
And the meaning is, "My painting
Makes me powerful over others."
  Then the figure seated, singing,
Playing on a drum of magic,
And the interpretation, "Listen!
'T is my voice you hear, my singing."
  Then the same red figure seated
In the shelter of a wigwam,
And the meaning of the symbol,
"I will come and sit beside you

In the mystery of my passion!"
    Then two figures, man and woman,
Standing hand in hand together,
With their hands so clasped together
That they seem in one united,
And the words thus represented
Are, "I see your heart within you,
And your cheeks are red with blushes!"
    Next the maiden on an island,
In the centre of an island;
And the song this shape suggested
Was, "Though you were at a distance,
Were upon some far-off island,
Such the spell I cast upon you,
Such the magic power of passion,
I could straightway draw you to me!"
    Then the figure of the maiden
Sleeping, and the lover near her,
Whispering to her in her slumbers,
Saying, "Though you were far from me
In the land of Sleep and Silence,
Still the voice of love would reach you!"
    And the last of all the figures
Was a heart within a circle,
Drawn within a magic circle;
And the image had this meaning:
"Naked lies your heart before me,
To your naked heart I whisper!"
    Thus it was that Hiawatha,
In his wisdom, taught the people
All the mysteries of painting,
All the art of Picture-Writing,
On the smooth bark of the birch-tree,
On the white skin of the reindeer,
On the grave-posts of the village.

XV.

HIAWATHA'S LAMENTATION.

In those days of Evil Spirits,
All the Manitos of mischief,
Fearing Hiawatha's wisdom,

And his love for Chibiabos,
Jealous of their faithful friendship,
And their noble words and actions,
Made at length a league against them,
To molest them and destroy them.
    Hiawatha, wise and wary,
Often said to Chibiabos,
"O my brother! do not leave me,
Lest the Evil Spirits harm you!"
Chibiabos, young and heedless,
Laughing shook his coal-black tresses,
Answered ever sweet and childlike,
"Do not fear for me, O brother!
Harm and evil come not near me!"
    Once when Peboan, the Winter,
Roofed with ice the Big-Sea-Water,
When the snow-flakes, whirling downward,
Hissed among the withered oak-leaves,
Changed the pine-trees into wigwams,
Covered all the earth with silence,—
Armed with arrows, shod with snow-shoes,
Heeding not his brother's warning,
Fearing not the Evil Spirits,
Forth to hunt the deer with antlers
All alone went Chibiabos.
    Right across the Big-Sea-Water
Sprang with speed the deer before him.
With the wind and snow he followed,
O'er the treacherous ice he followed,
Wild with all the fierce commotion
And the rapture of the hunting.
    But beneath, the Evil Spirits
Lay in ambush, waiting for him,
Broke the treacherous ice beneath him,
Dragged him downward to the bottom,
Buried in the sand his body.
Unktahee, the god of water,
He the god of the Dacotahs,
Drowned him in the deep abysses
Of the lake of Gitche Gumee.
    From the headlands Hiawatha
Sent forth such a wail of anguish,

Such a fearful lamentation,
That the bison paused to listen,
And the wolves howled from the prairies,
And the thunder in the distance
Starting answered "Baim-wawa!"
    Then his face with black he painted,
With his robe his head he covered,
In his wigwam sat lamenting,
Seven long weeks he sat lamenting,
Uttering still this moan of sorrow:—
    "He is dead, the sweet musician!
He the sweetest of all singers!
He has gone from us forever,
He has moved a little nearer
To the Master of all music,
To the Master of all singing!
O my brother, Chibiabos!"
    And the melancholy fir-trees
Waved their dark green fans above him,
Waved their purple cones above him,
Sighing with him to console him,
Mingling with his lamentation
Their complaining, their lamenting.
    Came the Spring, and all the forest
Looked in vain for Chibiabos;
Sighed the rivulet, Sebowisha,
Sighed the rushes in the meadow.
    From the tree-tops sang the blue-bird,
Sang the blue-bird, the Owaissa,
"Chibiabos! Chibiabos!
He is dead, the sweet musician!"
    From the wigwam sang the robin,
Sang the robin, the Opechee,
"Chibiabos! Chibiabos!
He is dead, the sweetest singer!"
    And at night through all the forest
Went the whippoorwill complaining,
Wailing went the Wawonaissa,
"Chibiabos! Chibiabos!
He is dead, the sweet musician!
He the sweetest of all singers!"
    Then the Medicine-men, the Medas,

The Magicians, the Wabenos,
And the Jossakeeds, the Prophets,
Came to visit Hiawatha;
Built a Sacred Lodge beside him,
To appease him, to console him,
Walked in silent, grave procession,
Bearing each a pouch of healing,
Skin of beaver, lynx, or otter,
Filled with magic roots and simples,
Filled with very potent medicines.

When he heard their steps approaching
Hiawatha ceased lamenting,
Called no more on Chibiabos;
Naught he questioned, naught he answered,
But his mournful head uncovered,
From his face the mourning colors
Washed he slowly and in silence,
Slowly and in silence followed
Onward to the Sacred Wigwam.

There a magic drink they gave him,
Made of Nahma-wusk, the spearmint,
And Wabeno-wusk, the yarrow,
Roots of power, and herbs of healing;
Beat their drums, and shook their rattles:
Chanted singly and in chorus,
Mystic songs like these, they chanted.

"I myself, myself! behold me!
'T is the great Gray Eagle talking;
Come, ye white crows, come and hear him!
The loud-speaking thunder helps me;
All the unseen spirits help me;
I can hear their voices calling,
All around the sky I hear them!
I can blow you strong, my brother,
I can heal you, Hiawatha!"

"Hi-au-ha!" replied the chorus,
"Way-ha-way!" the mystic chorus.

"Friends of mine are all the serpents!
Hear me shake my skin of hen-hawk!
Mahng, the white loon, I can kill him;
I can shoot your heart and kill it!

I can blow you strong, my brother,
I can heal you, Hiawatha!"
   "Hi-au-ha!" replied the chorus,
"Way-ha-way!" the mystic chorus.
   "I myself, myself! the prophet!
When I speak the wigwam trembles,
Shakes the Sacred Lodge with terror,
Hands unseen begin to shake it!
When I walk, the sky I tread on
Bends and makes a noise beneath me.
I can blow you strong, my brother!
Rise and speak, O Hiawatha!"
   "Hi-au-ha!" replied the chorus,
"Way-ha-way!" the mystic chorus.
   Then they shook their medicine-pouches
O'er the head of Hiawatha,
Danced their medicine-dance around him,
And upstarting wild and haggard,
Like a man from dreams awakened,
He was healed of all his madness.
As the clouds are swept from heaven,
Straightway from his brain departed
All his moody melancholy;
As the ice is swept from rivers,
Straightway from his heart departed
All his sorrow and affliction.
   Then they summoned Chibiabos
From his grave beneath the waters,
From the sands of Gitche Gumee
Summoned Hiawatha's brother.
And so mighty was the magic
Of that cry and invocation,
That he heard it as he lay there
Underneath the Big-Sea-Water;
From the sand he rose and listened,
Heard the music and the singing,
Came, obedient to the summons,
To the doorway of the wigwam,
But to enter they forbade him.
   Through a chink a coal they gave him,
Through the door a burning fire-brand;
Ruler in the Land of Spirits,

Ruler o'er the dead, they made him,
Telling him a fire to kindle
For all those that died thereafter,
Camp-fires for their night encampments
On their solitary journey
To the kingdom of Ponemah,
To the land of the Hereafter.

From the village of his childhood,
From the homes of those who knew him,
Passing silent through the forest,
Like a smoke-wreath wafted sideways,
Slowly vanished Chibiabos!
Where he passed, the branches moved not,
Where he trod, the grasses bent not,
And the fallen leaves of last year
Made no sound beneath his footsteps.

Four whole days he journeyed onward
Down the pathway of the dead men;
On the dead man's strawberry feasted,
Crossed the melancholy river,
On the swinging log he crossed it,
Came unto the Lake of Silver,
In the Stone Canoe was carried
To the Islands of the Blessed,
To the land of ghosts and shadows.

On that journey, moving slowly,
Many weary spirits saw he,
Panting under heavy burdens,
Laden with war-clubs, bows, and arrows,
Robes of fur, and pots and kettles,
And with food that friends had given
From that solitary journey.

"Ah! why do the living," said they,
"Lay such heavy burdens on us!
Better were it to go naked,
Better were it to go fasting,
Than to bear such heavy burdens
On our long and weary journey!"

Forth then issued Hiawatha,
Wandered eastward, wandered westward,
Teaching men the use of simples
And the antidotes for poisons,

And the cure of all diseases.
Thus was first made known to mortals
All the mystery of Medamin,
All the sacred art of healing.

XVI.

PAU-PUK-KEEWIS.

You shall hear how Pau-Puk-Keewis,
He, the handsome Yenadizze,
Whom the people called the Storm Fool,
Vexed the village with disturbance;
You shall hear of all his mischief,
And his flight from Hiawatha,
And his wondrous transmigrations,
And the end of his adventures.

On the shores of Gitche Gumee,
On the dunes of Nagow Wudjoo,
By the shining Big-Sea-Water
Stood the lodge of Pau-Puk-Keewis.
It was he who in his frenzy
Whirled these drifting sands together,
On the dunes of Nagow Wudjoo,
When, among the guests assembled,
He so merrily and madly
Danced at Hiawatha's wedding,
Danced the Beggar's Dance to please them.

Now, in search of new adventures,
From his lodge went Pau-Puk-Keewis,
Came with speed into the village,
Found the young men all assembled
In the lodge of old Iagoo,
Listening to his monstrous stories,
To his wonderful adventures.

He was telling them the story
Of Ojeeg, the Summer-Maker,
How he made a hole in heaven,
How he climbed up into heaven,
And let out the Summer-weather,
The perpetual, pleasant Summer;
How the Otter first essayed it;

How the Beaver, Lynx, and Badger
Tried in turn the great achievement,
From the summit of the mountain
Smote their fists against the heavens,
Smote against the sky their foreheads,
Cracked the sky, but could not break it;
How the Wolverine, uprising,
Made him ready for the encounter,
Bent his knees down, like a squirrel,
Drew his arms back, like a cricket.

"Once he leaped," said old Iagoo,
"Once he leaped, and lo! above him
Bent the sky, as ice in rivers
When the waters rise beneath it;
Twice he leaped, and lo! above him
Cracked the sky, as ice in rivers
When the freshet is at highest!
Thrice he leaped, and lo! above him
Broke the shattered sky asunder,
And he disappeared within it,
And Ojeeg, the Fisher Weasel,
With a bound went in behind him!"

"Hark you!" shouted Pau-Puk-Keewis,
As he entered at the doorway;
"I am tired of all this talking,
Tired of old Iagoo's stories,
Tired of Hiawatha's wisdom.
Here is something to amuse you,
Better than this endless talking."

Then from out his pouch of wolf-skin
Forth he drew, with solemn manner,
All the game of Bowl and Counters,
Pugasaing, with thirteen pieces.
White on one side were they painted,
And vermilion on the other;
Two Kenabeeks or great serpents,
Two Ininewug or wedge-men,
One great war-club, Pugamaugun,
And one slender fish, the Keego,
Four round pieces, Ozawabeeks,
And three Sheshebwug or ducklings.
All were made of bone and painted,

All except the Ozawabeeks;
These were brass, on one side burnished,
And were black upon the other.
　In a wooden bowl he placed them,
Shook and jostled them together,
Threw them on the ground before him,
Thus exclaiming and explaining:
"Red side up are all the pieces,
And one great Kenabeek standing
On the bright side of a brass piece,
On a burnished Ozawabeek;
Thirteen tens and eight are counted."
　Then again he shook the pieces,
Shook and jostled them together,
Threw them on the ground before him,
Still exclaiming and explaining:
"White are both the great Kenabeeks,
White the Ininewug, the wedge-men,
Red are all the other pieces;
Five tens and an eight are counted."
　Thus he taught the game of hazard,
Thus displayed it and explained it,
Running through its various chances,
Various changes, various meanings.
Twenty curious eyes stared at him,
Full of eagerness stared at him.
　"Many games," said old Iagoo,
"Many games of skill and hazard
Have I seen in different nations,
Have I played in different countries.
He who plays with old Iagoo
Must have very nimble fingers;
Though you think yourself so skilful,
I can beat you, Pau-Puk-Keewis,
I can even give you lessons
In your game of Bowl and Counters!"
　So they sat and played together,
All the old men and the young men,
Played for dresses, weapons, wampum,
Played till midnight, played till morning,
Played until the Yenadizze,
Till the cunning Pau-Puk-Keewis,

Of their treasures had despoiled them,
Of the best of all their dresses,
Shirts of deer-skin, robes of ermine,
Belts of wampum, crests of feathers,
Warlike weapons, pipes and pouches.
Twenty eyes glared wildly at him,
Like the eyes of wolves glared at him.
   Said the lucky Pau-Puk-Keewis:
"In my wigwam I am lonely,
In my wanderings and adventures
I have need of a companion,
Fain would have a Meshinauwa,
An attendant and pipe-bearer.
I will venture all these winnings,
All these garments heaped about me,
All this wampum, all these feathers,
On a single throw will venture
All against the young man yonder!"
'T was a youth of sixteen summers,
'T was a nephew of Iagoo;
Face-in-a-Mist, the people called him.
   As the fire burns in a pipe-head
Dusky red beneath the ashes,
So beneath his shaggy eyebrows
Glowed the eyes of old Iagoo.
"Ugh!" he answered very fiercely;
"Ugh!" they answered all and each one.
   Seized the wooden bowl the old man,
Closely in his bony fingers
Clutched the fatal bowl, Onagon,
Shook it fiercely and with fury,
Made the pieces ring together
As he threw them down before him.
   Red were both the great Kenabeeks,
Red the Ininewug, the wedge-men,
Red the Sheshebwug, the ducklings,
Black the four brass Ozawabeeks,
White alone the fish, the Keego;
Only five the pieces counted!
   Then the smiling Pau-Puk-Keewis
Shook the bowl and threw the pieces;
Lightly in the air he tossed them,

And they fell about him scattered;
Dark and bright the Ozawabeeks
Red and white the other pieces,
And upright among the others
One Ininewug was standing,
Even as crafty Pau-Puk-Keewis
Stood alone among the players
Saying, "Five tens! mine the game is!"
    Twenty eyes glared at him fiercely
Like the eyes of wolves glared at him,
As he turned and left the wigwam,
Followed by his Meshinauwa,
By the nephew of Iagoo,
By the tall and graceful stripling,
Bearing in his arms the winnings,
Shirts of deer-skin, robes of ermine,
Belts of wampum, pipes and weapons.
    "Carry them," said Pau-Puk-Keewis,
Pointing with his fan of feathers,
"To my wigwam far to eastward,
On the dunes of Nagow Wudjoo!"
    Hot and red with smoke and gambling
Were the eyes of Pau-Puk-Keewis
As he came forth to the freshness
Of the pleasant Summer morning.
All the birds were singing gayly,
All the streamlets flowing swiftly,
And the heart of Pau-Puk-Keewis
Sang with pleasure as the birds sing,
Beat with triumph like the streamlets,
As he wandered through the village,
In the early gray of morning,
With his fan of turkey-feathers,
With his plumes and tufts of swan's down,
Till he reached the farthest wigwam,
Reached the lodge of Hiawatha.
    Silent was it and deserted;
No one met him at the doorway,
No one came to bid him welcome;
But the birds were singing round it,
In and out and round the doorway,
Hopping, singing, fluttering, feeding,

And aloft upon the ridge-pole
Kahgahgee, the King of Ravens,
Sat with fiery eyes, and, screaming,
Flapped his wings at Pau-Puk-Keewis.
   "All are gone! the lodge is empty!"
Thus it was spake Pau-Puk-Keewis,
In his heart resolving mischief;
"Gone is wary Hiawatha,
Gone the silly Laughing Water,
Gone Nokomis, the old woman,
And the lodge is left unguarded!"
   By the neck he seized the raven,
Whirled it round him like a rattle,
Like a medicine-pouch he shook it,
Strangled Kahgahgee, the raven,
From the ridge-pole of the wigwam
Left its lifeless body hanging,
As an insult to its master,
As a taunt to Hiawatha.
   With a stealthy step he entered,
Round the lodge in wild disorder
Threw the household things about him,
Piled together in confusion
Bowls of wood and earthen kettles,
Robes of buffalo and beaver,
Skins of otter, lynx, and ermine,
As an insult to Nokomis,
As a taunt to Minnehaha.
   Then departed Pau-Puk-Keewis,
Whistling, singing through the forest,
Whistling gayly to the squirrels,
Who from hollow boughs above him
Dropped their acorn-shells upon him,
Singing gayly to the wood-birds,
Who from out the leafy darkness
Answered with a song as merry.
   Then he climbed the rocky head-lands,
Looking o'er the Gitche Gumee,
Perched himself upon their summit,
Waiting full of mirth and mischief
The return of Hiawatha.
   Stretched upon his back he lay there;

Far below him plashed the waters,
Plashed and washed the dreamy waters;
Far above him swam the heavens,
Swam the dizzy, dreamy heavens;
Round him hovered, fluttered, rustled,
Hiawatha's mountain chickens,
Flock-wise swept and wheeled about him,
Almost brushed him with their pinions.

And he killed them as he lay there,
Slaughtered them by tens and twenties,
Threw their bodies down the head-land,
Threw them on the beach below him,
Till at length Kayoshk, the sea-gull,
Perched upon a crag above them,
Shouted: "It is Pau-Puk-Keewis!
He is slaying us by hundreds!
Send a message to our brother,
Tidings send to Hiawatha!"

XVII.

THE HUNTING OF PAU-PUK-KEEWIS.

FULL of wrath was Hiawatha
When he came into the village,
Found the people in confusion,
Heard of all the misdemeanors,
All the malice and the mischief,
Of the cunning Pau-Puk-Keewis.

Hard his breath came through his nostrils,
Through his teeth he buzzed and muttered
Words of anger and resentment,
Hot and humming, like a hornet.
"I will slay this Pau-Puk-Keewis,
Slay this mischief-maker!" said he.
"Not so long and wide the world is,
Not so rude and rough the way is,
That my wrath shall not attain him,
That my vengeance shall not reach him!"

Then in swift pursuit departed
Hiawatha and the hunters
On the trail of Pau-Puk-Keewis.

Through the forest, where he passed it,
To the headlands where he rested;
But they found not Pau-Puk-Keewis.
Only in the trampled grasses,
In the whortleberry-bushes,
Found the couch where he had rested.
Found the impress of his body.

From the lowlands far beneath them,
From the Muskoday, the meadow,
Pau-Puk-Keewis, turning backward,
Made a gesture of defiance,
Made a gesture of derision;
And aloud cried Hiawatha,
From the summit of the mountain:
"Not so long and wide the world is,
Not so rude and rough the way is,
But my wrath shall overtake you,
And my vengeance shall attain you!"

Over rock and over river,
Through bush, and brake, and forest,
Ran the cunning Pau-Puk-Keewis;
Like an antelope he bounded,
Till he came unto a streamlet
In the middle of the forest,
To a streamlet still and tranquil,
That had overflowed its margin,
To a dam made by the beavers,
To a pond of quiet water,
Where knee-deep the trees were standing,
Where the water-lilies floated,
Where the rushes waved and whispered.

On the dam stood Pau-Puk-Keewis,
On the dam of trunks and branches.
Through whose chinks the water spouted,
O'er whose summit flowed the streamlet
From the bottom rose a beaver,
Looked with two great eyes of wonder,
Eyes that seemed to ask a question,
At the stranger, Pau-Puk-Keewis.

On the dam stood Pau-Puk-Keewis,
O'er his ankles flowed the streamlet,
Flowed the bright and silvery water,

And he spake unto the beaver,
With a smile he spake in this wise:
"O my friend Ahmeek, the beaver,
Cool and pleasant is the water;
Let me dive into the water,
Let me rest there in your lodges;
Change me, too, into a beaver!"
    Cautiously replied the beaver,
With reserve he thus made answer:
"Let me first consult the others,
Let me ask the other beavers."
Down he sank into the water,
Heavily sank he, as a stone sinks,
Down among the leaves and branches,
Brown and matted at the bottom.
    On the dam stood Pau-Puk-Keewis,
O'er his ankles flowed the streamlet,
Spouted through the chinks below him,
Dashed upon the stones beneath him,
Spread serene and calm before him,
And the sunshine and the shadows
Fell in flecks and gleams upon him,
Fell in little shining patches,
Through the waving, rustling branches.
    From the bottom rose the beavers,
Silently above the surface
Rose one head and then another,
Till the pond seemed full of beavers
Full of black and shining faces.
    To the beavers Pau-Puk-Keewis
Spake entreating, said in this wise:
"Very pleasant is your dwelling,
O my friends! and safe from danger;
Can you not with all your cunning,
All your wisdom and contrivance,
Change me, too, into a beaver?"
    "Yes!" replied Ahmeek, the beaver,
He the King of all the beavers,
"Let yourself slide down among us,
Down into the tranquil water."
    Down into the pond among them
Silently sank Pau-Puk-Keewis;

Black became his shirt of deer-skin,
Black his moccasins and leggings,
In a broad black tail behind him
Spread his fox-tails and his fringes;
He was changed into a beaver.
   "Make me large," said Pau-Puk-Keewis,
"Make me large and make me larger,
Larger than the other beavers."
   "Yes," the beaver chief responded,
"When our lodge below you enter,
In our wigwam we will make you
Ten times larger than the others."
   Thus into the clear, brown water
Silently sank Pau-Puk-Keewis;
Found the bottom covered over
With the trunks of trees and branches,
Hoards of food against the winter,
Piles and heaps against the famine,
Found the lodge with arching doorway,
Leading into spacious chambers.
   Here they made him large and larger,
Made him largest of the beavers,
Ten times larger than the others.
"You shall be our ruler," said they;
"Chief and king of all the beavers."
   But not long had Pau-Puk-Keewis
Sat in state among the beavers,
When there came a voice of warning
From the watchman at his station
In the water-flags and lilies,
Saying, "Here is Hiawatha!
Hiawatha with his hunters!"
   Then they heard a cry above them,
Heard a shouting and a tramping,
Heard a crashing and a rushing,
And the water round and o'er them
Sank and sucked away in eddies,
And they knew their dam was broken.
   On the lodge's roof the hunters
Leaped, and broke it all asunder;
Streamed the sunshine through the crevice,
Sprang the beavers through the doorway,

Hid themselves in deeper water,
In the channel of the streamlet;
But the mighty Pau-Puk-Keewis
Could not pass beneath the doorway;
He was puffed with pride and feeding,
He was swollen like a bladder.

Through the roof looked Hiawatha,
Cried aloud, "O Pau-Puk-Keewis!
Vain are all your craft and cunning,
Vain your manifold disguises!
Well I know you, Pau-Puk-Keewis!"

With their clubs they beat and bruised him,
Beat to death poor Pau-Puk-Keewis,
Pounded him as maize is pounded,
Till his skull was crushed to pieces.

Six tall hunters, lithe and limber,
Bore him home on poles and branches,
Bore the body of the beaver;
But the ghost, the Jeebi in him,
Thought and felt as Pau-Puk-Keewis,
Still lived on as Pau-Puk-Keewis.

And it fluttered, strove, and struggled,
Waving hither, waving thither,
As the curtains of a wigwam
Struggle with their thongs of deer-skin,
When the wintry wind is blowing;
Till it drew itself together,
Till it rose up from the body,
Till it took the form and features
Of the cunning Pau-Puk-Keewis,
Vanishing into the forest.

But the wary Hiawatha
Saw the figure ere it vanished,
Saw the form of Pau-Puk-Keewis
Glide into the soft blue shadow
Of the pine-trees of the forest;
Toward the squares of white beyond it,
Toward an opening in the forest,
Like a wind it rushed and panted,
Bending all the boughs before it,
And behind it, as the rain comes,
Came the steps of Hiawatha.

To a lake with many islands
Came the breathless Pau-Puk-Keewis,
Where among the water-lilies
Pishnekuh, the brant, were sailing;
Through the tufts of rushes floating,
Steering through the reedy islands.
Now their broad black beaks they lifted,
Now they plunged beneath the water,
Now they darkened in the shadow,
Now they brightened in the sunshine.
"Pishnekuh!" cried Pau-Puk-Keewis,
"Pishnekuh! my brothers!" said he,
"Change me to a brant with plumage,
With a shining neck and feathers,
Make me large, and make me larger,
Ten times larger than the others."
Straightway to a brant they changed him,
With two huge and dusky pinions,
With a bosom smooth and rounded.
With a bill like two great paddles,
Made him larger than the others,
Ten times larger than the largest,
Just as, shouting from the forest,
On the shore stood Hiawatha.
Up they rose with cry and clamor,
With a whir and beat of pinions,
Rose up from the reedy islands,
From the water-flags and lilies.
And they said to Pau-Puk-Keewis:
"In your flying, look not downward,
Take good heed, and look not downward,
Lest some strange mischance should happen,
Lest some great mishap befall you!"
Fast and far they fled to northward,
Fast and far through mist and sunshine,
Fed among the moors and fen-lands,
Slept among the reeds and rushes.
On the morrow as they journeyed,
Buoyed and lifted by the South-wind,
Wafted onward by the South-wind,
Blowing fresh and strong behind them,
Rose a sound of human voices,

Rose a clamor from beneath them,
From the lodges of a village,
From the people miles beneath them.
    For the people of the village
Saw the flock of brant with wonder,
Saw the wings of Pau-Puk-Keewis
Flapping far up in the ether,
Broader than two doorway curtains.
    Pau-Puk-Keewis heard the shouting,
Knew the voice of Hiawatha,
Knew the outcry of Iagoo,
And, forgetful of the warning,
Drew his neck in, and looked downward,
And the wind that blew behind him
Caught his mighty fan of feathers,
Sent him wheeling, whirling downward!
    All in vain did Pau-Puk-Keewis
Struggle to regain his balance!
Whirling round and round and downward,
He beheld in turn the village
And in turn the flock above him,
Saw the village coming nearer,
And the flock receding farther,
Heard the voices growing louder,
Heard the shouting and the laughter;
Saw no more the flock above him,
Only saw the earth beneath him;
Dead out of the empty heaven,
Dead among the shouting people,
With a heavy sound and sullen,
Fell the brant with broken pinions.
    But his soul, his ghost, his shadow,
Still survived as Pau-Puk-Keewis,
Took again the form and features
Of the handsome Yenadizze,
And again went rushing onward,
Followed fast by Hiawatha,
Crying: "Not so wide the world is,
Not so long and rough the way is,
But my wrath shall overtake you,
But my vengeance shall attain you!"
    And so near he came, so near him,

That his hand was stretched to seize him,
His right hand to seize and hold him,
When the cunning Pau-Puk-Keewis
Whirled and spun about in circles,
Fanned the air into a whirlwind,
Danced the dust and leaves about him,
And amid the whirling eddies
Sprang into a hollow oak-tree,
Changed himself into a serpent,
Gliding out through root and rubbish.
   With his right hand Hiawatha
Smote amain the hollow oak-tree,
Rent it into shreds and splinters,
Left it lying there in fragments.
But in vain; for Pau-Puk-Keewis,
Once again in human figure,
Full in sight ran on before him,
Sped away in gust and whirlwind,
On the shores of Gitche Gumee,
Westward by the Big-Sea-Water,
Came unto the rocky headlands,
To the Pictured Rocks of sandstone
Looking over lake and landscape.
   And the Old Man of the Mountain,
He the Manito of Mountains,
Opened wide his rocky doorways,
Opened wide his deep abysses,
Giving Pau-Puk-Keewis shelter
In his caverns dark and dreary,
Bidding Pau-Puk-Keewis welcome
To his gloomy lodge of sandstone.
   There without stood Hiawatha,
Found the doorways closed against him,
With his mittens, Minjekahwun,
Smote great caverns in the sandstone,
Cried aloud in tones of thunder,
"Open! I am Hiawatha!"
But the Old Man of the Mountain
Opened not, and made no answer
From the silent crags of sandstone,
From the gloomy rock abysses.
   Then he raised his hands to heaven,

Called imploring on the tempest,
Called Waymassimo, the lightning,
And the thunder, Annemeekee;
And they came with night and darkness,
Sweeping down the Big-Sea-Water
From the distant Thunder Mountains;
And the trembling Pau-Puk-Keewis
Heard the footsteps of the thunder,
Saw the red eyes of the lightning,
Was afraid, and crouched and trembled.

Then Waywassimo, the lightning,
Smote the doorways of the caverns,
With his war-club smote the doorways,
Smote the jutting crags of sandstone,
And the thunder, Annemeekee,
Shouted down into the caverns,
Saying, "Where is Pau-Puk-Keewis!"
And the crags fell, and beneath them
Dead among the rocky ruins
Lay the cunning Pau-Puk-Keewis,
Lay the handsome Yenadizze,
Slain in his own human figure.

Ended were his wild adventures,
Ended were his tricks and gambols,
Ended all his craft and cunning,
Ended all his mischief-making,
All his gambling and his dancing,
All his wooing of the maidens.

Then the noble Hiawatha
Took his soul, his ghost, his shadow,
Spake and said: "O Pau-Puk-Keewis!
Never more in human figure
Shall you search for new adventures;
Never more with jest and laughter
Dance the dust and leaves in whirlwinds;
But above there in the heavens
You shall soar and sail in circles;
I will change you to an eagle,
To Keneu, the great war-eagle,
Chief of all the fowls with feathers,
Chief of Hiawatha's chickens."

And the name of Pau-Puk-Keewis

Lingers still among the people,
Lingers still among the singers,
And among the story-tellers;
And in Winter, when the snow-flakes
Whirl in eddies round the lodges,
When the wind in gusty tumult
O'er the smoke-flue pipes and whistles,
"There," they cry, "comes Pau-Puk-Keewis;
He is dancing through the village,
He is gathering in his harvest!"

XVIII.

THE DEATH OF KWASIND.

FAR and wide among the nations
Spread the name and fame of Kwasind;
No man dared to strive with Kwasind,
No man could compete with Kwasind.
But the mischievous Puk-Wudjies,
They the envious Little People,
They the fairies and the pygmies,
Plotted and conspired against him.
   "If this hateful Kwasind," said they,
"If this great, outrageous fellow
Goes on thus a little longer,
Tearing everything he touches,
Rending everything to pieces,
Filling all the world with wonder,
What becomes of the Puk-Wudjies?
Who will care for the Puk-Wudjies?
He will tread us down like mushrooms,
Drive us all into the water,
Give our bodies to be eaten
By the wicked Nee-ba-naw-baigs,
By the Spirits of the water!"
   So the angry Little People
All conspired against the Strong Man,
All conspired to murder Kwasind,
Yes, to rid the world of Kwasind,
The audacious, overbearing,
Heartless, haughty, dangerous Kwasind!

Now this wondrous strength of Kwasind
In his crown alone was seated;
In his crown too was his weakness;
There alone could he be wounded,
Nowhere else could weapon pierce him,
Nowhere else could weapon harm him.

Even there the only weapon
That could wound him, that could slay him,
Was the seed-cone of the pine-tree,
Was the blue cone of the fir-tree.
This was Kwasind's fatal secret,
Known to no man among mortals;
But the cunning Little People,
The Puk-Wudjies, knew the secret,
Knew the only way to kill him.

So they gathered cones together,
Gathered seed-cones of the pine-tree,
Gathered blue cones of the fir-tree,
In the woods by Taquamenaw,
Brought them to the river's margin,
Heaped them in great piles together,
Where the red rocks from the margin
Jutting overhang the river.
There they lay in wait for Kwasind,
The malicious Little People.

'T was an afternoon in Summer;
Very hot and still the air was,
Very smooth the gliding river,
Motionless the sleeping shadows;
Insects glistened in the sunshine,
Insects skated on the water,
Filled the drowsy air with buzzing,
With a far-resounding war-cry.

Down the river came the Strong Man,
In his birch-canoe came Kwasind,
Floating slowly down the current
Of the sluggish Taquamenaw,
Very languid with the weather,
Very sleepy with the silence.

From the overhanging branches,
From the tassels of the birch-trees,
Soft the Spirit of Sleep descended;

By his airy hosts surrounded,
His invisible attendants,
Came the Spirit of Sleep, Nepahwin;
Like the burnished Dush-kwo-ne-she,
Like a dragon-fly, he hovered
O'er the drowsy head of Kwasind.

To his ear there came a murmur
As of waves upon a sea-shore,
As of far-off tumbling waters,
As of winds among the pine-trees;
And he felt upon his forehead
Blows of little airy war-clubs,
Wielded by the slumbrous legions
Of the Spirit of Sleep, Nepahwin,
As of some one breathing on him.

At the first blow of their war-clubs
Fell a drowsiness on Kwasind;
At the second blow they smote him,
Motionless his paddle rested;
At the third, before his vision,
Reeled the landscape into darkness,
Very sound asleep was Kwasind.

So he floated down the river,
Like a blind man seated upright,
Floated down the Taquamenaw,
Underneath the trembling birch-trees,
Underneath the wooded headlands,
Underneath the war encampment
Of the pygmies, the Puk-Wudjies.

There they stood, all armed and waiting,
Hurled the pine-cones down upon him,
Struck him on his brawny shoulders,
On his crown defenceless struck him.
"Death to Kwasind!" was the sudden
War-cry of the Little People.

And he sideways swayed and tumbled,
Sideways fell into the river,
Plunged beneath the sluggish water
Headlong, as an otter plunges;
And the birch-canoe, abandoned,
Drifted empty down the river,
Bottom upward swerved and drifted:

Nothing more was seen of Kwasind.
    But the memory of the Strong Man
Lingered long among the people,
And whenever through the forest
Raged and roared the wintry tempest,
And the branches, tossed and troubled,
Creaked and groaned and split asunder,
"Kwasind!" cried they; "that is Kwasind!
He is gathering in his fire-wood!"

XIX.

THE GHOSTS.

Never stoops the soaring vulture
On his quarry in the desert,
On the sick or wounded bison,
But another vulture, watching
From his high aerial look-out,
Sees the downward plunge, and follows;
And a third pursues the second,
Coming from the invisible ether,
First a speck, and then a vulture,
Till the air is dark with pinions.
    So disasters come not singly;
But as if they watched and waited,
Scanning one another's motions,
When the first descends, the others
Follow, follow, gathering flock-wise
Round their victim, sick and wounded,
First a shadow, then a sorrow,
Till the air is dark with anguish.
    Now, o'er all the dreary Northland,
Mighty Peboan, the Winter,
Breathing on the lakes and rivers,
Into stone had changed their waters.
From his hair he shook the snowflakes,
Till the plains were strewn with whiteness,
One uninterrupted level
As if, stooping, the Creator
With his hand had smoothed them over.
    Through the forest, wide and wailing,

Roamed the hunter on his snow-shoes;
In the village worked the women,
Pounded maize, or dressed the deer-skin;
And the young men played together
On the ice the noisy ball-play,
On the plain the dance of snow-shoes.

  One dark evening, after sundown,
In her wigwam Laughing Water
Sat with old Nokomis, waiting
For the steps of Hiawatha
Homeward from the hunt returning.

  On their faces gleamed the firelight,
Painting them with streaks of crimson,
In the eyes of old Nokomis
Glimmered like the watery moonlight,
In the eyes of Laughing Water
Glistened like the sun in water;
And behind them crouched their shadows
In the corners of the wigwam,
And the smoke in wreaths above them
Climbed and crowded through the smoke-flue.

  Then the curtain of the doorway
From without was slowly lifted;
Brighter glowed the fire a moment,
And a moment swerved the smoke-wreath,
As two women entered softly,
Passed the doorway uninvited,
Without word of salutation,
Without sign of recognition,
Sat down in the farthest corner,
Crouching low among the shadows.

  From their aspect and their garments,
Strangers seemed they in the village;
Very pale and haggard were they,
As they sat there sad and silent,
Trembling, cowering with the shadows.

  Was it the wind above the smoke-flue,
Muttering down into the wigwam?
Was it the owl, the Koko-koho,
Hooting from the dismal forest?
Sure a voice said in the silence:
"These are corpses clad in garments,

These are ghosts that come to haunt you,
From the kingdom of Ponemah,
From the land of the Hereafter!"
Homeward now came Hiawatha
From his hunting in the forest,
With the snow upon his tresses,
And the red deer on his shoulders.
At the feet of Laughing Water
Down he threw his lifeless burden;
Nobler, handsomer she thought him,
Than when first he came to woo her,
First threw down the deer before her,
As a token of his wishes,
As a promise of the future.

Then he turned and saw the strangers,
Cowering, crouching with the shadows;
Said within himself, "Who are they?
What strange guests has Minnehaha?"
But he questioned not the strangers,
Only spake to bid them welcome
To his lodge, his food, his fireside.

When the evening meal was ready,
And the deer had been divided,
Both the pallid guests, the strangers,
Springing from among the shadows,
Seized upon the choicest portions,
Seized the white fat of the roebuck,
Set apart for Laughing Water,
For the wife of Hiawatha;
Without asking, without thanking,
Eagerly devoured the morsels,
Flitted back among the shadows
In the corner of the wigwam.

Not a word spake Hiawatha,
Not a motion made Nokomis,
Not a gesture Laughing Water;
Not a change came o'er their features;
Only Minnehaha softly
Whispered, saying, "They are famished;
Let them do what best delights them;
Let them eat, for they are famished."

Many a daylight dawned and darkened.

Many a night shook off the daylight
As the pine shakes off the snow-flakes
From the midnight of its branches;
Day by day the guests unmoving
Sat there silent in the wigwam;
But by night, in storm or starlight,
Forth they went into the forest,
Bringing fire-wood to the wigwam,
Bringing pine-cones for the burning,
Always sad and always silent.

And whenever Hiawatha
Came from fishing or from hunting,
When the evening meal was ready,
And the food had been divided,
Gliding from their darksome corner,
Came the pallid guests, the strangers,
Seized upon the choicest portions
Set aside for Laughing Water,
And without rebuke or question
Flitted back among the shadows.

Never once had Hiawatha
By a word or look reproved them;
Never once had old Nokomis
Made a gesture of impatience;
Never once had Laughing Water
Shown resentment at the outrage.
All had they endured in silence,
That the rights of guest and stranger,
That the virtue of free-giving,
By a look might not be lessened,
By a word might not be broken.

Once at midnight Hiawatha,
Ever wakeful, ever watchful,
In the wigwam, dimly lighted
By the brands that still were burning,
By the glimmering, flickering firelight,
Heard a sighing, oft repeated,
Heard a sobbing, as of sorrow.

From his couch rose Hiawatha,
From his shaggy hides of bison,
Pushed aside the deer-skin curtain,
Saw the pallid guests, the shadows,

Sitting upright on their couches,
Weeping in the silent midnight.
 And he said: "O guests! why is it
That your hearts are so afflicted,
That you sob so in the midnight?
Has perchance the old Nokomis,
Has my wife, my Minnehaha,
Wronged or grieved you by unkindness,
Failed in hospitable duties?"
 Then the shadows ceased from weeping,
Ceased from sobbing and lamenting,
And they said, with gentle voices:
"We are ghosts of the departed,
Souls of those who once were with you.
From the realms of Chibiabos
Hither have we come to try you,
Hither have we come to warn you.
 "Cries of grief and lamentation
Reach us in the Blessed Islands;
Cries of anguish from the living,
Calling back their friends departed,
Sadden us with useless sorrow.
Therefore have we come to try you;
No one knows us, no one heeds us.
We are but a burden to you,
And we see that the departed
Have no place among the living.
 "Think of this, O Hiawatha!
Speak of it to all the people,
That henceforward and forever
They no more with lamentations
Sadden the souls of the departed
In the Islands of the Blessed.
 "Do not lay such heavy burdens
In the graves of those you bury,
Not such weight of furs and wampum,
Not such weight of pots and kettles,
For the spirits faint beneath them.
Only give them food to carry,
Only give them fire to light them.
 "Four days is the spirit's journey
To the land of ghosts and shadows,

Four its lonely night encampments;
Four times must their fires be lighted.
Therefore, when the dead are buried,
Let a fire, as night approaches,
Four times on the grave be kindled,
That the soul upon its journey
May not lack the cheerful fire-light,
May not grope about in darkness.
    "Farewell, noble Hiawatha!
We have put you to the trial,
To the proof have put your patience,
By the insult of our presence,
By the outrage of our actions,
We have found you great and noble,
Fail not in the greater trial,
Faint not in the harder struggle."
    When they ceased, a sudden darkness
Fell and filled the silent wigwam.
Hiawatha heard a rustle
As of garments trailing by him,
Heard the curtain of the doorway
Lifted by a hand he saw not,
Felt the cold breath of the night air,
For a moment saw the starlight;
But he saw the ghosts no longer,
Saw no more the wandering spirits
From the kingdom of Ponemah,
From the land of the Hereafter.

XX.

THE FAMINE.

O THE long and dreary Winter!
O the cold and cruel Winter!
Ever thicker, thicker, thicker
Froze the ice on lake and river,
Ever deeper, deeper, deeper
Fell the snow o'er all the landscape,
Fell the covering snow, and drifted
Through the forest, round the village.
    Hardly from his buried wigwam

Could the hunter force a passage;
With his mittens and his snow-shoes
Vainly walked he through the forest,
Sought for bird or beast and found none,
Saw no track of deer or rabbit,
In the snow beheld no footprints,
In the ghastly, gleaming forest
Fell, and could not rise from weakness,
Perished there from cold and hunger.

O the famine and the fever!
O the wasting of the famine!
O the blasting of the fever!
O the wailing of the children!
O the anguish of the women!

All the earth was sick and famished;
Hungry was the air around them,
Hungry was the sky above them,
And the hungry stars in heaven
Like the eyes of wolves glared at them!

Into Hiawatha's wigwam
Came two other guests, as silent
As the ghosts were, and as gloomy,
Waited not to be invited,
Did not parley at the doorway,
Sat there without word of welcome
In the seat of Laughing Water;
Looked with haggard eyes and hollow
At the face of Laughing Water.

And the foremost said: "Behold me!
I am Famine, Bukadawin!"
And the other said: "Behold me!
I am Fever, Ahkosewin!"

And the lovely Minnehaha
Shuddered as they looked upon her,
Shuddered at the words they uttered,
Lay down on her bed in silence,
Hid her face, but made no answer;
Lay there trembling, freezing, burning
At the looks they cast upon her,
At the fearful words they uttered.

Forth into the empty forest
Rushed the maddened Hiawatha;

In his heart was deadly sorrow,
In his face a stony firmness;
On his brow the sweat of anguish
Started, but it froze and fell not.
Wrapped in furs and armed for hunting,
With his mighty bow of ash-tree,
With his quiver full of arrows,
With his mittens, Minjekahwun,
Into the vast and vacant forest
On his snow-shoes strode he forward.
"Gitche Manito, the Mighty!"
Cried he with his face uplifted
In that bitter hour of anguish,
"Give your children food, O father!
Give us food, or we must perish!
Give me food for Minnehaha,
For my dying Minnehaha!"
Through the far-resounding forest,
Through the forest vast and vacant,
Rang that cry of desolation,
But there came no other answer
Than the echo of his crying,
Than the echo of the woodlands,
"Minnehaha! Minnehaha!"
All day long roved Hiawatha
In that melancholy forest,
Through the shadow of whose thickets,
In the pleasant days of Summer,
Of that ne'er forgotten Summer,
He had brought his young wife homeward
From the land of the Dacotahs;
When the birds sang in the thickets,
And the streamlets laughed and glistened,
And the air was full of fragrance,
And the lovely Laughing Water
Said with voice that did not tremble,
"I will follow you, my husband!"
In the wigwam with Nokomis,
With those gloomy guests, that watched her,
With the Famine and the Fever,
She was lying, the Beloved,
She the dying Minnehaha.

"Hark!" she said; "I hear a rushing,
Hear a roaring and a rushing,
Hear the Falls of Minnehaha
Calling to me from a distance!"
"No, my child!" said old Nokomis,
" 'T is the night-wind in the pine-trees!"

"Look!" she said; "I see my father
Standing lonely at his doorway,
Beckoning to me from his wigwam
In the land of the Dacotahs!"
"No, my child!" said old Nokomis,
" 'Tis the smoke, that waves and beckons!"

"Ah!" she said, "the eyes of Pauguk
Glare upon me in the darkness,
I can feel his icy fingers
Clasping mine amid the darkness!
Hiawatha! Hiawatha!"

And the desolate Hiawatha,
Far away amid the forest,
Miles away among the mountains,
Heard that sudden cry of anguish,
Heard the voice of Minnehaha
Calling to him in the darkness,
"Hiawatha! Hiawatha!"

Over snow-fields waste and pathless,
Under snow-encumbered branches,
Homeward hurried Hiawatha,
Empty-handed, heavy-hearted,
Heard Nokomis moaning, wailing:
"Wahonowin! Wahonowin!
Would that I had perished for you,
Would that I were dead as you are!
Wahonowin! Wahonowin!"

And he rushed into the wigwam,
Saw the old Nokomis slowly
Rocking to and fro and moaning,
Saw his lovely Minnehaha
Lying dead and cold before him,
And his bursting heart within him
Uttered such a cry of anguish,
That the forest moaned and shuddered,
That the very stars in heaven

Shook and trembled with his anguish.
    Then he sat down, still and speechless,
On the bed of Minnehaha,
At the feet of Laughing Water,
At those willing feet, that never
More would lightly run to meet him,
Never more would lightly follow.
    With both hands his face he covered,
Seven long days and nights he sat there,
As if in a swoon he sat there
Speechless, motionless, unconscious
Of the daylight or the darkness.
    Then they buried Minnehaha;
In the snow a grave they made her,
In the forest deep and darksome,
Underneath the moaning hemlocks;
Clothed her in her richest garments,
Wrapped her in her robes of ermine,
Covered her with snow, like ermine;
Thus they buried Minnehaha.
    And at night a fire was lighted,
On her grave four times was kindled,
For her soul upon its journey
To the Islands of the Blessed.
From his doorway Hiawatha
Saw it burning in the forest,
Lighting up the gloomy hemlocks;
From his sleepless bed uprising,
From the bed of Minnehaha,
Stood and watched it at the doorway,
That it might not be extinguished,
Might not leave her in the darkness.
    "Farewell!" said he, "Minnehaha!
Farewell, O my Laughing Water!
All my heart is buried with you,
All my thoughts go onward with you!
Come not back again to labor,
Come not back again to suffer,
Where the Famine and the Fever
Wear the heart and waste the body.
Soon my task will be completed.

Soon your footsteps I shall follow
To the Islands of the Blessed,
To the Kingdom of Ponemah,
To the Land of the Hereafter!"

XXI.

THE WHITE MAN'S FOOT.

In his lodge beside a river,
Close beside a frozen river,
Sat an old man, sad and lonely.
White his hair was as a snow-drift;
Dull and low his fire was burning,
And the old man shook and trembled,
Folded in his Waubewyon,
In his tattered white-skin-wrapper,
Hearing nothing but the tempest
As it roared along the forest,
Seeing nothing but the snow-storm,
As it whirled and hissed and drifted.
  All the coals were white with ashes
And the fire was slowly dying,
As a young man, walking lightly,
At the open doorway entered.
Red with blood of youth his cheeks were,
Soft his eyes, as stars in Spring-time,
Bound his forehead was with grasses;
Bound and plumed with scented grasses,
On his lips a smile of beauty,
Filling all the lodge with sunshine,
In his hand a bunch of blossoms
Filling all the lodge with sweetness.
  "Ah, my son!" exclaimed the old man,
"Happy are my eyes to see you.
Sit here on the mat beside me,
Sit here by the dying embers,
Let us pass the night together.
Tell me of your strange adventures,
Of the lands where you have travelled;
I will tell you of my prowess,
Of my many deeds of wonder."

From his pouch he drew his peace-pipe,
Very old and strangely fashioned;
Made of red stone was the pipe-head,
And the stem a reed with feathers;
Filled the pipe with bark of willow,
Placed a burning coal upon it,
Gave it to his guest, the stranger,
And began to speak in this wise:
"When I blow my breath about me,
When I breathe upon the landscape,
Motionless are all the rivers,
Hard as stone becomes the water!"
    And the young man answered, smiling:
"When I blow my breath about me,
When I breathe upon the landscape,
Flowers spring up o'er all the meadows,
Singing, onward rush the rivers!"
    "When I shake my hoary tresses,"
Said the old man, darkly frowning,
"All the land with snow is covered;
All the leaves from all the branches
Fall and fade and die and wither,
For I breathe, and lo! they are not.
From the waters and the marshes
Rise the wild goose and the heron,
Fly away to distant regions,
For I speak, and lo! they are not.
And where'er my foosteps wander,
All the wild beasts of the forest
Hide themselves in holes and caverns,
And the earth becomes as flint-stone!"
    "When I shake my flowing ringlets,"
Said the young man, softly laughing,
"Showers of rain fall warm and welcome,
Plants lift up their heads rejoicing,
Back unto their lakes and marshes
Come the wild goose and the heron,
Homeward shoots the arrowy swallow,
Sing the blue-bird and the robin,
And where'er my footsteps wander,
All the meadows wave with blossoms,
All the woodlands ring with music,

All the trees are dark with foliage!"
While they spake, the night departed;
From the distant realms of Wabun,
From his shining lodge of silver,
Like a warrior robed and painted,
Came the sun, and said, "Behold me!
Gheezis, the great sun, behold me!"
Then the old man's tongue was speechless,
And the air grew warm and pleasant,
And upon the wigwam sweetly
Sang the blue-bird and the robin,
And the stream began to murmur,
And a scent of growing grasses
Through the lodge was gently wafted.

And Segwun, the youthful stranger,
More distinctly in the daylight
Saw the icy face before him;
It was Peboan, the Winter!
From his eyes the tears were flowing,
As from melting lakes the streamlets,
And his body shrunk and dwindled
As the shouting sun ascended,
Till into the air it faded,
Till into the ground it vanished,
And the young man saw before him,
On the hearth-stone of the wigwam,
Where the fire had smoked and smouldered
Saw the earliest flower of Spring-time,
Saw the Beauty of the Spring-time,
Saw the Miskodeed in blossom.

Thus it was that in the Northland
After that unheard of coldness,
That intolerable Winter,
Came the Spring with all its splendor,
All its birds and all its blossoms,
All its flowers and leaves and grasses.

Sailing on the wind to northward,
Flying in great flocks, like arrows,
Like huge arrows shot through heaven,
Passed the swan, the Mahnahbezee,
Speaking almost as a man speaks;
And in long lines waving, bending

Like a bow-string snapped asunder,
Came the white goose, Waw-be-wawa;
And in pairs, or singly flying,
Mahng the loon, with clangorous pinions,
The blue heron, the Shuh-shuh-gah,
And the grouse, the Mushkodasa.
    In the thickets and the meadows
Piped the blue-bird, the Owaissa,
On the summit of the lodges
Sang the robin, the Opechee,
In the covert of the pine-trees
Cooed the pigeon, the Omeme,
And the sorrowing Hiawatha,
Speechless in his infinite sorrow,
Heard their voices calling to him,
Went forth from his gloomy doorway,
Stood and gazed into the heaven,
Gazed upon the earth and waters.
    From his wanderings far to eastward,
From the regions of the morning,
From the shining land of Wabun,
Homeward now returned Iagoo,
The great traveller, the great boaster,
Full of new and strange adventures,
Marvels many and many wonders.
    And the people of the village
Listened to him as he told them
Of his marvellous adventures,
Laughing answered him in this wise:
"Ugh! it is indeed Iagoo!
No one else beholds such wonders!"
    He had seen, he said, a water
Bigger than the Big-Sea-Water,
Broader than the Gitche Gumee,
Bitter so that none could drink it!
At each other looked the warriors,
Looked the women at each other,
Smiled, and said, "It cannot be so!
Kaw!" they said, "it cannot be so!"
    O'er it, said he, o'er this water
Came a great canoe with pinions,
A canoe with wings came flying,

Bigger than a grove of pine-trees,
Taller than the tallest tree-tops!
And the old men and the women
Looked and tittered at each other;
"Kaw!" they said, "we don't believe it!"
    From its mouth, he said, to greet him,
Came Waywassimo, the lightning,
Came the thunder, Annemeekee!
And the warriors and the women
Laughed aloud at poor Iagoo;
"Kaw!" they said, "what tales you tell us!"
    In it, said he, came a people,
In the great canoe with pinions
Came, he said, a hundred warriors;
Painted white were all their faces,
And with hair their chins were covered!
And the warriors and the women
Laughed and shouted in derision,
Like the ravens on the tree-tops,
Like the crows upon the hemlocks.
"Kaw!" they said, "what lies you tell us.
Do not think that we believe them!"
    Only Hiawatha laughed not,
But he gravely spake and answered
To their jeering and their jesting:
"True is all Iagoo tells us;
I have seen it in a vision,
Seen the great canoe with pinions,
Seen the people with white faces,
Seen the coming of this bearded
People of the wooden vessel
From the regions of the morning,
From the shining land of Wabun.
    "Gitche Manito, the Mighty,
The Great Spirit, the Creator,
Sends them hither on his errand,
Sends them to us with his message
Wheresoe'er they move, before them
Swarms the stinging fly, the Ahmo,
Swarms the bee, the honey-maker;
Wheresoe'er they tread, beneath them
Springs a flower unknown among us,

Springs the White-man's Foot in blossom.
"Let us welcome, then, the strangers,
Hail them as our friends and brothers,
And the heart's right hand of friendship
Give them when they come to see us.
Gitche Manito, the Mighty,
Said this to me in my vision.

"I beheld, too, in that vision,
All the secrets of the future,
Of the distant days that shall be.
I beheld the westward marches
Of the unknown, crowded nations.
All the land was full of people,
Restless, struggling, toiling, striving,
Speaking many tongues, yet feeling
But one heart-beat in their bosoms.
In the woodlands rang their axes,
Smoked their towns in all their valleys,
Over all the lakes and rivers
Rushed their great canoes of thunder.

"Then a darker, drearier vision,
Passed before me, vague and cloudlike.
I beheld our nations scattered,
All forgetful of my counsels,
Weakened, warring with each other;
Saw the remnants of our people
Sweeping westward, wild and woful,
Like the cloud-rack of a tempest,
Like the withered leaves of autumn!"

XXII.

HIAWATHA'S DEPARTURE.

By the shore of Gitche Gumee,
By the shining Big-Sea-Water,
At the doorway of his wigwam,
In the pleasant Summer morning,
Hiawatha stood and waited.

All the air was full of freshness,
All the earth was bright and joyous,
And before him, through the sunshine,

Westward toward the neighboring forest
Passed in golden swarms the Ahmo,
Passed the bees, the honey-makers,
Burning, singing in the sunshine.
　　Bright above him shone the heavens,
Level spread the lake before him;
From its bosom leaped the sturgeon,
Sparkling, flashing in the sunshine;
On its margin the great forest
Stood reflected in the water,
Every tree-top had its shadow,
Motionless beneath the water.
　　From the brow of Hiawatha
Gone was every trace of sorrow,
As the fog from off the water,
As the mist from off the meadow.
With a smile of joy and triumph,
With a look of exultation,
As of one who in a vision
Sees what is to be, but is not,
Stood and waited Hiawatha.
　　Toward the sun his hands were lifted,
Both the palms spread out against it,
And between the parted fingers
Fell the sunshine on his features,
Flecked with light his naked shoulders,
As it falls and flecks an oak-tree
Through the rifted leaves and branches.
　　O'er the water floating, flying,
Something in the hazy distance,
Something in the mists of morning,
Loomed and lifted from the water,
Now seemed floating, now seemed flying,
Coming nearer, nearer, nearer.
　　Was it Shingebis the diver?
Was it the pelican, the Shada?
Or the heron, the Shuh-shuh-gah?
Or the white goose, Waw-be-wawa,
With the water dripping, flashing
From its glossy neck and feathers?
　　It was neither goose nor diver,
Neither pelican nor heron,

O'er the water floating, flying,
Through the shining mist of morning,
But a birch-canoe with paddles,
Rising, sinking on the water,
Dripping, flashing in the sunshine,
And within it came a people
From the distant land of Wabun,
From the farthest realms of morning
Came the Black-Robe chief, the Prophet.
He the Priest of Prayer, the Pale-face,
With his guides and his companions.

And the noble Hiawatha,
With his hands aloft extended,
Held aloft in sign of welcome,
Waited, full of exultation,
Till the birch canoe with paddles
Grated on the shining pebbles,
Stranded on the sandy margin,
Till the Black-Robe chief, the Pale-face,
With the cross upon his bosom,
Landed on the sandy margin.

Then the joyous Hiawatha
Cried aloud and spake in this wise:
"Beautiful is the sun, O strangers,
When you come so far to see us!
All our town in peace awaits you,
All our doors stand open for you;
You shall enter all our wigwams,
For the heart's right hand we give you

"Never bloomed the earth so gayly,
Never shone the sun so brightly,
As to-day they shine and blossom
When you come so far to see us!
Never was our lake so tranquil,
Nor so free from rocks and sand-bars;
For your birch canoe in passing
Has removed both rock and sand-bar!

"Never before had our tobacco
Such a sweet and pleasant flavor,
Never the broad leaves of our corn-fields
Were so beautiful to look on,
As they seem to us this morning.

When you come so far to see us!"
    And the Black-Robe chief made answer,
Stammered in his speech a little,
Speaking words yet unfamiliar:
"Peace be with you, Hiawatha,
Peace be with you and your people,
Peace of prayer, and peace of pardon,
Peace of Christ, and joy of Mary!"
    Then the generous Hiawatha
Led the strangers to his wigwam,
Seated them on skins of bison,
Seated them on skins of ermine,
And the careful, old Nokomis
Brought them food in bowls of bass-wood,
Water brought in birchen dippers,
And the calumet, the peace-pipe,
Filled and lighted for their smoking.
    All the old men of the village,
All the warriors of the nation,
All the Jossakeeds, the prophets,
The magicians, the Wabenos,
And the medicine-men, the Medas,
Came to bid the strangers welcome;
"It is well," they said, "O brothers,
That you come so far to see us!"
    In a circle round the doorway,
With their pipes they sat in silence,
Waiting to behold the strangers,
Waiting to receive their message;
Till the Black-Robe chief, the Pale-face,
From the wigwam came to greet them,
Stammering in his speech a little,
Speaking words yet unfamiliar;
"It is well," they said, "O brother,
That you come so far to see us!"
    Then the Black-Robe chief, the prophet,
Told his message to the people,
Told the purport of his mission,
Told them of the Virgin Mary,
And her blessed Son, the Saviour,
How in distant lands and ages
He had lived on earth as we do;

How he fasted, prayed, and labored;
How the Jews, the tribe accursed,
Mocked him, scourged him, crucified him;
How he rose from where they laid him;
Walked again with his disciples,
And ascended into heaven.

And the chiefs made answer, saying:
"We have listened to your message,
We have heard your words of wisdom,
We will think on what you tell us.
It is well for us, O brothers,
That you come so far to see us!"

Then they rose up and departed
Each one homeward to his wigwam,
To the young men and the women
Told the story of the strangers
Whom the Master of Life had sent them
From the shining land of Wabun.

Heavy with the heat and silence
Grew the afternoon of Summer;
With a drowsy sound the forest
Whispered round the sultry wigwam,
With a sound of sleep the water
Rippled on the beach below it;
From the corn-fields shrill and ceaseless
Sang the grasshopper, Pah-Pukkeena;
And the guests of Hiawatha,
Weary with the heat of Summer,
Slumbered in the sultry wigwam.

Slowly o'er the simmering landscape
Fell the evening's dusk and coolness,
And the long and level sunbeams
Shot their spears into the forest,
Breaking through its shields of shadow,
Rushed into each secret ambush,
Searched each thicket, dingle, hollow;
Still the guests of Hiawatha
Slumbered in the silent wigwam.

From his place rose Hiawatha,
Bade farewell to old Nokomis,
Spake in whispers, spake in this wise,
Did not wake the guests, that slumbered:

"I am going, O Nokomis,
On a long and distant journey,
To the portals of the Sunset,
To the regions of the home-wind,
Of the Northwest-Wind, Keewaydin.
But these guests I leave behind me,
In your watch and ward I leave them.
See that never harm comes near them,
See that never fear molests them,
Never danger nor suspicion,
Never want of food or shelter,
In the lodge of Hiawatha!"

Forth into the village went he,
Bade farewell to all the warriors,
Bade farewell to all the young men,
Spake persuading, spake in this wise:

"I am going, O my people,
On a long and distant journey;
Many moons and many winters
Will have come, and will have vanished,
Ere I come again to see you.
But my guests I leave behind me;
Listen to their words of wisdom,
Listen to the truth they tell you,
For the Master of Life has sent them
From the land of light and morning!"

On the shore stood Hiawatha,
Turned and waved his hand at parting;
On the clear and luminous water
Launched his birch-canoe for sailing,
From the pebbles of the margin
Shoved it forth into the water;
Whispered to it, "Westward! westward!"
And with speed it darted forward.

And the evening sun descending
Set the clouds on fire with redness,
Burned the broad sky, like a prairie,
Left upon the level water
One long track and trail of splendor,
Down whose stream, as down a river,
Westward, westward Hiawatha
Sailed into the fiery sunset.

Sailed into the purple vapors,
Sailed into the dusk of evening.
  And the people from the margin,
Watched him floating, rising, sinking,
Till the birch-canoe seemed lifted
High into that sea of splendor,
Till it sank into the vapors
Like the new moon slowly, slowly
Sinking in the purple distance.
  And they said, "Farewell forever!"
Said, "Farewell, O Hiawatha!"
And the forests, dark and lonely,
Moved through all their depths of darkness,
Sighed, "Farewell, O Hiawatha!"
And the waves upon the margin
Rising, rippling on the pebbles,
Sobbed, "Farewell, O Hiawatha!"
And the heron, the Shuh-shuh-gah,
From her haunts among the fen-lands,
Screamed, "Farewell, O Hiawatha!"
  Thus departed Hiawatha,
Hiawatha the Beloved,
In the glory of the sunset,
In the purple mists of evening,
To the regions of the home-wind,
Of the Northwest-Wind, Keewaydin,
To the Islands of the Blessed,
To the kingdom of Ponemah,
To the land of the Hereafter!

THE COURTSHIP OF MILES STANDISH, 1858.

I.

MILES STANDISH.

In the Old Colony days, in Plymouth the land of the Pil-
  grims,
To and fro in a room of his simple and primitive dwelling,
Clad in doublet and hose, and boots of Cordovan leather,
Strode, with a martial air, Miles Standish the Puritan Cap
  tain.

Buried in thought he seemed, with his hands behind him, and
   pausing
Ever and anon to behold his glittering weapons of warfare,
Hanging in shining array along the walls of the chamber,—
Cutlass and corselet of steel, and his trusty sword of Damas-
   cus,
Curved at the point and inscribed with its mystical Arabic
   sentence,
While underneath, in a corner, were fowling-piece, musket,
   and matchlock.
Short of stature he was, but strongly built and athletic,
Broad in the shoulders, deep-chested, with muscles and sinews
   of iron;
Brown as a nut was his face, but his russet beard was already
Flaked with patches of snow, as hedges sometimes in Novem-
   ber.
Near him was seated John Alden, his friend and household
   companion,
Writing with diligent speed at a table of pine by the window;
Fair-haired, azure-eyed, with delicate Saxon complexion,
Having the dew of his youth, and the beauty thereof, as the
   captives
Whom Saint Gregory saw, and exclaimed, "Not Angles but
   Angels."
Youngest of all was he of the men who came in the May
   Flower.

  Suddenly breaking the silence, the diligent scribe inter-
   rupting,
Spake, in the pride of his heart, Miles Standish the Captain
   of Plymouth.
"Look at these arms," he said, "the warlike weapons that hang
   here,
Burnished and bright and clean, as if for parade or inspection!
This is the sword of Damascus I fought with in Flanders;
   this breastplate,
Well I remember the day! once saved my life in a skirmish;
Here in front you can see the very dint of the bullet
Fired point-blank at my heart by a Spanish arcabucero.
Had it not been of sheer steel, the forgotten bones of Miles
   Standish

Would at this moment be mould, in their grave in the
     Flemish morasses."
Thereupon answered John Alden, but looked not up from his
     writing:
"Truly the breath of the Lord hath slackened the speed of
     the bullet;
He in his mercy preserved you, to be our shield and our
     weapon!"
Still the Captain continued, unheeding the words of the
     stripling:
"See, how bright they are burnished, as if in an arsenal hanging;
That is because I have done it myself, and not left it to
     others.
Serve yourself, would you be well served, is an excellent
     adage;
So I take care of my arms, as you of your pens and your
     inkhorn.
Then, too, there are my soldiers, my great, invincible army,
Twelve men, all equipped, having each his rest and his match-
     lock,
Eighteen shillings a month, together with diet and pillage,
And, like Cæsar, I know the name of each of my soldiers!"
This he said with a smile, that danced in his eyes, as the
     sunbeams
Dance on the waves of the sea, and vanish again in a moment.
Alden laughed as he wrote, and still the Captain continued:
"Look! you can see from this window my brazen howitzer
     planted
High on the roof of the church, a preacher who speaks to the
     purpose,
Steady, straight-forward, and strong, with irresistible logic,
Orthodox, flashing conviction right into the hearts of the
     heathen.
Now we are ready, I think, for any assault of the Indians;
Let them come, if they like, and the sooner they try it the
     better,—
Let them come if they like, be it sagamore, sachem, or pow-
     wow,
Aspinet, Samoset, Corbitant, Squanto, or Tokamahamon!"

     Long at the window he stood, and wistfully gazed on the
     landscape,

Washed with a cold gray mist, the vapory breath of the
    east-wind,
Forest and meadow and hill, and the steel-blue rim of the
    ocean,
Lying silent and sad, in the afternoon shadows and sunshine.
Over his countenance flitted a shadow like those on the
    landscape,
Gloom intermingled with light; and his voice was subdued
    with emotion,
Tenderness, pity, regret, as after a pause he proceeded:
"Yonder there, on the hill by the sea, lies buried Rose
    Standish;
Beautiful rose of love, that bloomed for me by the wayside!
She was the first to die of all who came in the May Flower!
Green above her is growing the field of wheat we have sown
    there,
Better to hide from the Indian scouts the graves of our
    people,
Lest they should count them and see how many already have
    perished!"
Sadly his face he averted, and strode up and down, and was
    thoughtful.

Fixed to the opposite wall was a shelf of books, and among
    them
Prominent three, distinguished alike for bulk and for binding;
Bariffe's Artillery Guide, and the Commentaries of Cæsar,
Out of the Latin translated by Arthur Goldinge of London,
And, as if guarded by these, between them was standing the
    Bible.
Musing a moment before them, Miles Standish paused, as if
    doubtful
Which of the three he should choose for his consolation and
    comfort,
Whether the wars of the Hebrews, the famous campaigns of
    the Romans,
Or the Artillery practice, designed for belligerent Christians.
Finally down from its shelf he dragged the ponderous Roman,
Seated himself at the window, and opened the book, and in
    silence
Turned o'er the well-worn leaves, where thumb-marks thick
    on the margin,

Like the trample of feet, proclaimed the battle was hottest.
Nothing was heard in the room but the hurrying pen of the
    stripling,
Busily writing epistles important, to go by the May Flower,
Ready to sail on the morrow, or next day at latest, God
    willing!
Homeward bound with the tidings of all that terrible winter,
Letters written by Alden, and full of the name of Priscilla,
Full of the name and the fame of the Puritan maiden Pris-
    cilla!

II.

LOVE AND FRIENDSHIP.

NOTHING was heard in the room but the hurrying pen of the
    stripling,
Or an occasional sigh from the laboring heart of the Captain,
Reading the marvellous words and achievements of Julius
    Cæsar.
After a while he exclaimed, as he smote with his hand, palm
    downwards,
Heavily on the page: "A wonderful man was this Cæsar!
You are a writer, and I am a fighter, but here is a fellow
Who could both write and fight, and in both was equally
    skilful!"
Straightway answered and spake John Alden, the comely, the
    youthful:
"Yes, he was equally skilled, as you say, with his pen and his
    weapons.
Somewhere have I read, but where I forget, he could dictate
Seven letters at once, at the same time writing his memoirs."
"Truly," continued the Captain, not heeding or hearing the
    other,
"Truly a wonderful man was Caius Julius Cæsar!
Better be first, he said, in a little Iberian village,
Than be second in Rome, and I think he was right when he
    said it.
Twice was he married before he was twenty, and many times
    after;
Battles five hundred he fought, and a thousand cities he
    conquered;

He, too, fought in Flanders, as he himself has recorded;
Finally he was stabbed by his friend, the orator Brutus!
Now, do you know what he did on a certain occasion in
    Flanders,
When the rear-guard of his army retreated, the front giving
    way too,
And the immortal Twelfth Legion was crowded so closely
    together
There was no room for their swords? Why, he seized a shield
    from a soldier,
Put himself straight at the head of his troops, and commanded
    the captains,
Calling on each by his name, to order forward the ensigns;
Then to widen the ranks, and give more room for their
    weapons;
So he won the day, the battle of something-or-other.
That's what I always say; if you wish a thing to be well done,
You must do it yourself, you must not leave it to others!"

All was silent again; the Captain continued his reading.
Nothing was heard in the room but the hurrying pen of the
    stripling
Writing epistles important to go next day by the May Flower,
Filled with the name and the fame of the Puritan maiden
    Priscilla;
Every sentence began or closed with the name of Priscilla,
Till the treacherous pen, to which he confided the secret,
Strove to betray it by singing and shouting the name of
    Priscilla!
Finally closing his book, with a bang of the ponderous cover,
Sudden and loud as the sound of a soldier grounding his
    musket,
Thus to the young man spake Miles Standish the Captain of
    Plymouth:
"When you have finished your work, I have something im-
    portant to tell you.
Be not however in haste; I can wait; I shall not be impa-
    tient!"
Straightway Alden replied, as he folded the last of his letters,
Pushing his papers aside, and giving respectful attention:
"Speak; for whenever you speak, I am always ready to listen,
Always ready to hear whatever pertains to Miles Standish."

Thereupon answered the Captain, embarrassed, and culling his
    phrases:
" 'Tis not good for a man to be alone, say the Scriptures.
This I have said before, and again and again I repeat it;
Every hour in the day, I think it, and feel it, and say it.
Since Rose Standish died, my life has been weary and dreary;
Sick at heart have I been, beyond the healing of friendship.
Oft in my lonely hours have I thought of the maiden Pris-
    cilla.
She is alone in the world; her father and mother and brother
Died in the winter together; I saw her going and coming,
Now to the grave of the dead, and now to the bed of the
    dying,
Patient, courageous, and strong, and said to myself, that if
    ever
There were angels on earth, as there are angels in heaven,
Two have I seen and known; and the angel whose name is
    Priscilla
Holds in my desolate life the place which the other aban-
    doned.
Long have I cherished the thought, but never have dared to
    reveal it,
Being a coward in this, though valiant enough for the most
    part.
Go to the damsel Priscilla, the loveliest maiden of Plymouth,
Say that a blunt old Captain, a man not of words but of
    actions,
Offers his hand and his heart, the hand and heart of a soldier.
Not in these words, you know, but this in short is my mean-
    ing;
I am a maker of war, and not a maker of phrases.
You, who are bred as a scholar, can say it in elegant language,
Such as you read in your books of the pleadings and wooings
    of lovers,
Such as you think best adapted to win the heart of a
    maiden."

  When he had spoken, John Alden, the fair-haired taciturn
    stripling,
All aghast at his words, surprised, embarrassed, bewildered,
Trying to mask his dismay by treating the subject with light-
    ness,

Trying to smile, and yet feeling his heart stand still in his
  bosom,
Just as a timepiece stops in a house that is stricken by
  lightning,
Thus made answer and spake, or rather stammered than
  answered:
"Such a message as that I am sure I should mangle and mar
  it;
If you would have it well done,—I am only repeating your
  maxim,—
You must do it yourself, you must not leave it to others!"
But with the air of a man whom nothing can turn from his
  purpose,
Gravely shaking his head, made answer the Captain of
  Plymouth:
"Truly the maxim is good, and I do not mean to gainsay it;
But we must use it discreetly, and not waste powder for
  nothing.
Now, as I said before, I was never a maker of phrases.
I can march up to a fortress and summon the place to sur-
  render,
But march up to a woman with such a proposal, I dare not.
I'm not afraid of bullets, nor shot from the mouth of a
  cannon,
But of a thundering 'No!' point-blank from the mouth of a
  woman,
That I confess I'm afraid of, nor am I ashamed to confess it!
So you must grant my request, for you are an elegant scholar,
Having the graces of speech, and skill in the turning of
  phrases."
Taking the hand of his friend, who still was reluctant and
  doubtful,
Holding it long in his own, and pressing it kindly, he added:
"Though I have spoken thus lightly, yet deep is the feeling
  that prompts me;
Surely you cannot refuse what I ask in the name of our
  friendship!"
Then made answer John Alden: "The name of friendship is
  sacred;
What you demand in that name, I have not the power to
  deny you!"

So the strong will prevailed, subduing and moulding the gentler,
Friendship prevailed over love, and Alden went on his errand.

III.

THE LOVER'S ERRAND.

So THE strong will prevailed, and Alden went on his errand,
Out of the street of the village, and into the paths of the forest,
Into the tranquil woods, where bluebirds and robins were building
Towns in the populous trees, with hanging gardens of verdure,
Peaceful, aerial cities of joy and affection and freedom.
All around him was calm, but within him commotion and conflict,
Love contending with friendship, and self with each generous impulse.
To and fro in his breast his thoughts were heaving and dashing,
As in a foundering ship, with every roll of the vessel,
Washes the bitter sea, the merciless surge of the ocean!
"Must I relinquish it all," he cried with a wild lamentation,
"Must I relinquish it all, the joy, the hope, the illusion?
Was it for this I have loved, and waited, and worshipped in silence?
Was it for this I have followed the flying feet and the shadow
Over the wintry sea, to the desolate shores of New England?
Truly the heart is deceitful, and out of its depths of corruption
Rise, like an exhalation, the misty phantoms of passion;
Angels of light they seem, but are only delusions of Satan.
All is clear to me now; I feel it, I see it distinctly!
This is the hand of the Lord; it is laid upon me in anger,
For I have followed too much the heart's desires and devices,
Worshipping Astaroth blindly, and impious idols of Baal.
This is the cross I must bear; the sin and the swift retribution."

So through the Plymouth woods John Alden went on his errand;

Crossing the brook at the ford, where it brawled over pebble
    and shallow,
Gathering still, as he went, the May flowers blooming around
    him,
Fragrant, filling the air with a strange and wonderful sweet-
    ness,
Children lost in the woods, and covered with leaves in their
    slumber.
"Puritan flowers," he said, "and the type of Puritan maidens,
Modest and simple and sweet, the very type of Priscilla!
So I will take them to her; to Priscilla the May-flower of
    Plymouth,
Modest and simple and sweet, as a parting gift will I take
    them;
Breathing their silent farewells, as they fade and wither and
    perish.
Soon to be thrown away as is the heart of the giver."
So through the Plymouth woods John Alden went on his
    errand;
Came to an open space, and saw the disk of the ocean,
Sailless, sombre and cold with the comfortless breath of the
    east-wind;
Saw the new-built house, and people at work in a meadow;
Heard, as he drew near the door, the musical voice of Priscilla
Singing the hundredth Psalm, the grand old Puritan anthem,
Music that Luther sang to the sacred words of the Psalmist,
Full of the breath of the Lord, consoling and comforting
    many.
Then, as he opened the door, he beheld the form of the
    maiden
Seated beside her wheel, and the carded wool like a snow-
    drift
Piled at her knee, her white hands feeding the ravenous
    spindle,
While with her foot on the treadle she guided the wheel in
    its motion.
Open wide on her lap lay the well-worn psalm-book of Ains-
    worth,
Printed in Amsterdam, the words and the music together,
Rough-hewn, angular notes, like stones in the wall of a
    churchyard,
Darkened and overhung by the running vine of the verses.

Such was the book from whose pages she sang the old Puritan anthem,

She, the Puritan girl, in the solitude of the forest,

Making the humble house and the modest apparel of home-spun

Beautiful with her beauty, and rich with the wealth of her being!

Over him rushed, like a wind that is keen and cold and relentless,

Thoughts of what might have been, and the weight and woe of his errand;

All the dreams that had faded, and all the hopes that had vanished,

All his life henceforth a dreary and tenantless mansion,

Haunted by vain regrets, and pallid, sorrowful faces.

Still he said to himself, and almost fiercely he said it,

"Let not him that putteth his hand to the plough look backwards;

Though the ploughshare cut through the flowers of life to its fountains,

Though it pass o'er the graves of the dead and the hearts of the living,

It is the will of the Lord; and his mercy endureth forever!"

So he entered the house: and the hum of the wheel and the singing

Suddenly ceased; for Priscilla, aroused by his step on the threshold,

Rose as he entered, and gave him her hand, in signal of welcome,

Saying, "I knew it was you, when I heard your step in the passage;

For I was thinking of you, as I sat there singing and spinning."

Awkward and dumb with delight, that a thought of him had been mingled

Thus in the sacred psalm, that came from the heart of the maiden,

Silent before her he stood, and gave her the flowers for an answer,

Finding no words for his thought. He remembered that day in the winter,

After the first great snow when he broke a path from the village,
Reeling and plunging along through the drifts that encumbered the doorway,
Stamping the snow from his feet as he entered the house, and Priscilla
Laughed at his snowy locks, and gave him a seat by the fireside,
Grateful and pleased to know he had thought of her in the snow-storm.
Had he but spoken then! perhaps not in vain had he spoken;
Now it was all too late; the golden moment had vanished!
So he stood there abashed, and gave her the flowers for an answer.

Then they sat down and talked of the birds and the beautiful Springtime,
Talked of their friends at home, and the May Flower that sailed on the morrow.
"I have been thinking all day," said gently the Puritan maiden,
"Dreaming all night, and thinking all day, of the hedge-rows of England,—
They are in blossom now, and the country is all like a garden;
Thinking of lanes and fields, and the song of the lark and the linnet,
Seeing the village street, and familiar faces of neighbors
Going about as of old, and stopping to gossip together,
And, at the end of the street, the village church, with the ivy
Climbing the old gray tower, and the quiet graves in the churchyard.
Kind are the people I live with, and dear to me my religion;
Still my heart is so sad, that I wish myself back in Old England.
You will say it is wrong, but I cannot help it: I almost
Wish myself back in Old England, I feel so lonely and wretched."

Thereupon answered the youth:—"Indeed I do not condemn you;
Stouter hearts than a woman's have quailed in this terrible winter.
Yours is tender and trusting, and needs a stronger to lean on;

So I have come to you now, with an offer and proffer ot
    marriage
Made by a good man and true, Miles Standish the Captain
    of Plymouth!"

    Thus he delivered his message, the dexterous writer of
    letters,—
Did not embellish the theme, nor array it in beautiful phrases,
But came straight to the point, and blurted it out like a
    schoolboy;
Even the Captain himself could hardly have said it more
    bluntly.
Mute with amazement and sorrow, Priscilla the Puritan
    maiden
Looked into Alden's face, her eyes dilated with wonder,
Feeling his words like a blow, that stunned her and rendered
    her speechless;
Till at length she exclaimed, interrupting the ominous silence:
"If the great Captain of Plymouth is so very eager to wed me,
Why does he not come himself, and take the trouble to woo
    me?
If I am not worth the wooing, I surely am not worth the
    winning!"
Then John Alden began explaining and smoothing the matter,
Making it worse as he went, by saying the Captain was
    busy,—
Had no time for such things;—such things! the words grating
    harshly
Fell on the ear of Priscilla; and swift as a flash she made
    answer:
"Has he no time for such things, as you call it, before he is
    married,
Would he be likely to find it, or make it, after the wedding?
That is the way with you men; you don't understand us, you
    cannot.
When you have made up your minds, after thinking of this
    one and that one,
Choosing, selecting, rejecting, comparing one with another,
Then you make known your desire, with abrupt and sudden
    avowal,
And are offended and hurt, and indignant perhaps, that a
    woman

Does not respond at once to a love that she never suspected,
Does not attain at a bound the height to which you have
 been climbing.
This is not right nor just: for surely a woman's affection
Is not a thing to be asked for, and had for only the asking.
When one is truly in love, one not only says it, but shows it.
Had he but waited awhile, had he only showed that he loved
 me,
Even this Captain of yours—who knows?—at last might have
 won me,
Old and rough as he is; but now it never can happen."

Still John Alden went on, unheeding the words of Priscilla,
Urging the suit of his friend, explaining, persuading, expand-
 ing;
Spoke of his courage and skill, and of all his battles in
 Flanders,
How with the people of God he had chosen to suffer affliction,
How, in return for his zeal, they had made him Captain of
 Plymouth;
He was a gentleman born, could trace his pedigree plainly
Back to Hugh Standish of Duxbury Hall, in Lancashire,
 England,
Who was the son of Ralph, and the grandson of Thurston de
 Standish;
Heir unto vast estates, of which he was basely defrauded,
Still bore the family arms, and had for his crest a cock argent
Combed and wattled gules, and all the rest of the blazon.
He was a man of honor, of noble and generous nature;
Though he was rough, he was kindly; she knew how during
 the winter
He had attended the sick, with a hand as gentle as woman's;
Somewhat hasty and hot, he could not deny it, and head-
 strong,
Stern as a soldier might be, but hearty, and placable always,
Not to be laughed at and scorned, because he was little of
 stature;
For he was great of heart, magnanimous, courtly, courageous;
Any woman in Plymouth, nay any woman in England,
Might be happy and proud to be called the wife of Miles
 Standish!

But as he warmed and glowed, in his simple and eloquent
    language,
Quite forgetful of self, and full of the praise of his rival,
Archly the maiden smiled, and, with eyes overrunning with
    laughter,
Said, in a tremulous voice, "Why don't you speak for yourself,
    John?"

IV.

JOHN ALDEN.

INTO the open air John Alden, perplexed and bewildered,
Rushed like a man insane, and wandered alone by the sea-
    side;
Paced up and down the sands, and bared his head to the
    east-wind,
Cooling his heated brow, and the fire and fever within him.
Slowly as out of the heavens, with apocalyptical splendors,
Sank the City of God, in the vision of John the Apostle,
So, with its cloudy walls of chrysolite, jasper, and sapphire,
Sank the broad red sun, and over its turrets uplifted
Glimmered the golden reed of the angel who measured the
    city.

  "Welcome, O wind of the East!" he exclaimed in his wild
    exultation.
"Welcome, O wind of the East, from the caves of the misty
    Atlantic!
Blowing o'er fields of dulse, and measureless meadows of sea-
    grass,
Blowing o'er rocky wastes, and the grottos and gardens of
    ocean!
Lay thy cold, moist hand on my burning forehead, and wrap
    me
Close in thy garments of mist, to allay the fever within me!"

  Like an awakened conscience, the sea was moaning and
    tossing,
Beating remorseful and loud the mutable sands of the sea-
    shore.
Fierce in his soul was the struggle and tumult of passions
    contending;

Love triumphant and crowned, and friendship wounded and
    bleeding,
Passionate cries of desire, and importunate pleadings of duty!
"Is it my fault," he said, "that the maiden has chosen between
    us?
Is it my fault that he failed,—my fault that I am the victor?"
Then within him there thundered a voice, like the voice of
    the Prophet:
"It hath displeased the Lord!"—and he thought of David's
    transgression,
Bathsheba's beautiful face, and his friend in the front of the
    battle!
Shame and confusion of guilt, and abasement and self-
    condemnation,
Overwhelmed him at once; and he cried in the deepest con-
    trition:
"It hath displeased the Lord! It is the temptation of Satan!"

Then, uplifting his head, he looked at the sea, and beheld
    there
Dimly the shadowy form of the May Flower riding at anchor,
Rocked on the rising tide, and ready to sail on the morrow;
Heard the voices of men through the mist, the rattle of
    cordage
Thrown on the deck, the shouts of the mate, and the sailors'
    "Ay, ay, Sir!"
Clear and distinct, but not loud, in the dripping air of the
    twilight.
Still for a moment he stood, and listened, and stared at the
    vessel,
Then went hurriedly on, as one who, seeing a phantom,
Stops, then quickens his pace, and follows the beckoning
    shadow.
"Yes, it is plain to me now," he murmured; "the hand of
    the Lord is
Leading me out of the land of darkness, the bondage of error,
Through the sea, that shall lift the walls of its waters around me,
Hiding me, cutting me off, from the cruel thoughts that
    pursue me.
Back will I go o'er the ocean, this dreary land will abandon,
Her whom I may not love, and him whom my heart has
    offended.

Better to be in my grave in the green old churchyard in
    England,
Close by my mother's side, and among the dust of my
    kindred;
Better be dead and forgotten, than living in shame and
    dishonor!
Sacred and safe and unseen, in the dark of the narrow
    chamber
With me my secret shall lie, like a buried jewel that glimmers
Bright on the hand that is dust, in the chambers of silence
    and darkness,—
Yes, as the marriage ring of the great espousal hereafter!"

    Thus as he spake, he turned, in the strength of his strong
    resolution,
Leaving behind him the shore, and hurried along in the
    twilight,
Through the congenial gloom of the forest silent and sombre,
Till he beheld the lights in the seven houses of Plymouth,
Shining like seven stars in the dusk and mist of the evening.
Soon he entered his door, and found the redoubtable Captain
Sitting alone, and absorbed in the martial pages of Cæsar,
Fighting some great campaign in Hainault or Brabant or
    Flanders.
"Long have you been on your errand," he said with a cheery
    demeanor,
Even as one who is waiting an answer, and fears not the issue.
"Not far off is the house, although the woods are between us;
But you have lingered so long, that while you were going
    and coming
I have fought ten battles and sacked and demolished a city.
Come, sit down, and in order relate to me all that has
    happened."

    Then John Alden spake, and related the wondrous adven-
    ture,
From beginning to end, minutely, just as it happened;
How he had seen Priscilla, and how he had sped in his
    courtship,
Only smoothing a little, and softening down her refusal.
But when he came at length to the words Priscilla had spoken,
Words so tender and cruel: "Why don't you speak for your-
    self, John?"

Up leaped the Captain of Plymouth, and stamped on the
floor, till his armor
Clanged on the wall, where it hung, with a sound of sinister
omen.
All his pent-up wrath burst forth in a sudden explosion,
Even as a hand-grenade, that scatters destruction around it.
Wildly he shouted, and loud: "John Alden! you have be-
trayed me!
Me, Miles Standish, your friend! have supplanted, defrauded,
betrayed me!
One of my ancestors ran his sword through the heart of Wat
Tyler;
Who shall prevent me from running my own through the
heart of a traitor?
Yours is the greater treason, for yours is a treason to friend-
ship!
You, who lived under my roof, whom I cherished and loved
as a brother;
You, who have fed at my board, and drunk at my cup, to
whose keeping
I have intrusted my honor, my thoughts the most sacred and
secret,—
You too, Brutus! ah woe to the name of friendship hereafter!
Brutus was Cæsar's friend, and you were mine, but hence-
forward
Let there be nothing between us save war, and implacable
hatred!"

So spake the Captain of Plymouth, and strode about in
the chamber,
Chafing and choking with rage; like cords were the veins on
his temples.
But in the midst of his anger a man appeared at the doorway,
Bringing in uttermost haste a message of urgent importance,
Rumors of danger and war and hostile incursions of Indians!
Straightway the Captain paused, and, without further ques-
tion or parley,
Took from the nail on the wall his sword with its scabbard
of iron,
Buckled the belt round his waist, and, frowning fiercely,
departed.
Alden was left alone. He heard the clank of the scabbard

Growing fainter and fainter, and dying away in the distance.
Then he arose from his seat, and looked forth into the dark-
    ness,
Felt the cool air blow on his cheek, that was hot with the
    insult,
Lifted his eyes to the heavens, and, folding his hands as in
    childhood,
Prayed in the silence of night to the Father who seeth in
    secret.

    Meanwhile the choleric Captain strode wrathful away to
    the council,
Found it already assembled, impatiently waiting his coming;
Men in the middle of life, austere and grave in deportment,
Only one of them old, the hill that was nearest to heaven,
Covered with snow, but erect, the excellent Elder of Plym-
    outh.
God had sifted three kingdoms to find the wheat for this
    planting,
Then had sifted the wheat, as the living seed of a nation;
So say the chronicles old, and such is the faith of the people!
Near them was standing an Indian, in attitude stern and
    defiant,
Naked down to the waist, and grim and ferocious in aspect;
While on the table before them was lying unopened a Bible,
Ponderous, bound in leather, brass-studded, printed in Holland,
And beside it outstretched the skin of a rattlesnake glittered,
Filled, like a quiver, with arrows; a signal and challenge of
    warfare,
Brought by the Indian, and speaking with arrowy tongues of
    defiance.
This Miles Standish beheld, as he entered, and heard them
    debating
What were an answer befitting the hostile message and
    menace,
Talking of this and of that, contriving, suggesting, objecting;
One voice only for peace, and that the voice of the Elder,
Judging it wise and well that some at least were converted,
Rather than any were slain, for this was but Christian be-
    havior!
Then outspake Miles Standish, the stalwart Captain of Plym-
    outh,

Muttering deep in his throat, for his voice was husky with
   anger:
"What! do you mean to make war with milk and the water
   of roses?
Is it to shoot red squirrels you have your howitzer planted
There on the roof of the church, or is it to shoot red devils?
Truly the only tongue that is understood by a savage
Must be the tongue of fire that speaks from the mouth of the
   cannon!"
Thereupon answered and said the excellent Elder of Plym-
   outh,
Somewhat amazed and alarmed at this irreverent language:
"Not so thought Saint Paul, nor yet the other Apostles;
Not from the cannon's mouth were the tongues of fire they
   spake with!"
But unheeded fell this mild rebuke on the Captain,
Who had advanced to the table, and thus continued dis-
   coursing:
"Leave this matter to me, for to me by right it pertaineth.
War is a terrible trade; but in the cause that is righteous,
Sweet is the smell of powder; and thus I answer the chal-
   lenge!"

Then from the rattlesnake's skin, with a sudden, contempt-
   uous gesture,
Jerking the Indian arrows, he filled it with powder and bullets
Full to the very jaws, and handed it back to the savage,
Saying, in thundering tones: "Here, take it! this is your
   answer!"
Silently out of the room then glided the glistening savage,
Bearing the serpent's skin, and seeming himself like a serpent,
Winding his sinuous way in the dark to the depths of the
   forest.

V.

THE SAILING OF THE MAY FLOWER.

Just in the gray of the dawn, as the mists uprose from the
   meadows,
There was a stir and a sound in the slumbering village of
   Plymouth;
Clanging and clicking of arms, and the order imperative,
   "Forward!"

Given in tone suppressed, a tramp of feet, and then silence.
Figures ten, in the mist, marched slowly out of the village.
Standish the stalwart it was, with eight of his valorous army,
Led by their Indian guide, by Hobomok, friend of the white
    men,
Northward marching to quell the sudden revolt of the savage.
Giants they seemed in the mist, or the mighty men of King
    David;
Giants in heart they were, who believed in God and the
    Bible,—
Ay, who believed in the smiting of Midianites and Philistines.
Over them gleamed far off the crimson banners of morning;
Under them loud on the sands, the serried billows, advancing,
Fired along the line, and in regular order retreated.

Many a mile had they marched, when at length the village
    of Plymouth
Woke from its sleep, and arose, intent on its manifold labors.
Sweet was the air and soft; and slowly the smoke from the
    chimneys
Rose over roofs of thatch, and pointed steadily eastward;
Men came forth from the doors, and paused and talked of
    the weather,
Said that the wind had changed, and was blowing fair for the
    May Flower;
Talked of their Captain's departure, and all the dangers that
    menaced,
He being gone, the town, and what should be done in his
    absence.
Merrily sang the birds, and the tender voices of women
Consecrated with hymns the common cares of the household.
Out of the sea rose the sun, and the billows rejoiced at his
    coming;
Beautiful were his feet on the purple tops of the mountains;
Beautiful on the sails of the May Flower riding at anchor,
Battered and blackened and worn by all the storms of the
    winter.
Loosely against her masts was hanging and flapping her
    canvas,
Rent by so many gales, and patched by the hands of the
    sailors.

Suddenly from her side, as the sun rose over the ocean,
Darted a puff of smoke, and floated seaward; anon rang
Loud over field and forest the cannon's roar, and the echoes
Heard and repeated the sound, the signal-gun of departure!
Ah! but with louder echoes replied the hearts of the people!
Meekly, in voices subdued, the chapter was read from the
    Bible,
Meekly the prayer was begun, but ended in fervent entreaty!
Then from their houses in haste came forth the Pilgrims of
    Plymouth,
Men and women and children, all hurrying down to the sea-
    shore,
Eager, with tearful eyes, to say farewell to the May Flower,
Homeward bound o'er the sea, and leaving them here in the
    desert.

  Foremost among them was Alden. All night he had lain
    without slumber,
Turning and tossing about in the heat and unrest of his fever.
He had beheld Miles Standish, who came back late from the
    council,
Stalking into the room, and heard him mutter and murmur,
Sometimes it seemed a prayer, and sometimes it sounded like
    swearing.
Once he had come to the bed, and stood there a moment in
    silence;
Then he had turned away, and said: "I will not awake him;
Let him sleep on, it is best; for what is the use of more
    talking!"
Then he extinguished the light, and threw himself down on
    his pallet,
Dressed as he was, and ready to start at the break of the
    morning,—
Covered himself with the cloak he had worn in his campaigns
    in Flanders,—
Slept as a soldier sleeps in his bivouac, ready for action.
But with the dawn he arose; in the twilight Alden beheld him
Put on his corselet of steel, and all the rest of his armor,
Buckle about his waist his trusty blade of Damascus,
Take from the corner his musket, and so stride out of the
    chamber.

Often the heart of the youth had burned and yearned to
    embrace him,
Often his lips had essayed to speak, imploring for pardon,
All the old friendship came back, with its tender and grateful
    emotions.
But his pride overmastered the noble nature within him,—
Pride, and the sense of his wrong, and the burning fire of the
    insult.
So he beheld his friend departing in anger, but spake not,
Saw him go forth to danger, perhaps to death, and he spake
    not!
Then he arose from his bed, and heard what the people were
    saying,
Joined in the talk at the door, with Stephen and Richard and
    Gilbert,
Joined in the morning prayer, and in the reading of Scripture,
And, with the others, in haste went hurrying down to the
    sea-shore,
Down to the Plymouth Rock, that had been to their feet as a
    doorstep
Into a world unknown,—the corner-stone of a nation!

There with his boat was the Master, already a little im-
    patient
Lest he should lose the tide, or the wind might shift to the
    eastward,
Square-built, hearty, and strong, with an odor of ocean about
    him,
Speaking with this one and that, and cramming letters and
    parcels
Into his pockets capacious, and messages mingled together
Into his narrow brain, till at last he was wholly bewildered.
Nearer the boat stood Alden, with one foot placed on the
    gunwale,
One still firm on the rock, and talking at times with the
    sailors,
Seated erect on the thwarts, all ready and eager for starting.
He too was eager to go, and thus put an end to his anguish,
Thinking to fly from despair, that swifter than keel is or
    canvas,
Thinking to drown in the sea the ghost that would rise and
    pursue him.

But as he gazed on the crowd, he beheld the form of Priscilla
Standing dejected among them, unconscious of all that was
    passing.
Fixed were her eyes upon his, as if she divined his intention,
Fixed with a look so sad, so reproachful, imploring, and
    patient,
That with a sudden revulsion his heart recoiled from its
    purpose,
As from the verge of a crag, where one step more is destruc-
    tion.
Strange is the heart of man, with its quick, mysterious
    instincts!
Strange is the life of man, and fatal or fated are moments,
Whereupon turn, as on hinges, the gates of the wall ada-
    mantine!
"Here I remain!" he exclaimed, as he looked at the heavens
    above him,
Thanking the Lord whose breath had scattered the mist and
    the madness,
Wherein, blind and lost, to death he was staggering headlong.
"Yonder snow-white cloud, that floats in the ether above me,
Seems like a hand that is pointing and beckoning over the
    ocean.
There is another hand, that is not so spectral and ghost-like,
Holding me, drawing me back, and clasping mine for protec-
    tion.
Float, O hand of cloud, and vanish away in the ether!
Roll thyself up like a fist, to threaten and daunt me; I heed
    not
Either your warning or menace or any omen of evil!
There is no land so sacred, no air so pure and so wholesome,
As is the air she breathes, and the soil that is pressed by her
    footsteps.
Here for her sake will I stay, and like an invisible presence
Hover around her forever, protecting, supporting her weakness;
Yes! as my foot was the first that stepped on this rock at the
    landing,
So, with the blessing of God, shall it be the last at the
    leaving!"

Meanwhile the Master alert, but with dignified air and
    important,

Scanning with watchful eye the tide and the wind and the
    weather,
Walked about on the sands; and the people crowded around
    him
Saying a few last words, and enforcing his careful remem-
    brance.
Then, taking each by the hand, as if he were grasping a tiller,
Into the boat he sprang, and in haste shoved off to his vessel,
Glad in his heart to get rid of all this worry and flurry,
Glad to be gone from a land of sand and sickness and sorrow,
Short allowance of victual, and plenty of nothing but Gospel!
Lost in the sound of the oars was the last farewell of the
    Pilgrims.
O strong hearts and true! not one went back in the May
    Flower!
No, not one looked back, who had set his hand to this
    ploughing!

  Soon were heard on board the shouts and songs of the
    sailors
Heaving the windlass round, and hoisting the ponderous
    anchor.
Then the yards were braced, and all sails set to the west-
    wind,
Blowing steady and strong; and the May Flower sailed from
    the harbor,
Rounded the point of the Gurnet, and leaving far to the
    southward
Island and cape of sand, and the Field of the First Encounter,
Took the wind on her quarter, and stood for the open Atlantic,
Borne on the send of the sea, and the swelling hearts of the
    Pilgrims.

  Long in silence they watched the receding sail of the vessel,
Much endeared to them all, as something living and human;
Then, as if filled with the spirit, and wrapt in a vision
    prophetic,
Baring his hoary head, the excellent Elder of Plymouth
Said, "Let us pray!" and they prayed and thanked the Lord
    and took courage.
Mournfully sobbed the waves at the base of the rock, and
    above them

Bowed and whispered the wheat on the hill of death, and
their kindred
Seemed to awake in their graves, and to join in the prayer
that they uttered.
Sun-illumined and white, on the eastern verge of the ocean
Gleamed the departing sail, like a marble slab in a graveyard;
Buried beneath it lay forever all hope of escaping.
Lo! as they turned to depart, they saw the form of an Indian,
Watching them from the hill; but while they spake with each
other,
Pointing with outstretched hands, and saying, "Look!" he had
vanished.
So they returned to their homes; but Alden lingered a little,
Musing alone on the shore, and watching the wash of the
billows
Round the base of the rock, and the sparkle and flash of the
sunshine,
Like the spirit of God, moving visibly over the waters.

VI.

PRISCILLA.

Thus for a while he stood, and mused by the shore of the
ocean,
Thinking of many things, and most of all of Priscilla;
And as if thought had the power to draw to itself, like the
loadstone,
Whatsoever it touches, by subtile laws of its nature,
Lo! as he turned to depart, Priscilla was standing beside him.

"Are you so much offended, you will not speak to me?"
said she.
"Am I so much to blame, that yesterday, when you were
pleading
Warmly the cause of another, my heart, impulsive and wayward,
Pleaded your own, and spake out, forgetful perhaps of
decorum?
Certainly you can forgive me for speaking so frankly, for
saying

What I ought not to have said, yet now I can never unsay it;
For there are moments in life, when the heart is so full of
    emotion,
That if by chance it be shaken, or into its depths like a
    pebble
Drops some careless word, it overflows, and its secret,
Spilt on the ground like water, can never be gathered together.
Yesterday I was shocked, when I heard you speak of Miles
    Standish,
Praising his virtues, transforming his very defects into virtues,
Praising his courage and strength, and even his fighting in
    Flanders,
As if by fighting alone you could win the heart of a woman,
Quite overlooking yourself and the rest, in exalting your hero.
Therefore I spake as I did, by an irresistible impulse.
You will forgive me, I hope, for the sake of the friendship
    between us,
Which is too true and too sacred to be so easily broken!"
Thereupon answered John Alden, the scholar, the friend of
    Miles Standish:
"I was not angry with you, with myself alone I was angry,
Seeing how badly I managed the matter I had in my keep-
    ing."
"No!" interrupted the maiden, with answer prompt and
    decisive;
"No; you are angry with me, for speaking so frankly and
    freely.
It was wrong, I acknowledge; for it is the fate of a woman
Long to be patient and silent, to wait like a ghost that is
    speechless,
Till some questioning voice dissolves the spell of its silence.
Hence is the inner life of so many suffering women
Sunless and silent and deep, like subterranean rivers
Running through caverns of darkness, unheard, unseen, and
    unfruitful,
Chafing their channels of stone, with endless and profitless
    murmurs."
Thereupon answered John Alden, the young man, the lover of
    women:
"Heaven forbid it, Priscilla; and truly they seem to be always
More like the beautiful rivers that watered the garden of
    Eden,

More like the river Euphrates, through deserts of Havilah
    flowing,
Filling the land with delight, and memories sweet of the
    garden!"
"Ah, by these words, I can see," again interrupted the maiden,
"How very little you prize me, or care for what I am saying.
When from the depths of my heart, in pain and with secret
    misgiving,
Frankly I speak to you, asking for sympathy only and kind-
    ness,
Straightway you take up my words, that are plain and direct
    and in earnest,
Turn them away from their meaning, and answer with flat-
    tering phrases.
This is not right, is not just, is not true to the best that is in
    you;
For I know and esteem you, and feel that your nature is
    noble,
Lifting mine up to a higher, a more ethereal level.
Therefore I value your friendship, and feel it perhaps the
    more keenly
If you say aught that implies I am only as one among many,
If you make use of those common and complimentary phrases
Most men think so fine, in dealing and speaking with women,
But which women reject as insipid, if not as insulting."

Mute and amazed was Alden; and listened and looked at
    Priscilla,
Thinking he never had seen her more fair, more divine in her
    beauty.
He who but yesterday pleaded so glibly the cause of another,
Stood there embarrassed and silent, and seeking in vain for an
    answer.
So the maiden went on, and little divined or imagined
What was at work in his heart, that made him so awkward
    and speechless.
"Let us, then, be what we are, and speak what we think, and
    in all things
Keep ourselves loyal to truth, and the sacred professions of
    friendship.
It is no secret I tell you, nor am I ashamed to declare it:

I have liked to be with you, to see you, to speak with you
    always.
So I was hurt at your words, and a little affronted to hear you
Urge me to marry your friend, though he were the Captain
    Miles Standish.
For I must tell you the truth: much more to me is your
    friendship
Than all the love he could give, were he twice the hero you
    think him."
Then she extended her hand, and Alden, who eagerly grasped
    it,
Felt all the wounds in his heart, that were aching and bleed-
    ing so sorely,
Healed by the touch of that hand, and he said, with a voice
    full of feeling:
"Yes, we must ever be friends; and of all who offer you
    friendship
Let me be ever the first, the truest, the nearest and dearest!"

Casting a farewell look at the glimmering sail of the May
    Flower,
Distant, but still in sight, and sinking below the horizon,
Homeward together they walked, with a strange, indefinite
    feeling,
That all the rest had departed and left them alone in the
    desert.
But, as they went through the fields in the blessing and smile
    of the sunshine,
Lighter grew their hearts, and Priscilla said very archly:
"Now that our terrible Captain has gone in pursuit of the
    Indians,
Where he is happier far than he would be commanding a
    household,
You may speak boldly, and tell me of all that happened
    between you,
When you returned last night, and said how ungrateful you
    found me."
Thereupon answered John Alden, and told her the whole of
    the story,—
Told her his own despair, and the direful wrath of Miles
    Standish.

Whereat the maiden smiled, and said between laughing and
    earnest,
"He is a little chimney, and heated hot in a moment!"
But as he gently rebuked her, and told her how much he had
    suffered,—
How he had even determined to sail that day in the May
    Flower,
And had remained for her sake, on hearing the dangers that
    threatened,—
All her manner was changed, and she said with a faltering
    accent,
"Truly I thank you for this: how good you have been to me
    always!"

Thus, as a pilgrim devout, who toward Jerusalem journeys,
Taking three steps in advance, and one reluctantly backward,
Urged by importunate zeal, and withheld by pangs of con-
    trition;
Slowly but steadily onward, receding yet ever advancing,
Journeyed this Puritan youth to the Holy Land of his long-
    ings,
Urged by the fervor of love, and withheld by remorseful
    misgivings.

VII.

THE MARCH OF MILES STANDISH.

MEANWHILE the stalwart Miles Standish was marching stead-
    ily northward,
Winding through forest and swamp, and along the trend of
    the seashore,
All day long, with hardly a halt, the fire of his anger
Burning and crackling within, and the sulphurous odor of
    powder
Seeming more sweet to his nostrils than all the scents of the
    forest.
Silent and moody he went, and much he revolved his dis-
    comfort;
He who was used to success, and to easy victories always,
Thus to be flouted, rejected, and laughed to scorn by a
    maiden,
Thus to be mocked and betrayed by the friend whom most
    he had trusted!

Ah! 't was too much to be borne, and he fretted and chafed
in his armor!

"I alone am to blame," he muttered, "for mine was the
folly.
What has a rough old soldier, grown grim and gray in the
harness,
Used to the camp and its ways, to do with the wooing of
maidens?
'T was but a dream,—let it pass,—let it vanish like so many
others!
What I thought was a flower, is only a weed, and is worthless;
Out of my heart will I pluck it, and throw it away, and
henceforward
Be but a fighter of battles, a lover and wooer of dangers!"
Thus he revolved in his mind his sorry defeat and discomfort,
While he was marching by day or lying at night in the forest,
Looking up at the trees, and the constellations beyond them.

After a three days' march he came to an Indian encamp-
ment
Pitched on the edge of a meadow between the sea and the
forest;
Women at work by the tents, and the warriors, horrid with
war-paint,
Seated about a fire, and smoking and talking together;
Who, when they saw from afar the sudden approach of the
white men,
Saw the flash of the sun on breastplate and sabre and musket,
Straightway leaped to their feet, and two, from among them
advancing,
Came to parley with Standish, and offer him furs as a present;
Friendship was in their looks, but in their hearts there was
hatred.
Braves of the tribe were these, and brothers gigantic in
stature,
Huge as Goliath of Gath, or the terrible Og, king of Bashan;
One was Pecksuot named, and the other was called Watta-
wamat.
Round their necks were suspended their knives in scabbards
of wampum,
Two-edged, trenchant knives, with points as sharp as a needle.

Other arms had they none, for they were cunning and crafty.
"Welcome, English!" they said,—these words they had
    learned from the traders
Touching at times on the coast, to barter and chaffer for
    peltries.
Then in their native tongue they began to parley with
    Standish,
Through his guide and interpreter, Hobomok, friend of the
    white man.
Begging for blankets and knives, but mostly for muskets and
    powder,
Kept by the white man, they said, concealed, with the plague,
    in his cellars,
Ready to be let loose, and destroy his brother the red man!
But when Standish refused, and said he would give them the
    Bible,
Suddenly changing their tone, they began to boast and to
    bluster.
Then Wattawamat advanced with a stride in front of the
    other,
And, with a lofty demeanor, thus vauntingly spake to the
    Captain:
"Now Wattawamat can see, by the fiery eyes of the Captain,
Angry is he in his heart; but the heart of the brave Watta-
    wamat
Is not afraid at the sight. He was not born of a woman,
But on a mountain, at night, from an oak-tree riven by
    lightning,
Forth he sprang at a bound, with all his weapons about him.
Shouting, 'Who is there here to fight with the brave
    Wattawamat?'"
Then he unsheathed his knife, and, whetting the blade on his
    left hand,
Held it aloft and displayed a woman's face on the handle,
Saying, with bitter expression and look of sinister meaning:
"I have another at home, with the face of a man on the
    handle;
By and by they shall marry; and there will be plenty of
    children!"

Then stood Pecksuot forth, self-vaunting, insulting Miles
    Standish:

While with his fingers he patted the knife that hung at his
    bosom,
Drawing it half from its sheath, and plunging it back, as he
    muttered:
"By and by it shall see; it shall eat; ah, ha! but shall speak
    not!
This is the mighty Captain the white men have sent to
    destroy us!
He is a little man; let him go and work with the women!"

  Meanwhile Standish had noted the faces and figures of
    Indians
Peeping and creeping about from bush to tree in the forest,
Feigning to look for game, with arrows set on their bow-
    strings,
Drawing about him still closer and closer the net of their
    ambush.
But undaunted he stood, and dissembled and treated them
    smoothly;
So the old chronicles say, that were writ in the days of the
    fathers.
But when he heard their defiance, the boast, the taunt, and
    the insult,
All the hot blood of his race, of Sir Hugh and of Thurston de
    Standish,
Boiled and beat in his heart, and swelled in the veins of his
    temples.
Headlong he leaped on the boaster, and, snatching his knife
    from its scabbard,
Plunged it into his heart, and, reeling backward, the savage
Fell with his face to the sky, and a fiendlike fierceness upon it.
Straight there arose from the forest the awful sound of the
    war-whoop,
And, like a flurry of snow on the whistling wind of December,
Swift and sudden and keen came a flight of feathery arrows.
Then came a cloud of smoke, and out of the cloud came the
    lightning,
Out of the lightning thunder; and death unseen ran before it.
Frightened, the savages fled for shelter in swamp and in
    thicket,
Hotly pursued and beset; but their sachem, the brave Watta-
    wamat,

Fled not; he was dead. Unswerving and swift had a bullet
Passed through his brain, and he fell with both hands clutch-
ing the greensward,
Seeming in death to hold back from his foe the land of his
fathers.

There on the flowers of the meadow the warriors lay, and
above them,
Silent, with folded arms, stood Hobomok, friend of the white
man.
Smiling at length he exclaimed to the stalwart Captain of
Plymouth:
"Pecksuot bragged very loud, of his courage, his strength, and
his stature,—
Mocked the great Captain, and called him a little man; but
I see now
Big enough have you been to lay him speechless before you!"

Thus the first battle was fought and won by the stalwart
Miles Standish.
When the tidings thereof were brought to the village of
Plymouth,
And as a trophy of war the head of the brave Wattawamat
Scowled from the roof of the fort, which at once was a church
and a fortress,
All who beheld it rejoiced, and praised the Lord, and took
courage.
Only Priscilla averted her face from this spectre of terror,
Thanking God in her heart that she had not married Miles
Standish;
Shrinking, fearing almost, lest, coming home from his battles,
He should lay claim to her hand, as the prize and reward
of his valor.

VIII.

THE SPINNING-WHEEL.

MONTH after month passed away, and in Autumn the ships
of the merchants
Came with kindred and friends, with cattle and corn for the
Pilgrims.
All in the village was peace; the men were intent on their
labors,

Busy with hewing and building, with garden-plot and with
    merestead,
Busy with breaking the glebe, and mowing the grass in the
    meadows,
Searching the sea for its fish, and hunting the deer in the forest.
All in the village was peace; but at times the rumor of
    warfare
Filled the air with alarm, and the apprehension of danger.
Bravely the stalwart Miles Standish was scouring the land
    with his forces,
Waxing valiant in fight and defeating the alien armies,
Till his name had become a sound of fear to the nations.
Anger was still in his heart, but at times the remorse and
    contrition
Which in all noble natures succeed the passionate outbreak,
Came like a rising tide, that encounters the rush of a river,
Staying its current awhile, but making it bitter and brackish.

Meanwhile Alden at home had built him a new habitation,
Solid, substantial, of timber rough-hewn from the firs of the
    forest.
Wooden-barred was the door, and the roof was covered with
    rushes;
Latticed the windows were, and the window-panes were of
    paper,
Oiled to admit the light, while wind and rain were excluded.
There too he dug a well, and around it planted an orchard:
Still may be seen to this day some trace of the well and the
    orchard.
Close to the house was the stall, where, safe and secure from
    annoyance,
Raghorn, the snow-white bull, that had fallen to Alden's
    allotment
In the division of cattle, might ruminate in the night-time
Over the pastures he cropped, made fragrant by sweet penny-
    royal.

Oft when his labor was finished, with eager feet would the
    dreamer
Follow the pathway that ran through the woods to the house
    of Priscilla,

Led by illusions romantic and subtile deceptions of fancy,
Pleasure disguised as duty, and love in the semblance of
    friendship.
Ever of her he thought, when he fashioned the walls of his
    dwelling;
Ever of her he thought, when he delved in the soil of his
    garden;
Ever of her he thought, when he read in his Bible on Sunday
Praise of the virtuous woman, as she is described in the
    Proverbs,—
How the heart of her husband doth safely trust in her always,
How all the days of her life she will do him good, and not
    evil,
How she seeketh the wool and the flax and worketh with
    gladness,
How she layeth her hand to the spindle and holdeth the
    distaff,
How she is not afraid of the snow for herself or her house-
    hold,
Knowing her household are clothed with the scarlet cloth of
    her weaving!

So as she sat at her wheel one afternoon in the Autumn,
Alden, who opposite sat, and was watching her dexterous
    fingers,
As if the thread she was spinning were that of his life and his
    fortune,
After a pause in their talk, thus spake to the sound of the
    spindle.
"Truly, Priscilla," he said, "when I see you spinning and
    spinning,
Never idle a moment, but thrifty and thoughtful of others,
Suddenly you are transformed, are visibly changed in a mo-
    ment;
You are no longer Priscilla, but Bertha the Beautiful Spinner."
Here the light foot on the treadle grew swifter and swifter;
    the spindle
Uttered an angry snarl, and the thread snapped short in her
    fingers;
While the impetuous speaker, not heeding the mischief, con-
    tinued:

"You are the beautiful Bertha, the spinner, the queen of
    Helvetia;
She whose story I read at a stall in the streets of Southamp-
    ton,
Who, as she rode on her palfrey, o'er valley and meadow and
    mountain,
Ever was spinning her thread from a distaff fixed to her
    saddle.
She was so thrifty and good, that her name passed into a
    proverb.
So shall it be with your own, when the spinning-wheel shall
    no longer
Hum in the house of the farmer, and fill its chambers with
    music.
Then shall the mothers, reproving, relate how it was in their
    childhood,
Praising the good old times, and the days of Priscilla the
    spinner!"
Straight uprose from her wheel the beautiful Puritan maiden,
Pleased with the praise of her thrift from him whose praise
    was the sweetest,
Drew from the reel on the table a snowy skein of her spinning,
Thus making answer, meanwhile, to the flattering phrases of
    Alden:
"Come, you must not be idle; if I am a pattern for house-
    wives,
Show yourself equally worthy of being the model of husbands.
Hold this skein on your hands, while I wind it, ready for
    knitting;
Then who knows but hereafter, when fashions have changed
    and the manners,
Fathers may talk to their sons of the good old times of John
    Alden!"
Thus, with a jest and a laugh, the skein on his hands she
    adjusted,
He sitting awkwardly there, with his arms extended before
    him,
She standing graceful, erect, and winding the thread from his
    fingers,

Sometimes chiding a little his clumsy manner of holding,
Sometimes touching his hands, as she disentangled expertly
Twist or knot in the yarn, unawares—for how could she help
    it?—
Sending electrical thrills through every nerve in his body.

  Lo! in the midst of this scene, a breathless messenger
    entered,
Bringing in hurry and heat the terrible news from the village.
Yes; Miles Standish was dead!—an Indian had brought them
    the tidings,—
Slain by a poisoned arrow, shot down in the front of the
    battle,
Into an ambush beguiled, cut off with the whole of his forces;
All the town would be burned, and all the people be mur-
    dered!
Such were the tidings of evil that burst on the hearts of the
    hearers.
Silent and statue-like stood Priscilla, her face looking back-
    ward
Still at the face of the speaker, her arms uplifted in horror;
But John Alden, upstarting, as if the barb of the arrow
Piercing the heart of his friend had struck his own, and had
    sundered
Once and forever the bonds that held him bound as a captive,
Wild with excess of sensation, the awful delight of his free-
    dom,
Mingled with pain and regret, unconscious of what he was
    doing,
Clasped, almost with a groan, the motionless form of Priscilla,
Pressing her close to his heart, as forever his own, and
    exclaiming:
"Those whom the Lord hath united, let no man put them
    asunder!"

  Even as rivulets twain, from distant and separate sources,
Seeing each other afar, as they leap from the rocks, and
    pursuing
Each one its devious path, but drawing nearer and nearer,
Rush together at last, at their trysting-place in the forest;

So these lives that had run thus far in separate channels,
Coming in sight of each other, then swerving and flowing
    asunder,
Parted by barriers strong, but drawing nearer and nearer,
Rushed together at last, and one was lost in the other.

IX.

THE WEDDING-DAY.

FORTH from the curtain of clouds, from the tent of purple and
    scarlet,
Issued the sun, the great High-Priest, in his garments resplen-
    dent,
Holiness unto the Lord, in letters of light, on his forehead,
Round the hem of his robe the golden bells and pomegranates.
Blessing the world he came, and the bars of vapor beneath
    him
Gleamed like a grate of brass, and the sea at his feet was a
    laver!

This was the wedding morn of Priscilla the Puritan maiden.
Friends were assembled together; the Elder and Magistrate
    also
Graced the scene with their presence, and stood like the Law
    and the Gospel,
One with the sanction of earth and one with the blessing of
    heaven.
Simple and brief was the wedding, as that of Ruth and of
    Boaz.
Softly the youth and the maiden repeated the words of
    betrothal,
Taking each other for husband and wife in the Magistrate's
    presence,
After the Puritan way, and the laudable custom of Holland.
Fervently then, and devoutly, the excellent Elder of Plym-
    outh
Prayed for the hearth and the home, that were founded that
    day in affection,
Speaking of life and of death, and imploring divine benedic-
    tions.

Lo! when the service was ended, a form appeared on the threshold,
Clad in armor of steel, a sombre and sorrowful figure!
Why does the bridegroom start and stare at the strange apparition?
Why does the bride turn pale, and hide her face on his shoulder?
Is it a phantom of air,—a bodiless, spectral illusion?
Is it a ghost from the grave, that has come to forbid the betrothal?
Long had it stood there unseen, a guest uninvited, unwelcomed;
Over its clouded eyes there had passed at times an expression
Softening the gloom and revealing the warm heart hidden beneath them,
As when across the sky the driving rack of the rain-cloud
Grows for a moment thin, and betrays the sun by its brightness.
Once it had lifted its hand, and moved its lips, but was silent,
As if an iron will had mastered the fleeting intention.
But when were ended the troth and the prayer and the last benediction,
Into the room it strode, and the people beheld with amazement
Bodily there in his armor Miles Standish, the Captain of Plymouth!
Grasping the bridegroom's hand, he said with emotion, "Forgive me!
I have been angry and hurt,—too long have I cherished the feeling;
I have been cruel and hard, but now, thank God! it is ended.
Mine is the same hot blood that leaped in the veins of Hugh Standish,
Sensitive, swift to resent, but as swift in atoning for error.
Never so much as now was Miles Standish the friend of John Alden."
Thereupon answered the bridegroom: "Let all be forgotten between us,—
All save the dear, old friendship, and that shall grow older and dearer!"
Then the Captain advanced, and, bowing, saluted Priscilla,

Gravely, and after the manner of old-fashioned gentry in
England,
Something of camp and of court, of town and of country,
commingled,
Wishing her joy of her wedding, and loudly lauding her
husband.
Then he said with a smile: "I should have remembered the
adage,—
If you would be well served, you must serve yourself; and
moreover,
No man can gather cherries in Kent at the season of Christ-
mas!"

Great was the people's amazement, and greater yet their
rejoicing,
Thus to behold once more the sunburnt face of their Captain,
Whom they had mourned as dead; and they gathered and
crowded about him,
Eager to see him and hear him, forgetful of bride and bride-
groom,
Questioning, answering, laughing, and each interrupting the
other,
Till the good Captain declared, being quite overpowered and
bewildered,
He had rather by far break into an Indian encampment,
Than come again to a wedding to which he had not been
invited.

Meanwhile the bridegroom went forth and stood with the
bride at the doorway,
Breathing the perfumed air of that warm and beautiful morn-
ing.
Touched with autumnal tints, but lonely and sad in the
sunshine,
Lay extended before them the land of toil and privation;
There were the graves of the dead, and the barren waste of
the seashore,
There the familiar fields, the groves of pine, and the meadows;
But to their eyes transfigured, it seemed as the Garden of
Eden,
Filled with the presence of God, whose voice was the sound
of the ocean.

Soon was their vision disturbed by the noise and stir of
    departure,
Friends coming forth from the house, and impatient of longer
    delaying,
Each with his plan for the day, and the work that was left
    uncompleted.
Then from a stall near at hand, amid exclamations of wonder,
Alden the thoughtful, the careful, so happy, so proud of
    Priscilla,
Brought out his snow-white bull, obeying the hand of its
    master,
Led by a cord that was tied to an iron ring in its nostrils,
Covered with crimson cloth, and a cushion placed for a saddle.
She should not walk, he said, through the dust and heat of the
    noonday;
Nay, she should ride like a queen, not plod along like a
    peasant.
Somewhat alarmed at first, but reassured by the others,
Placing her hand on the cushion, her foot in the hand of her
    husband,
Gayly, with joyous laugh, Priscilla mounted her palfrey.
"Nothing is wanting now," he said with a smile, "but the
    distaff;
Then you would be in truth my queen, my beautiful Bertha!"

Onward the bridal procession now moved to their new
    habitation,
Happy husband and wife, and friends conversing together.
Pleasantly murmured the brook, as they crossed the ford in
    the forest,
Pleased with the image that passed, like a dream of love
    through its bosom,
Tremulous, floating in air, o'er the depths of the azure abysses.
Down through the golden leaves the sun was pouring his
    splendors,
Gleaming on purple grapes, that, from branches above them
    suspended,
Mingled their odorous breath with the balm of the pine and
    the fir-tree,
Wild and sweet as the clusters that grew in the valley of
    Eshcol.
Like a picture it seemed of the primitive, pastoral ages,

Fresh with the youth of the world, and recalling Rebecca and
    Isaac,
Old and yet ever new, and simple and beautiful always,
Love immortal and young in the endless succession of lovers.
So through the Plymouth woods passed onward the bridal
    procession.

THE VILLAGE BLACKSMITH.

UNDER a spreading chestnut tree
    The village smithy stands;
The smith, a mighty man is he,
    With large and sinewy hands;
And the muscles of his brawny arms
    Are strong as iron bands.

His hair is crisp, and black, and long,
    His face is like the tan;
His brow is wet with honest sweat,
    He earns whate'er he can,
And looks the whole world in the face,
    For he owes not any man.

Week in, week out, from morn till night,
    You can hear his bellows blow;
You can hear him swing his heavy sledge,
    With measured beat and slow,
Like a sexton ringing the village bell,
    When the evening sun is low.

And children coming home from school
    Look in at the open door;
They love to see the flaming forge,
    And hear the bellows roar,
And catch the burning sparks that fly
    Like chaff from a threshing floor.

He goes on Sunday to the church,
    And sits among his boys:

He hears the parson pray and preach,
　　He hears his daughter's voice,
Singing in the village choir,
　　And it makes his heart rejoice.

It sounds to him like her mother's voice,
　　Singing in Paradise!
He needs must think of her once more,
　　How in the grave she lies;
And with his hard, rough hand he wipes
　　A tear out of his eyes.

Toiling,—rejoicing,—sorrowing,
　　Onward through life he goes;
Each morning sees some task begin,
　　Each evening sees it close;
Something attempted, something done,
　　Has earned a night's repose.

Thanks, thanks to thee, my worthy friend,
　　For the lesson thou hast taught!
Thus at the flaming forge of life
　　Our fortunes must be wrought;
Thus on its sounding anvil shaped
　　Each burning deed and thought!

ENDYMION.

THE rising moon has hid the stars;
Her level rays, like golden bars,
　　Lie on the landscape green,
　　With shadows brown between.

And silver white the river gleams,
As if Diana, in her dreams,
　　Had dropt her silver bow
　　Upon the meadows low.

On such a tranquil night as this,
She woke Endymion with a kiss,
　　When, sleeping in the grove,
　　He dreamed not of her love.

Like Dian's kiss, unasked, unsought,
Love gives itself, but is not bought;
   Nor voice, nor sound betrays
   Its deep, impassioned gaze.

It comes,—the beautiful, the free,
The crown of all humanity,—
   In silence and alone
   To seek the elected one.

It lifts the boughs, whose shadows deep,
Are Life's oblivion, the soul's sleep,
   And kisses the closed eyes
   Of him, who slumbering lies

O, weary hearts! O, slumbering eyes!
O, drooping souls, whose destinies
   Are fraught with fear and pain,
   Ye shall be loved again!

No one is so accursed by fate,
No one so utterly desolate,
   But some heart, though unknown,
   Responds unto his own.

Responds,—as if with unseen wings,
An angel touched its quivering strings;
   And whispers, in its song,
   "Where hast thou stayed so long!"

EXCELSIOR.

THE shades of night were falling fast,
As through an Alpine village passed
A youth, who bore, 'mid snow and ice,
A banner with the strange device,
   Excelsior!

His brow was sad; his eye beneath,
Flashed like a falchion from its sheath,
And like a silver clarion rung
The accents of that unknown tongue,
   Excelsior!

In happy homes he saw the light
Of household fires gleam warm and bright;
Above, the spectral glaciers shone,
And from his lips escaped a groan,
Excelsior!

"Try not the Pass!" the old man said;
"Dark lowers the tempest overhead,
The roaring torrent is deep and wide!"
And loud that clarion voice replied,
Excelsior!

"O stay," the maiden said, "and rest
Thy weary head upon this breast!"
A tear stood in his bright blue eye,
But still he answered, with a sigh,
Excelsior!

"Beware the pine tree's withered branch!
Beware the awful avalanche!"
This was the peasant's last Good-night,
A voice replied, far up the height,
Excelsior!

At break of day, as heavenward
The pious monks of Saint Bernard
Uttered the oft-repeated prayer,
A voice cried through the startled air,
Excelsior!

A traveller, by the faithful hound,
Half-buried in the snow was found,
Still grasping in his hand of ice
That banner with the strange device,
Excelsior!

There in the twilight cold and gray,
Lifeless, but beautiful, he lay,
And from the sky, serene and far,
A voice fell, like a falling star,
Excelsior!

THE BRIDGE.

I stood on the bridge at midnight,
  As the clocks were striking the hour,
And the moon rose o'er the city,
  Behind the dark church-tower.

I saw her bright reflection
  In the waters under me,
Like a golden goblet falling
  And sinking into the sea.

And far in the hazy distance
  Of that lovely night in June,
The blaze of the flaming furnace
  Gleamed redder than the moon.

Among the long, black rafters
  The wavering shadows lay,
And the current that came from the ocean
  Seemed to lift and bear them away;

As, sweeping and eddying through them,
  Rose the belated tide,
And, streaming into the moonlight,
  The seaweed floated wide.

And like those waters rushing
  Among the wooden piers,
A flood of thoughts came o'er me
  That filled my eyes with tears.

How often, O, how often,
  In the days that had gone by,
I had stood on that bridge at midnight
  And gazed on that wave and sky!

How often, O, how often,
  I had wished that the ebbing tide
Would bear me away on its bosom
  O'er the ocean wild and wide!

For my heart was hot and restless,
　And my life was full of care,
And the burden laid upon me
　Seemed greater than I could bear.

But now it has fallen from me,
　It is buried in the sea;
And only the sorrow of others
　Throws its shadow over me.

Yet whenever I cross the river
　On its bridge with wooden piers,
Like the odor of brine from the ocean,
　Comes the thought of other years.

And I think how many thousands
　Of care-encumbered men,
Each bearing his burden of sorrow,
　Have crossed the bridge since then.

I see the long procession
　Still passing to and fro,
The young heart hot and restless,
　And the old subdued and slow!

And forever and forever,
　As long as the river flows,
As long as the heart has passions,
　As long as life has woes;

The moon and its broken reflection
　And its shadows shall appear,
As the symbol of love in heaven,
　And its wavering image here.

A PSALM OF LIFE.

WHAT THE HEART OF THE YOUNG MAN
SAID TO THE PSALMIST.

TELL me not, in mournful numbers,
　"Life is but an empty dream!"
For the soul is dead that slumbers,
　And things are not what they seem.

Life is real! Life is earnest!
  And the grave is not its goal;
"Dust thou art, to dust returnest,"
  Was not spoken of the soul.

Not enjoyment, and not sorrow,
  Is our destined end or way;
But to act, that each to-morrow
  Find us farther than to-day.

Art is long, and Time is fleeting,
  And our hearts, though stout and **brave,**
Still, like muffled drums, are beating
  Funeral marches to the grave.

In the world's broad field of battle,
  In the bivouac of Life,
Be not like dumb, driven cattle;
  Be a hero in the strife!

Trust no Future, howe'er pleasant!
  Let the dead Past bury its dead!
Act,—act in the living Present!
  Heart within, and God o'erhead!

Lives of great men all remind us
  We can make our lives sublime,
And, departing, leave behind us
  Footprints on the sands of time;

Footprints, that perhaps another,
  Sailing o'er life's solemn main,
A forlorn and shipwrecked brother,
  Seeing, shall take heart again.

Let us, then, be up and doing,
  With a heart for any fate;
Still achieving, still pursuing,
  Learn to labor and to **wait.**

THE WRECK OF THE HESPERUS.

It was the schooner Hesperus,
  That sailed the wintry sea;
And the skipper had taken his little daughtèr,
  To bear him company.

Blue were her eyes as the fairy-flax,
  Her cheeks like the dawn of day,
And her bosom white as the hawthorn buds,
  That ope in the month of May.

The skipper he stood beside the helm,
  His pipe was in his mouth,
And he watched how the veering flaw did blow
  The smoke now West, now South.

Then up and spake an old Sailor,
  Had sailed the Spanish Main,
"I pray thee, put into yonder port,
  For I fear a hurricane.

"Last night, the moon had a golden ring,
  And to-night no moon we see!"
The skipper, he blew a whiff from his pipe,
  And a scornful laugh laughed he.

Colder and louder blew the wind,
  A gale from the Northeast;
The snow fell hissing in the brine,
  And the billows frothed like yeast.

Down came the storm, and smote amain,
  The vessel in its strength;
She shuddered and paused, like a frighted steed,
  Then leaped her cable's length.

"Come hither! come hither! my little daughtèr,
  And do not tremble so;
For I can weather the roughest gale,
  That ever wind did blow."

He wrapped her warm in his seaman's coat
   Against the stinging blast;
He cut a rope from a broken spar,
   And bound her to the mast.

"O father! I hear the church-bells ring,
   O say, what may it be?"
" 'T is a fog-bell on a rock-bound coast!"—
   And he steered for the open sea.

"O father! I hear the sound of guns,
   O say, what may it be?"
"Some ship in distress, that cannot live
   In such an angry sea!"

"O father! I see a gleaming light,
   O say, what may it be?"
But the father answered never a word,
   A frozen corpse was he.

Lashed to the helm, all stiff and stark,
   With his face turned to the skies,
The lantern gleamed through the gleaming snow
   On his fixed and glassy eyes.

Then the maiden clasped her hands and prayed
   That savèd she might be;
And she thought of Christ, who stilled the wave,
   On the Lake of Galilee.

And fast through the midnight dark and drear,
   Through the whistling sleet and snow,
Like a sheeted ghost, the vessel swept
   Towards the reef of Norman's Woe.

And ever the fitful gusts between,
   A sound came from the land;
It was the sound of the trampling surf,
   On the rocks and the hard sea-sand.

The breakers were right beneath her bows,
   She drifted a dreary wreck,
And a whooping billow swept the crew
   Like icicles from her deck.

She struck where the white and fleecy waves
　　Looked soft as carded wool,
But the cruel rocks, they gored her side
　　Like the horns of an angry bull.

Her rattling shrouds, all sheathed in ice,
　　With the masts went by the board;
Like a vessel of glass, she stove and sank,
　　Ho! ho! the breakers roared!

At daybreak on the bleak sea-beach,
　　A fisherman stood aghast,
To see the form of a maiden fair,
　　Lashed close to a drifting mast.

The salt-sea was frozen on her breast,
　　The salt tears in her eyes;
And he saw her hair, like the brown sea-weed,
　　On the billows fall and rise.

Such was the wreck of the Hesperus
　　In the midnight and the snow!
Christ save us all from a death like this,
　　On the reef of Norman's Woe!

THE DAY IS DONE.

The day is done, and the darkness,
　　Falls from the wings of Night,
As a feather is wafted downward
　　From an eagle in his flight.

I see the lights of the village
　　Gleam through the rain and the mist,
And a feeling of sadness comes o'er me,
　　That my soul cannot resist:

A feeling of sadness and longing,
　　That is not akin to pain,
And resembles sorrow only
　　As the mist resembles the rain.

THE DAY IS DONE.

Come, read to me some poem,
  Some simple and heartfelt lay,
That shall soothe this restless feeling,
  And banish the thoughts of day.

Not from the grand old masters,
  Not from the bards sublime,
Whose distant footsteps echo
  Through the corridors of Time.

For, like strains of martial music,
  Their mighty thoughts suggest
Life's endless toil and endeavor;
  And to-night I long for rest.

Read from some humbler poet,
  Whose songs gushed from his heart,
As showers from the clouds of summer,
  Or tears from the eyelids start;

Who, through long days of labor,
  And nights devoid of ease,
Still heard in his soul the music
  Of wonderful melodies.

Such songs have power to quiet
  The restless pulse of care,
And come like the benediction
  That follows after prayer.

Then read from the treasured volume
  The poem of thy choice,
And lend to the rhyme of the poet
  The beauty of thy voice.

And the night shall be filled with music,
  And the cares, that infest the day,
Shall fold their tents, like the Arabs,
  And as silently steal away.

DRINKING SONG.

DRINKING SONG.

INSCRIPTION FOR AN ANTIQUE PITCHER.

COME, old friend! sit down and listen!
    From the pitcher, placed between us,
How the waters laugh and glisten
    In the head of old Silenus!

Old Silenus, bloated, drunken,
    Led by his inebriate Satyrs;
On his breast his head is sunken,
    Vacantly he leers and chatters.

Fauns with youthful Bacchus follow;
    Ivy crowns that brow supernal
As the forehead of Apollo,
    And possessing youth eternal.

Round about him, fair Bacchantes,
    Bearing cymbals, flutes, and thyrses,
Wild from Naxian groves, or Zante's
    Vineyards, sing delirious verses.

Thus he won, through all the nations,
    Bloodless victories, and the farmer
Bore, as trophies and oblations,
    Vines for banners, ploughs for armor.

Judged by no o'erzealous rigor,
    Much this mystic throng expresses:
Bacchus was the type of vigor,
    And Silenus of excesses.

These are ancient ethnic revels,
    Of a faith long since forsaken;
Now the Satyrs, changed to devils,
    Frighten mortals wine-o'ertaken.

Now to rivulets from the mountains
    Point the rods of fortune-tellers;
Youth perpetual dwells in fountains,—
    Not in flasks, and casks, and cellars.

Claudius, though he sang of flagons
  And huge tankards filled with Rhenish,
From that fiery blood of dragons
  Never would his own replenish.

Even Redi, though he chaunted
  Bacchus in the Tuscan valleys,
Never drank the wine he vaunted
  In his dithyrambic sallies.

Then with water fill the pitcher
  Wreathed about with classic fables,
Ne'er Falernian threw a richer
  Light upon Lucullus' tables.

Come, old friend, sit down and listen!
  As it passes thus between us,
How its wavelets laugh and glisten
  In the head of old Silenus!

THE ARROW AND THE SONG.

I SHOT an arrow into the air,
It fell to earth, I knew not where;
For, so swiftly it flew, the sight
Could not follow it in its flight.

I breathed a song into the air,
It fell to earth, I knew not where;
For who has sight so keen and strong,
That it can follow the flight of song?

Long, long afterward, in an oak
I found the arrow, still unbroke;
And the song, from beginning to end,
I found again in the heart of a friend.

VOICES OF THE NIGHT, 1839.

PRELUDE.

PLEASANT it was, when woods were green,
  And winds were soft and low,
To lie amid some sylvan scene,
Where, the long drooping boughs between,
Shadows dark and sunlight sheen
  Alternate come and go;

Or where the denser grove receives
  No sunlight from above,
But the dark foliage interweaves
In one unbroken roof of leaves,
Underneath whose sloping eaves
  The shadows hardly move.

Beneath some patriarchal tree
  I lay upon the ground;
His hoary arms uplifted he,
And all the broad leaves over me
Clapped their little hands in glee,
  With one continuous sound;—

A slumberous sound,—a sound that brings
  The feelings of a dream,—
As of innumerable wings,
As, when a bell no longer swings,
Faint the hollow murmur rings
  O'er meadow, lake, and stream.

And dreams of that which cannot die,
  Bright visions, came to me,
As lapped in thought I used to lie,
And gaze into the summer sky,
Where the sailing clouds went by,
  Like ships upon the sea;

Dreams that the soul of youth engage
  Ere Fancy has been quelled;
Old legends of the monkish page,
Traditions of the saint and sage,
Tales that have the rime of age,
  And chronicles of Eld.

And, loving still these quaint old themes,
  Even in the city's throng
I feel the freshness of the streams,
That, crossed by shades and sunny gleams,
Water the green land of dreams,
  The holy land of song.

Therefore, at Pentecost, which brings
  The Spring, clothed like a bride,
When nestling buds unfold their wings,
And bishop's-caps have golden rings,
Musing upon many things,
  I sought the woodlands wide.

The green trees whispered low and mild,
  It was a sound of joy!
They were my playmates when a child,
And rocked me in their arms so wild!
Still they looked at me and smiled,
  As if I were a boy;

And ever whispered, mild and low,
  "Come, be a child once more!"
And waved their long arms to and fro,
And beckoned solemnly and slow;
O, I could not choose but go
  Into the woodlands hoar;

Into the blithe and breathing air,
  Into the solemn wood,
Solemn and silent everywhere!
Nature with folded hands seemed there,
Kneeling at her evening prayer!
  Like one in prayer I stood.

Before me rose an avenue
  Of tall and sombrous pines;
Abroad their fan-like branches grew,
And, where the sunshine darted through,
Spread a vapor soft and blue,
  In long and sloping lines.

And, falling on my weary brain,
  Like a fast-falling shower,
The dreams of youth came back again,
Low lispings of the summer rain,
Dropping on the ripened grain,
  As once upon the flower.

Visions of childhood! Stay, O stay!
  Ye were so sweet and wild!
And distant voices seemed to say,
"It cannot be! They pass away!
Other themes demand thy lay;
  Thou art no more a child!

"The land of Song within thee lies,
  Watered by living springs;
The lids of Fancy's sleepless eyes
Are gates unto that Paradise;
Holy thoughts, like stars, arise,
  Its clouds are angels' wings.

"Learn, that henceforth thy song shall be,
  Not mountains capped with snow,
Nor forests sounding like the sea,
Nor rivers flowing ceaselessly,
Where the woodlands bend to see
  The bending heavens below.

"There is a forest where the din
  Of iron branches sounds!
A mighty river roars between,
And whosoever looks therein,
Sees the heavens all black with sin,—
  Sees not its depths, nor bounds.

"Athwart the swinging branches cast,
    Soft rays of sunshine pour;
Then comes the fearful wintry blast;
Our hopes, like withered leaves, fall fast;
Pallid lips say, 'It is past!
    We can return no more!'

"Look, then, into thine heart, and write!
    Yes, into Life's deep stream!
All forms of sorrow and delight,
All solemn Voices of the Night,
That can soothe thee, or affright,—
    Be these henceforth thy theme."

HYMN TO THE NIGHT.

Ἀσπασίη, τρίχλιστος

I HEARD the trailing garments of the Night
    Sweep through her marble halls!
I saw her sable skirts all fringed with light
    From the celestial walls!

I felt her presence, by its spell of might,
    Stoop o'er me from above;
The calm, majestic presence of the Night,
    As of the one I love.

I heard the sounds of sorrow and delight,
    The manifold, soft chimes,
That fill the haunted chambers of the Night,
    Like some old poet's rhymes.

From the cool cisterns of the midnight air
    My spirit drank repose;
The fountain of perpetual peace flows there—
    From those deep cisterns flows.

O holy Night! from thee I learn to bear
    What man has borne before!
Thou layest thy finger on the lips of Care,
    And they complain no more.

Peace! Peace! Orestes-like I breathe this prayer!
  Descend with broad-winged flight,
The welcome, the thrice-prayed for, the most fair,
  The best-beloved Night!

THE REAPER AND THE FLOWERS.

THERE is a Reaper whose name is Death,
  And, with his sickle keen,
He reaps the bearded grain at a breath,
  And the flowers that grow between.

"Shall I have nought that is fair?" saith he;
  "Have nought but the bearded grain?
Though the breath of these flowers is sweet to me.
  I will give them all back again."

He gazed at the flowers with tearful eyes,
  He kissed their drooping leaves;
It was for the Lord of Paradise
  He bound them in his sheaves.

"My Lord has need of these flowerets gay,"
  The Reaper said, and smiled;
"Dear tokens of the earth are they,
  Where he was once a child.

"They shall all bloom in fields of light,
  Transplanted by my care,
And saints, upon their garments white,
  These sacred blossoms wear."

And the mother gave, in tears and pain,
  The flowers she most did love;
She knew she should find them all again
  In the fields of light above.

O, not in cruelty, not in wrath,
  The Reaper came that day;
'T was an angel visited the green earth,
  And took the flowers away.

THE LIGHT OF STARS.

THE night is come, but not too soon;
  And sinking silently,
All silently, the little moon
  Drops down behind the sky.

There is no light in earth or heaven,
  But the cold light of stars;
And the first watch of night is given
  To the red planet Mars.

Is it the tender star of love?
  The star of love and dreams?
O no! from that blue tent above,
  A hero's armor gleams.

And earnest thoughts within me rise,
  When I behold afar,
Suspended in the evening skies,
  The shield of that red star.

O star of strength! I see thee stand
  And smile upon my pain;
Thou beckonest with thy mailed hand,
  And I am strong again.

Within my breast there is no light,
  But the cold light of stars;
I give the first watch of the night
  To the red planet Mars.

The star of the unconquered will,
  He rises in my breast,
Serene, and resolute, and still,
  And calm, and self-possessed.

And thou, too, whosoe'er thou art,
  That readest this brief psalm,
As one by one thy hopes depart,
  Be resolute and calm.

O fear not in a world like this,
    And thou shalt know ere long,
Know how sublime a thing it is
    To suffer and be strong.

FOOTSTEPS OF ANGELS.

WHEN the hours of Day are numbered,
    And the voices of the Night
Wake the better soul, that slumbered,
    To a holy, calm delight;

Ere the evening lamps are lighted,
    And, like phantoms grim and tall,
Shadows from the fitful fire-light
    Dance upon the parlor wall;

Then the forms of the departed
    Enter at the open door;
The beloved, the true-hearted,
    Come to visit me once more;

He, the young and strong, who cherished
    Noble longings for the strife,
By the road-side fell and perished,
    Weary with the march of life!

They, the holy ones and weakly,
    Who the cross of suffering bore,
Folded their pale hands so meekly,
    Spake with us on earth no more!

And with them the Being Beauteous,
    Who unto my youth was given,
More than all things else to love me,
    And is now a saint in heaven.

With a slow and noiseless footstep
    Comes that messenger divine,
Takes the vacant chair beside me,
    Lays her gentle hand in mine.

And she sits and gazes at me
  With those deep and tender eyes,
Like the stars, so still and saint-like,
  Looking downward from the skies.

Uttered not, yet comprehended,
Is the spirit's voiceless prayer,
Soft rebukes, in blessings ended,
  Breathing from her lips of air.

O, though oft depressed and lonely,
  All my fears are laid aside,
If I but remember only
  Such as these have lived and died!

FLOWERS.

SPAKE full well, in language quaint and olden,
  One who dwelleth by the castled Rhine,
When he called the flowers, so blue and golden,
  Stars, that in earth's firmament do shine.

Stars they are, wherein we read our history,
  As astrologers and seers of eld;
Yet not wrapped about with awful mystery,
  Like the burning stars, which they beheld.

Wondrous truths, and manifold as wondrous,
  God hath written in those stars above;
But not less in the bright flowerets under us
  Stands the revelation of his love.

Bright and glorious is that revelation,
  Written all over this great world of ours;
Making evident our own creation,
  In these stars of earth,—these golden flowers.

And the Poet, faithful and far-seeing,
  Sees, alike in stars and flowers, a part
Of the self-same, universal being,
  Which is throbbing in his brain and heart.

Gorgeous flowerets in the sunlight shining,
  Blossoms flaunting in the eye of day,
Tremulous leaves, with soft and silver lining,
  Buds that open only to decay;

Brilliant hopes, all woven in gorgeous tissues,
  Flaunting gayly in the golden light,
Large desires, with most uncertain issues,
  Tender wishes, blossoming at night!

These in flowers and men are more than seeming,
  Workings are they of the self-same powers
Which the Poet, in no idle dreaming,
  Seeth in himself and in the flowers.

Everywhere about us are they glowing,
  Some like stars, to tell us Spring is born;
Others, their blue eyes with tears o'erflowing,
  Stand like Ruth amid the golden corn;

Not alone in Spring's armorial bearing,
  And in Summer's green-emblazoned field,
But in arms of brave old Autumn's wearing,
  In the centre of his brazen shield;

Not alone in meadows and green alleys,
  On the mountain-top, and by the brink
Of sequestered pools in woodland valleys,
  Where the slaves of Nature stoop to drink;

Not alone in her vast dome of glory,
  Not on graves of bird and beast alone,
But in old cathedrals, high and hoary,
  On the tombs of heroes, carved in stone;

In the cottage of the rudest peasant,
  In ancestral homes, whose crumbling towers,
Speaking of the Past unto the Present,
  Tell us of the ancient Games of Flowers;

In all places, then, and in all seasons,
  Flowers expand their light and soul-like wings,
Teaching us, by most persuasive reasons,
  How akin they are to human things.

And with childlike, credulous affection
  We behold their tender buds expand;
Emblems of our own great resurrection,
  Emblems of the bright and better land.

THE BELEAGUERED CITY.

I HAVE read, in some old marvellous tale,
  Some legend strange and vague,
That a midnight host of spectres pale
  Beleaguered the walls of Prague.

Beside the Moldau's rushing stream,
  With the wan moon overhead,
There stood, as in an awful dream,
  The army of the dead.

White as a sea-fog, landward bound,
  The spectral camp was seen,
And, with a sorrowful, deep sound,
  The river flowed between.

No other voice nor sound was there,
  No drum, nor sentry's pace;
The mistlike banners clasped the air,
  As clouds with clouds embrace.

But, when the old cathedral bell
  Proclaimed the morning prayer,
The white pavilions rose and fell
  On the alarmed air.

Down the broad valley fast and far
  The troubled army fled;
Up rose the glorious morning star,
  The ghastly host was dead.

I have read, in the marvellous heart of man,
  That strange and mystic scroll,
That an army of phantoms vast and wan
  Beleaguer the human soul.

Encamped beside Life's rushing stream,
　In Fancy's misty light,
Gigantic shapes and shadows gleam,
　Portentous through the night.

Upon its midnight battle-ground
　The spectral camp is seen,
And, with a sorrowful, deep sound,
　Flows the River of Life between.

No other voice, nor sound is there,
　In the army of the grave;
No other challenge breaks the air,
　But the rushing of Life's wave.

And, when the solemn and deep church-bell
　Entreats the soul to pray,
The midnight phantoms feel the spell,
　The shadows sweep away.

Down the broad Vale of Tears afar
　The spectral camp is fled;
Faith shineth as a morning star,
　Our ghastly fears are dead.

MIDNIGHT MASS FOR THE DYING YEAR.

Yes, the Year is growing old,
　And his eye is pale and bleared!
Death, with frosty hand and cold,
　Plucks the old man by the beard,
　　Sorely,—sorely!

The leaves are falling, falling,
　Solemnly and slow;
Caw! caw! the rooks are calling,
　It is a sound of woe,
　　A sound of woe!

Through woods and mountain passes
　The winds, like anthems, roll;
They are chanting solemn masses,
　Singing: "Pray for this poor soul,
　　Pray,—pray!"

And the hooded clouds, like friars,
　Tell their beads in drops of rain,
And patter their doleful prayers!—
　But their prayers are all in vain,
　　All in vain!

There he stands in the foul weather,
　The foolish, fond Old Year,
Crowned with wild flowers and with heather,
　Like weak, despised Lear,
　　A king,—a king!

Then comes the summer-like day,
　Bids the old man rejoice!
His joy! his last! O, the old man gray,
　Loveth that ever-soft voice,
　　Gentle and low.

To the crimson woods he saith,—
　To the voice gentle and low
Of the soft air, like a daughter's breath,—
　"Pray do not mock me so!
　　Do not laugh at me!"

And now the sweet day is dead;
　Cold in his arms it lies;
No stain from its breath is spread
　Over the glassy skies,
　　No mist or stain!

Then, too, the Old Year dieth,
　And the forests utter a moan,
Like the voice of one who crieth
　In the wilderness alone,
　　"Vex not his ghost!"

Then comes, with an awful roar,
   Gathering and sounding on,
The storm-wind from Labrador,
   The wind Euroclydon,
      The storm-wind!

Howl! howl! and from the forest
   Sweep the red leaves away!
Would the sins that thou abhorrest,
   O Soul! could thus decay,
      And be swept away!

For there shall come a mightier blast,
   There shall be a darker day;
And the stars, from heaven downcast,
   Like red leaves be swept away!
      Kyrie, eleyson!
      Christe, eleyson!

EARLIER POEMS.

[These poems were written for the most part during my college life, and all of them before the age of nineteen. Some have found their way into schools, and seem to be successful. Others lead a vagabond and precarious existence in the corners of newspapers, or have changed their names and run away to seek their fortunes beyond the sea. I say, with the Bishop of Avranches, on a similar occasion: "I cannot be displeased to see these children of mine which I have neglected, and almost exposed, brought from their wanderings in lanes and alleys, and safely lodged, in order to go forth into the world together in a more decorous garb."]

AN APRIL DAY.

WHEN the warm sun, that brings
Seed-time and harvest, has returned again,
'T is sweet to visit the still wood, where springs
   The first flower of the plain.

I love the season well,
When forest glades are teeming with bright forms,
Nor dark and many-folded clouds foretell
   The coming-on of storms.

From the earth's loosened mould
The sapling draws its sustenance, and thrives;
Though stricken to the heart with winter's cold,
    The drooping tree revives.

The softly-warbled song
Comes from the pleasant woods, and colored wings
Glance quick in the bright sun, that moves along
    The forest openings.

When the bright sunset fills
The silver woods with light, the green slope throws
Its shadows in the hollows of the hills,
    And wide the upland glows.

And, when the eve is born,
In the blue lake the sky, o'er-reaching far,
Is hollowed out, and the moon dips her horn,
    And twinkles many a star.

Inverted in the tide,
Stand the gray rocks, and trembling shadows throw,
And the fair trees look over, side by side,
    And see themselves below.

Sweet April!—many a thought
Is wedded unto thee, as hearts are wed;
Nor shall they fail, till, to its autumn brought,
    Life's golden fruit is shed.

AUTUMN.

WITH what a glory comes and goes the year!
The buds of spring, those beautiful harbingers
Of sunny skies and cloudless times, enjoy
Life's newness, and earth's garniture spread out.
And when the silver habit of the clouds
Comes down upon the autumn sun, and with
A sober gladness the old year takes up
His bright inheritance of golden fruits,
A pomp and pageant fill the splendid scene.

There is a beautiful spirit breathing now
Its mellow richness on the clustered trees,
And, from a beaker full of richest dyes,
Pouring new glory on the autumn woods,
And dipping in warm light the pillared clouds
Morn on the mountain, like a summer bird,
Lifts up her purple wing, and in the vales
The gentle wind, a sweet and passionate wooer,
Kisses the blushing leaf, and stirs up life
Within the solemn woods of ash deep-crimsoned,
And silver beech, and maple yellow-leaved,
Where autumn, like a faint old man, sits down
By the wayside a-weary. Through the trees
The golden robin moves. The purple finch,
That on wild cherry and red cedar feeds,
A winter bird, comes with its plaintive whistle,
And pecks by the witch-hazel, whilst aloud
From cottage roofs the warbling bluebird sings,
And merrily, with oft-repeated stroke,
Sounds from the threshing-floor the busy flail.

O what a glory doth this world put on
For him who, with a fervent heart, goes forth
Under the bright and glorious sky, and looks
On duties well performed, and days well spent!
For him the wind, ay, and the yellow leaves
Shall have a voice, and give him eloquent teachings.
He shall so hear the solemn hymn, that Death
Has lifted up for all, that he shall go
To his long resting-place without a tear.

WOODS IN WINTER.

When winter winds are piercing chill,
    And through the hawthorns blows the gale,
With solemn feet I tread the hill,
    That overbrows the lonely vale.

O'er the bare upland, and away
    Through the long reach of desert woods,
The embracing sunbeams chastely play,
    And gladden these deep solitudes.

Where, twisted round the barren oak,
  The summer vine in beauty clung,
And summer winds the stillness broke,
  The crystal icicle is hung.

Where, from their frozen urns, mute springs
  Pour out the river's gradual tide,
Shrilly the skater's iron rings,
  And voices fill the woodland side.

Alas! how changed from the fair scene,
  When birds sang out their mellow lay,
And winds were soft, and woods were green,
  And the song ceased not with the day.

But still wild music is abroad,
  Pale, desert woods! within your crowd;
And gathering winds, in hoarse accord,
  Amid the vocal reeds pipe loud.

Chill airs and wintry winds! my ear
  Has grown familiar with your song;
I hear it in the opening year,—
  I listen, and it cheers me long.

HYMN OF THE MORAVIAN NUNS OF BETH-LEHEM AT THE CONSECRATION OF PULASKI'S BANNER.

When the dying flame of day
Through the chancel shot its ray,
Far the glimmering tapers shed
Faint light on the cowled head;
And the censer burning swung,
Where, before the altar, hung
The blood-red banner, that with prayer
Had been consecrated there.

And the nun's sweet hymn was heard the while,
Sung low in the dim, mysterious aisle:
"Take thy banner! May it wave
Proudly o'er the good and brave;
When the battle's distant wail
Breaks the sabbath of our vale,
When the clarion's music thrills
To the hearts of these lone hills,
When the spear in conflict shakes,
And the strong lance shivering breaks.

"Take thy banner! and, beneath
The battle-cloud's encircling wreath,
Guard it!—till our homes are free!
Guard it!—God will prosper thee!
In the dark and trying hour,
In the breaking forth of power,
In the rush of steeds and men,
His right hand will shield thee then.

"Take thy banner! But, when night
Closes round the ghastly fight,
If the vanquished warrior bow,
Spare him!—By our holy vow,
By our prayers and many tears,
By the mercy that endears,
Spare him!—he our love hath shared!
Spare him!—as thou wouldst be spared!

"Take thy banner!—and if e'er
Thou shouldst press the soldier's bier,
And the muffled drum should beat
To the tread of mournful feet,
Then this crimson flag shall be
Martial cloak and shroud for thee."

The warrior took that banner proud,
And it was his martial cloak and shroud!

SUNRISE ON THE HILLS.

I stood upon the hills, when heaven's wide arch
Was glorious with the sun's returning march,
And woods were brightened, and soft gales
Went forth to kiss the sun-clad vales.
The clouds were far beneath me;—bathed in light,
They gathered mid-way round the wooded height,
And, in their fading-glory, shone
Like hosts in battle overthrown,
As many a pinnacle, with shifting glance,
Through the gray mist thrust up its shattered lance,
And rocking on the cliff was left
The dark pine blasted, bare, and cleft.
The veil of cloud was lifted, and below
Glowed the rich valley, and the river's flow
Was darkened by the forest's shade
Or glistened in the white cascade;
Where upward, in the mellow blush of day,
The noisy bittern wheeled his spiral way.

I heard the distant waters dash,
I saw the current whirl and flash,—
And richly, by the blue lake's silver beach,
The woods were bending with a silent reach.
Then o'er the vale, with gentle swell,
The music of the village bell
Came sweetly to the echo-giving hills;
And the wild horn, whose voice the woodland fills,
Was ringing to the merry shout,
That faint and far the glen sent out,
Where, answering to the sudden shot, thin smoke,
Through thick-leaved branches, from the dingle broke.

If thou art worn and hard beset
With sorrows, that thou wouldst forget,
If thou wouldst read a lesson, that will keep
Thy heart from fainting and thy soul from sleep,
Go to the woods and hills!—No tears
Dim the sweet look that Nature wears.

THE SPIRIT OF POETRY.

THERE is a quiet spirit in these woods,
That dwells where'er the gentle south wind blows;
Where, underneath the white-thorn, in the glade,
The wild flowers bloom, or, kissing the soft air,
The leaves above their sunny palms outspread.
With what a tender and impassioned voice
It fills the nice and delicate ear of thought,
When the fast-ushering star of morning comes
O'er-riding the gray hills with golden scarf;
Or when the cowled and dusky-sandaled Eve,
In mourning weeds, from out the western gate,
Departs with silent pace! That spirit moves
In the green valley, where the silver brook,
From its full laver, pours the white cascade;
And, babbling low amid the tangled woods,
Slips down through moss-grown stones with endless laughter.
And frequent, on the everlasting hills,
Its feet go forth, when it doth wrap itself
In all the dark embroidery of the storm,
And shouts the stern, strong wind. And here, amid
The silent majesty of these deep woods,
Its presence shall uplift thy thoughts from earth,
As to the sunshine and the pure, bright air
Their tops the green trees lift. Hence gifted bards
Have ever loved the calm and quiet shades.
For them there was an eloquent voice in all
The sylvan pomp of woods, the golden sun,
The flowers, the leaves, the river on its way,
Blue skies, and silver clouds, and gentle winds,—
The swelling upland, where the sidelong sun
Aslant the wooded slope, at evening, goes,—
Groves, through whose broken roof the sky looks in,
Mountain, and shattered cliff, and sunny vale,
The distant lake, fountains,—and mighty trees,
In many a lazy syllable, repeating
Their old poetic legends to the wind.

And this is the sweet spirit, that doth fill
The world: and, in these wayward days of youth,

My busy fancy oft embodies it,
As a bright image of the light and beauty
That dwell in nature,—of the heavenly forms
We worship in our dreams, and the soft hues
That stain the wild bird's wing, and flush the clouds
When the sun sets. Within her eye
The heaven of April, with its changing light,
And when it wears the blue of May, is hung,
And on her lip the rich, red rose. Her hair
Is like the summer tresses of the trees,
When twilight makes them brown, and on her cheek
Blushes the richness of an autumn sky,
With ever-shifting beauty. Then her breath,
It is so like the gentle air of Spring,
As, from the morning's dewy flowers, it comes
Full of their fragrance, that it is a joy
To have it round us,—and her silver voice
Is the rich music of a summer bird,
Heard in the still night, with its passionate cadence.

BURIAL OF THE MINNISINK.

On sunny slope and beechen swell,
The shadowed light of evening fell;
And, where the maple's leaf was brown,
With soft and silent lapse came down
The glory, that the wood receives,
At sunset, in its brazen leaves.

Far upward in the mellow light
Rose the blue hills. One cloud of white,
Around a far uplifted cone,
In the warm blush of evening shone;
An image of the silver lakes,
By which the Indian's soul awakes.

But soon a funeral hymn was heard
Where the soft breath of evening stirred
The tall, gray forest; and a band

Of stern in heart, and strong in hand,
Came winding down beside the wave,
To lay the red chief in his grave.

They sang, that by his native bowers
He stood, in the last moon of flowers,
And thirty snows had not yet shed
Their glory on the warrior's head;
But, as the summer fruit decays,
So died he in those naked days.

A dark cloak of the roebuck's skin
Covered the warrior, and within
Its heavy folds the weapons, made
For the hard toils of war, were laid;
The cuirass, woven of plaited reeds,
And the broad belt of shells and beads.

Before, a dark-haired virgin train
Chanted the death dirge of the slain;
Behind, the long procession came
Of hoary men and chiefs of fame,
With heavy hearts, and eyes of grief,
Leading the war-horse of their chief.

Stripped of his proud and martial dress,
Uncurbed, unreined, and riderless,
With darting eye, and nostril spread,
And heavy and impatient tread,
He came; and oft that eye so proud
Asked for his rider in the crowd.

They buried the dark chief; they freed
Beside the grave his battle steed;
And swift an arrow cleaved its way
To his stern heart! One piercing neigh
Arose,—and, on the dead man's plain,
The rider grasps his steed again.

TRANSLATIONS.

[Don Jorge Manrique, the author of the following poem, flourished in the last half of the fifteenth century. He followed the profession of arms, and died on the field of battle. Mariana, in his "History of Spain," makes honorable mention of him, as being present at the siege of Uclés, and speaks of him as "a youth of estimable qualities, who in this war gave brilliant proofs of his valor. He died young, and was thus cut off from long exercising his great virtues and exhibiting to the world the light of his genius, which was already known to fame." He was mortally wounded in a skirmish near Cañavete, in the year 1479.

The name of Rodrigo Manrique, the father of the poet, Conde de Paredes and Maestre de Santiago, is well known in Spanish history and song. He died in 1476; according to Mariana, in the town of Uclés; but, according to the poem of his son, in Ocaña. It was his death that called forth the poem upon which rests the literary reputation of the younger Manrique. In the language of his historian, "Don Jorge Manrique, in an elegant Ode, full of poetic beauties, rich embellishments of genius, and high moral reflections, mourned the death of his father as with a funeral hymn." This praise is not exaggerated. The poem is a model in its kind. Its conception is solemn and beautiful; and, in accordance with it, the style moves on—calm, dignified, and majestic.]

COPLAS DE MANRIQUE.

FROM THE SPANISH.

O LET the soul her slumbers break,
Let thought be quickened, and awake;
Awake to see
How soon this life is past and gone,
And death comes softly stealing on,
How silently!

Swiftly our pleasures glide away,
Our hearts recall the distant day
With many sighs;
The moments that are speeding fast
We heed not, but the past,—the past,—
More highly prize.

Onward its course the present keeps,
Onward the constant current sweeps,
Till life is done;
And, did we judge of time aright,
The past and future in their flight
Would be as one.

Let no one fondly dream again,
That Hope and all her shadowy train
Will not decay;
Fleeting as were the dreams of old,
Remembered like a tale that's told,
They pass away.

Our lives are rivers, gliding free
To that unfathomed, boundless sea,
The silent grave!
Thither all earthly pomp and boast
Roll, to be swallowed up and lost
In one dark wave.

Thither the mighty torrents stray,
Thither the brook pursues its way,
And tinkling rill.
They all are equal. Side by side
The poor man and the son of pride
Lie calm and still.

I will not here invoke the throng
Of orators and sons of song,
The deathless few;
Fiction entices and deceives,
And, sprinkled o'er her fragrant leaves,
Lies poisonous dew.

To One alone my thoughts arise,
The Eternal Truth,—the Good and Wise,—
To Him I cry,
Who shared on earth our common lot,
But the world comprehended not
His deity.

This world is but the rugged road
Which leads us to the bright abode
Of peace above;
So let us choose that narrow way,
Which leads no traveller's foot astray
From realms of love.

Our cradle is the starting-place,
In life we run the onward race,
And reach the goal;
When, in the mansions of the blest,
Death leaves to its eternal rest
The weary soul.

Did we but use it as we ought,
This world would school each wandering thought
To its high state.
Faith wings the soul beyond the sky,
Up to that better world on high,
For which we wait.

Yes,—the glad messenger of love,
To guide us to our home above,
The Saviour came;
Born amid mortal cares and fears,
He suffered in this vale of tears
A death of shame.

Behold of what delusive worth
The bubbles we pursue on earth,
The shapes we chase,
Amid a world of treachery!
They vanish ere death shuts the eye
And leave no trace.

Time steals them from us,—chance strange,
Disastrous accidents, and change,
That come to all;
Even in the most exalted state,
Relentless sweeps the stroke of fate,
The strongest fall.

Tell me,—the charms that lovers seek
In the clear eye and blushing cheek,
The hues that play
O'er rosy lip and brow of snow,
When hoary age approaches slow,
Ah, where are they?

The cunning skill, the curious arts,
The glorious strength that youth imparts
In life's first stage;
These shall become a heavy weight,
When Time swings wide his outward gate
To weary age.

The noble blood of Gothic name,
Heroes emblazoned high to fame,
In long array;
How, in the onward course of time,
The landmarks of that race sublime
Were swept away!

Some, the degraded slaves of lust,
Prostrate and trampled in the dust,
Shall rise no more;
Others, by guilt and crime, maintain
The scutcheon, that, without a stain,
Their fathers bore.

Wealth and the high estate of pride,
With what untimely speed they glide,
How soon depart!
Bid not the shadowy phantoms stay,
The vassals of a mistress they,
Of fickle heart.

These gifts in Fortune's hands are found;
Her swift revolving wheel turns round,
And they are gone!
No rest the inconstant goddess knows,
But changing, and without repose,
Still hurries on.

Even could the hand of avarice save
Its gilded baubles, till the grave
Reclaimed its prey,
Let none on such poor hopes rely;
Life, like an empty dream, flits by,
And where are they?

Earthly desires and sensual lust
Are passions springing from the dust,—
They fade and die;
But, in the life beyond the tomb,
They seal the immortal spirit's doom
Eternally!

The pleasures and delights, which mask
In treacherous smiles life's serious task,
What are they, all,
But the fleet coursers of the chase,
And death an ambush in the race,
Wherein we fall?

No foe, no dangerous pass, we heed,
Brook no delay,—but onward speed
With loosened rein;
And, when the fatal snare is near,
We strive to check our mad career,
But strive in vain.

Could we new charms to age impart,
And fashion with a cunning art
The human face,
As we can clothe the soul with light,
And make the glorious spirit bright
With heavenly grace,—

How busily each passing hour
Should we exert that magic power.
What ardor show,
To deck the sensual slave of sin,
Yet leave the freeborn soul within,
In weeds of woe!

Monarchs, the powerful and the strong,
Famous in history and in song
Of olden time,
Saw, by the stern decrees of fate,
Their kingdoms lost, and desolate
Their race sublime.

Who is the champion? who the strong?
Pontiff and priest, and sceptred throng?
On these shall fall
As heavily the hand of Death,
As when it stays the shepherd's breath
Beside his stall.

I speak not of the Trojan name,
Neither its glory nor its shame
Has met our eyes;
Nor of Rome's great and glorious dead,
Though we have heard so oft, and read,
Their histories.

Little avails it now to know
Of ages passed so long ago,
Nor how they rolled;
Our theme shall be of yesterday,
Which to oblivion sweeps away,
Like days of old.

Where is the King, Don Juan? Where
Each royal prince and noble heir
Of Aragon?
Where are the courtly gallantries?
The deeds of love and high emprise,
In battle done?

Tourney and joust, that charmed the eye,
And scarf, and gorgeous panoply,
And nodding plume,—
What were they but a pageant scene?
What but the garlands, gay and green,
That deck the tomb?

Where are the high-born dames, and where
Their gay attire, and jewelled hair,
And odors sweet?
Where are the gentle knights, that came
To kneel, and breathe love's ardent flame,
Low at their feet?

Where is the song of Troubadour?
Where are the lute and gay tambour
They loved of yore?
Where is the mazy dance of old,
The flowing robes, inwrought with gold,
The dancers wore?

And he who next the sceptre swayed,
Henry, whose royal court displayed
Such power and pride;
O, in what winning smiles arrayed,
The world its various pleasures laid
His throne beside!

But O! how false and full of guile
That world, which wore so soft a smile
But to betray!
She, that had been his friend before,
Now from the fated monarch tore
Her charms away.

The countless gifts,—the stately walls,
The royal palaces, and halls,
All filled with gold;
Plate with armorial bearings wrought,
Chambers with ample treasures fraught
Of wealth untold;

The noble steeds, and harness bright,
The gallant lord, and stalwart knight,
In rich array,—
Where shall we seek them now? Alas!
Like the bright dewdrops on the grass,
They passed away.

His brother, too, whose factious zeal
Usurped the sceptre of Castile,
Unskilled to reign;
What a gay, brilliant court had he,
When all the flower of chivalry
Was in his train!

But he was mortal; and the breath,
That flamed from the hot forge of Death,
Blasted his years;
Judgment of God! that flame by thee,
When raging fierce and fearfully,
Was quenched in tears!

Spain's haughty Constable,—the true
And gallant Master, whom we knew
Most loved of all.
Breathe not a whisper of his pride,—
He on the gloomy scaffold died,
Ignoble fall!

The countless treasures of his care,
His hamlets green, and cities fair,
His mighty power,—
What were they all but grief and shame,
Tears and a broken heart, when came
The parting hour?

His other brothers, proud and high,
Masters, who, in prosperity,
Might rival kings;
Who made the bravest and the best
The bondsmen of their high behest,
Their underlings;

What was their prosperous estate,
When high exalted and elate
With power and pride?
What, but a transient gleam of light,
A flame, which, glaring at its height,
Grew dim and died?

So many a duke of royal name,
Marquis and count of spotless fame,
And baron brave,
That might the sword of empire wield,
All these, O Death, hast thou concealed
In the dark grave.

Their deeds of mercy and of arms,
In peaceful days, of war's alarms,
When thou dost show,
O Death, thy stern and angry face,
One stroke of thy all-powerful mace
Can overthrow.

Unnumbered hosts, that threaten nigh,
Pennon and standard flaunting high,
And flag displayed;
High battlements intrenched around,
Bastion, and moated wall, and mound
And palisade,

And covered trench, secure and deep,—
All these cannot one victim keep,
O Death, from thee,
When thou dost battle in thy wrath,
And thy strong shafts pursue their path
Unerringly.

O World! so few the years we live,
Would that the life which thou dost give
Were life indeed!
Alas! thy sorrows fall so fast,
Our happiest hour is when at last
The soul is freed.

Our days are covered o'er with grief,
And sorrows neither few nor brief
Veil all in gloom;
Left desolate of real good,
Within this cheerless solitude
No pleasures bloom.

Thy pilgrimage begins in tears,
And ends in bitter doubts and fears,
Or dark despair;
Midway so many toils appear,
That he who lingers longest here
Knows most of care.

Thy goods are bought with many a groan
By the hot sweat of toil alone,
And weary hearts;
Fleet-footed is the approach of woe,
But with a lingering step and slow
Its form departs.

And he, the good man's shield and shade,
To whom all hearts their homage paid,
As Virtue's son,—
Roderic Manrique,—he whose name
Is written on the scroll of Fame,
Spain's champion;

His signal deeds and prowess high
Demand no pompous eulogy,—
Ye saw his deeds!
Why should their praise in verse be sung?
The name, that dwells on every tongue,
No minstrel needs.

To friends a friend;—how kind to all
The vassals of this ancient hall
And feudal fief!
To foes how stern a foe was he!
And to the valiant and the free
How brave a chief!

What prudence with the old and wise;
What grace in youthful gayeties;
In all how sage!
Benignant to the serf and slave,
He showed the base and falsely brave
A lion's rage.

His was Octavian's prosperous star,
The rush of Cæsar's conquering car

At battle's call;
His, Scipio's virtue; his, the skill
And the indomitable will
Of Hannibal.

His was a Trajan's goodness,—his
A Titus' noble charities
And righteous laws;
The arm of Hector, and the might
Of Tully, to maintain the right
In truth's just cause;

The clemency of Antonine,
Aurelius' countenance divine,
Firm, gentle, still;
The eloquence of Adrian,
And Theodosius' love to man,
And generous will;

In tented field and bloody fray,
An Alexander's vigorous sway
And stern command;
The faith of Constantine; ay, more,
The fervent love Camillus bore
His native land.

He left no well-filled treasury,
He heaped no pile of riches high,
Nor massive plate;
He fought the Moors,—and, in their fall,
City and tower and castled wall
Were his estate.

Upon the hard-fought battle-ground,
Brave steeds and gallant riders found
A common grave;
And there the warrior's hand did gain
The rents, and the long vassal train,
That conquest gave.

And if, of old, his halls displayed
The honored and exalted grade
His worth had gained,
So, in the dark, disastrous hour,

Brothers and bondsmen of his power
His hand sustained.

After high deeds, not left untold,
In the stern warfare, which of old
'T was his to share,
Such noble leagues he made, that more
And fairer regions, than before,
His guerdon were.

These are the records, half effaced,
Which, with the hand of youth, he traced
On history's page;
But with fresh victories he drew
Each fading character anew
In his old age.

By his unrivalled skill, by great
And veteran service to the state,
By worth adored,
He stood, in his high dignity,
The proudest knight of chivalry,
Knight of the Sword.

He found his cities and domains
Beneath a tyrant's galling chains
And cruel power;
But, by fierce battle and blockade,
Soon his own banner was displayed
From every tower.

By the tried valor of his hand,
His monarch and his native land
Were nobly served;—
Let Portugal repeat the story,
And proud Castile, who shared the glory
His arms deserved.

And when so oft, for weal or woe,
His life upon the fatal throw
Had been cast down;
When he had served, with patriot zeal,
Beneath the banner of Castile,
His sovereign's crown;

And done such deeds of valor strong,
That neither history nor song
Can count them all;
Then, on Ocaña's castled rock,
Death at his portal came to knock,
With sudden call,—

Saying, "Good Cavalier, prepare
To leave this world of toil and care
With joyful mien;
Let thy strong heart of steel this day
Put on its armor for the fray,—
The closing scene.

"Since thou hast been, in battle-strife,
So prodigal of health and life,
For earthly fame,
Let virtue nerve thy heart again;
Loud on the last stern battle-plain
They call thy name.

"Think not the struggle that draws near
Too terrible for man,—nor fear
To meet the foe;
Nor let thy noble spirit grieve,
Its life of glorious fame to leave
On earth below.

"A life of honor and of worth
Has no eternity on earth,
'T is but a name;
And yet its glory far exceeds
That base and sensual life, which leads
To want and shame.

"The eternal life, beyond the sky,
Wealth cannot purchase, nor the high
And proud estate;
The soul in dalliance laid,—the spirit
Corrupt with sin,—shall not inherit
A joy so great.

"But the good monk, in cloistered cell,
Shall gain it by his book and bell,

His prayers and tears;
And the brave knight, whose arm endures
Fierce battle, and against the Moors
His standard rears.

"And thou, brave knight, whose hand has poured
The life-blood of the Pagan horde
O'er all the land,
In heaven shalt thou receive, at length,
The guerdon of thine earthly strength
And dauntless hand.

"Cheered onward by this promise sure,
Strong in the faith entire and pure
Thou dost profess,
Depart,—thy hope is certainty,—
The third—the better life on high
Shalt thou possess."

"O Death, no more, no more delay,
My spirit longs to flee away,
And be at rest;
The will of Heaven my will shall be,—
I bow to the divine decree,
To God's behest.

"My soul is ready to depart,
No thought rebels, the obedient heart
Breathes forth no sigh;
The wish on earth to linger still
Were vain, when 't is God's sovereign will
That we shall die.

"O thou, that for our sins didst take
A human form, and humbly make
Thy home on earth;
Thou, that to thy divinity
A human nature didst ally
By mortal birth,

"And in that form didst suffer here
Torment, and agony, and fear,
So patiently;
By thy redeeming grace alone,

And not for merits of my own,
O, pardon me!"

As thus the dying warrior prayed,
Without one gathering mist or shade
Upon his mind;
Encircled by his family,
Watched by affection's gentle eye
So soft and kind;

His soul to Him, who gave it, rose;
God lead it to its long repose,
Its glorious rest!
And, though the warrior's sun has set,
Its light shall linger round us yet,
Bright, radiant, blest.[1]

[1] This poem of Manrique is a great favorite in Spain. No less than four poetic Glosses, or running commentaries, upon it have been published, no one of which, however, possesses great poetic merit. That of the Carthusian monk, Rodrigo de Valdepeñas, is the best. It is known as the *Glosa del Cartujo.* There is also a prose Commentary by Luis de Aranda.

The following stanzas of the poem were found in the author's pocket, after his death on the field of battle.

"O World! so few the years we live,
Would that the life which thou dost give
Were life indeed!
Alas! thy sorrows fall so fast,
Our happiest hour is when at last
The soul is freed.

"Our days are covered o'er with grief,
And sorrows neither few nor brief
Veil all in gloom;
Left desolate of real good,
Within this cheerless solitude
No pleasures bloom.

"Thy pilgrimage begins in tears,
And ends in bitter doubts and fears,
Or dark despair;
Midway so many toils appear,
That he who lingers longest here
Knows most of care.

"Thy goods are bought with many a groan,
By the hot sweat of toil alone,
And weary hearts;
Fleet-footed is the approach of woe,
But with a lingering step and slow
Its form departs."

THE GOOD SHEPHERD.

FROM THE SPANISH OF LOPE DE VEGA.

SHEPHERD! that with thine amorous, sylvan song
Hast broken the slumber which encompassed me,—
That mad'st thy crook from the accursed tree,
On which thy powerful arms were stretched so long!
Lead me to mercy's ever-flowing fountains;
For thou my shepherd, guard, and guide shalt be.
I will obey thy voice, and wait to see
Thy feet all beautiful upon the mountains.
Hear, Shepherd! thou who for thy flock art dying,
O, wash away these scarlet sins, for thou
Rejoicest at the contrite sinner's vow.
O, wait!—to thee my weary soul is crying,—
Wait for me!—Yet why ask it, when I see,
With feet nailed to the cross, thou 'rt waiting still for me.

TO-MORROW.

FROM THE SPANISH OF LOPE DE VEGA.

LORD, what am I, that, with unceasing care,
Thou didst seek after me,—that thou didst wait,
Wet with unhealthy dews, before my gate,
And pass the gloomy nights of winter there?
O strange delusion!—that I did not greet
Thy blest approach, and O, to Heaven how lost,
If my ingratitude's unkindly frost
Has chilled the bleeding wounds upon thy feet.
How oft my guardian angel gently cried,
"Soul, from thy casement look, and thou shalt see
How he persists to knock and wait for thee!"
And, O! how often to that voice of sorrow,
"To-morrow we will open," I replied,
And when the morrow came I answered still, "To-morrow."

THE NATIVE LAND.

FROM THE SPANISH OF FRANCISCO DE ALDANA.

CLEAR fount of light! my native land on high
Bright with a glory that shall never fade!
Mansion of truth! without a veil or shade,
Thy holy quiet meets the spirit's eye.
There dwells the soul in its ethereal essence,
Gasping no longer for life's feeble breath;
But, sentinelled in heaven, its glorious presence
With pitying eye beholds, yet fears not, death.
Beloved country! banished from thy shore,
A stranger in this prison-house of clay,
The exiled spirit weeps and sighs for thee!
Heavenward the bright perfections I adore
Direct, and the sure promise cheers the way,
That, whither love aspires, there shall my dwelling be.

THE IMAGE OF GOD.

FROM THE SPANISH OF FRANCISCO DE ALDANA.

O LORD! that seest, from yon starry height,
Centred in one the future and the past,
Fashioned in thine own image, see how fast
The world obscures in me what once was bright!
Eternal Sun! the warmth which thou hast given,
To cheer life's flowery April, fast decays;
Yet, in the hoary winter of my days,
Forever green shall be my trust in Heaven.
Celestial King! O let thy presence pass
Before my spirit, and an image fair
Shall meet that look of mercy from on high,
As the reflected image in a glass
Doth meet the look of him who seeks it there,
And owes its being to the gazer's eye.

THE BROOK.

FROM THE SPANISH.

LAUGH of the mountain!—lyre of bird and tree!
Pomp of the meadow! mirror of the morn!
The soul of April, unto whom are born
The rose and jessamine, leaps wild in thee!
Although, where'er thy devious current strays,
The lap of earth with gold and silver teems,
To me thy clear proceeding brighter seems
Than golden sands, that charm each shepherd's gaze.
How without guile thy bosom, all transparent
As the pure crystal, lets the curious eye
Thy secrets scan, thy smooth, round pebbles count!
How, without malice murmuring, glides thy current!
O sweet simplicity of days gone by!
Thou shun'st the haunts of man, to dwell in limpid fount!

THE CELESTIAL PILOT.

FROM DANTE.   PURGATORIO II.

AND now, behold! as at the approach of morning,
Through the gross vapors, Mars grows fiery red
Down in the west upon the ocean floor,

Appeared to me,—may I again behold it!—
A light along the sea, so swiftly coming,
Its motion by no flight of wing is equalled.

And when therefrom I had withdrawn a little
Mine eyes, that I might question my conductor,
Again I saw it brighter grown and larger.

Thereafter, on all sides of it, appeared
I knew not what of white, and underneath,
Little by little, there came forth another.

My master yet had uttered not a word,
While the first brightness into wings unfolded!
But, when he clearly recognized the pilot,

He cried aloud: "Quick, quick, and bow the knee!
Behold the Angel of God! fold up thy hands!
Henceforward shalt thou see such officers!

"See, how he scorns all human arguments,
So that no oar he wants, nor other sail
Than his own wings, between so distant shores!

"See, how he holds them, pointed straight to heaven,
Fanning the air with the eternal pinions,
That do not moult themselves like mortal hair!"

And then, as nearer and more near us came
The Bird of Heaven, more glorious he appeared,
So that the eye could not sustain his presence,

But down I cast it; and he came to shore
With a small vessel, gliding swift and light,
So that the water swallowed nought thereof.

Upon the stern stood the Celestial Pilot!
Beatitude seemed written in his face!
And more than a hundred spirits sat within.

"*In exitu Israel* out of Egypt!"
Thus sang they all together in one voice,
With whatso in that Psalm is after written.

Then made he sign of holy rood upon them,
Whereat all cast themselves upon the shore,
And he departed swiftly as he came.

THE TERRESTRIAL PARADISE.

FROM DANTE.   PURGATORIO XXVIII.

LONGING already to search in and round
The heavenly forest, dense and living-green,
Which to the eyes tempered the new-born day,

Withouten more delay I left the bank,
Crossing the level country slowly, slowly,
Over the soil, that everywhere breathed fragrance.

A gently breathing air, that no mutation
Had in itself, smote me upon the forehead,
No heavier blow, than of a pleasant breeze,

Whereat the tremulous branches readily
Did all of them bow downward towards that side
Where its first shadow casts the Holy Mountain;

Yet not from their upright direction bent
So that the little birds upon their tops
Should cease the practice of their tuneful art;

But, with full-throated joy, the hours of prime
Singing received they in the midst of foliage
That made monotonous burden to their rhymes,

Even as from branch to branch it gathering swells,
Through the pine forests on the shore of Chiassi,
When Æolus unlooses the Sirocco.

Already my slow steps had led me on
Into the ancient wood so far, that I
Could see no more the place where I had entered.

And lo! my farther course cut off a river,
Which, towards the left hand, with its little waves,
Bent down the grass, that on its margin sprang.

All waters that on earth most limpid are,
Would seem to have within themselves some mixture,
Compared with that, which nothing doth conceal,

Although it moves on with a brown, brown current,
Under the shade perpetual, that never
Ray of the sun lets in, nor of the moon.

BEATRICE.

FROM DANTE. PURGATORIO XXX., XXXI.

EVEN as the Blessed, in the new covenant,
Shall rise up quickened, each one from his grave,
Wearing again the garments of the flesh,

So, upon that celestial chariot,
A hundred rose *ad vocem tanti senis,*
Ministers and messengers of life eternal.

They all were saying: *"Benedictus qui venis,"*
And scattering flowers above and round about,
"Manibus o date lilia plenis."

I once beheld, at the approach of day,
The orient sky all stained with roseate hues,
And the other heaven with light serene adorned.

And the sun's face uprising, overshadowed,
So that, by temperate influence of vapors,
The eye sustaining his aspect for long while;

Thus in the bosom of a cloud of flowers,
Which from those hands angelic were thrown up,
And down descended inside and without,

With crown of olive o'er a snow-white veil,
Appeared a lady, under a green mantle,
Vested in colors of the living flame.

    *   *   *   *   *

Even as the snow, among the living rafters
Upon the back of Italy, congeals,
Blown on and beaten by Sclavonian winds,

And then, dissolving, filters through itself,
Whene'er the land, that loses shadow, breathes,
Like as a taper melts before a fire,

Even such I was, without a sigh or tear,
Before the song of those who chime forever
After the chiming of the eternal spheres;

But, when I heard in those sweet melodies
Compassion for me, more than had they said,
"O wherefore, lady, dost thou thus consume him?"

The ice, that was about my heart congealed,
To air and water changed, and, in my anguish,
Through lips and eyes came gushing from my breast.

*   *   *   *   *

Confusion and dismay, together mingled,
Forced such a feeble "Yes!" out of my mouth,
To understand it one had need of sight.

Even as a cross-bow breaks, when 't is discharged,
Too tensely drawn the bow-string and the bow,
And with less force the arrow hits the mark;

So I gave way under this heavy burden,
Gushing forth into bitter tears and sighs,
And the voice, fainting, flagged upon its passage.

SPRING.

FROM THE FRENCH OF CHARLES D'ORLEANS.
XV. CENTURY.

GENTLE Spring!—in sunshine clad,
    Well dost thou thy power display!
For Winter maketh the light heart sad,
    And thou,—thou makest the sad heart gay.
He sees thee, and calls to his gloomy train,
    The sleet, and the snow, and the wind, and the rain;
And they shrink away, and they flee in fear,
    When thy merry step draws near.

Winter giveth the fields and the trees, so old,
　Their beards of icicles and snow;
And the rain, it raineth so fast and cold,
　We must cower over the embers low;
And, snugly housed from the wind and weather,
Mope like birds that are changing feather.
But the storm retires, and the sky grows clear,
　When thy merry step draws near.

Winter maketh the sun in the gloomy sky
　Wrap him round with a mantle of cloud;
But, Heaven be praised, thy step is nigh;
　Thou tearest away the mournful shroud,
And the earth looks bright, and Winter surly,
Who has toiled for nought both late and early,
Is banished afar by the new-born year,
　When thy merry step draws near.

THE CHILD ASLEEP.

FROM THE FRENCH.

Sweet babe! true portrait of thy father's face,
　Sleep on the bosom that thy lips have pressed!
Sleep, little one; and closely, gently place
　Thy drowsy eyelid on thy mother's breast.

Upon that tender eye, my little friend,
　Soft sleep shall come, that cometh not to me!
I watch to see thee, nourish thee, defend;—
　'T is sweet to watch for thee,—alone for thee!

His arms fall down; sleep sits upon his brow;
　His eye is closed; he sleeps, nor dreams of harm.
Wore not his cheek the apple's ruddy glow,
　Would you not say he slept on Death's cold arm?

Awake, my boy!—I tremble with affright!
　Awake, and chase this fatal thought!—Unclose
Thine eye but for one moment on the light!
　Even at the price of thine, give me repose!

Sweet error!—he but slept,—I breathe again;—
    Come, gentle dreams, the hour of sleep beguile.
O! when shall he, for whom I sigh in vain,
    Beside me watch to see thy waking smile?

THE GRAVE.

FROM THE ANGLO-SAXON.

For thee was a house built
Ere thou wast born,
For thee was a mould meant
Ere thou of mother camest.
But it is not made ready,
Nor its depth measured,
Nor is it seen
How long it shall be.
Now I bring thee
Where thou shalt be;
Now I shall measure thee,
And the mould afterwards.

Thy house is not
Highly timbered,
It is unhigh and low;
When thou art therein,
The heel-ways are low,
The side-ways unhigh.
The roof is built
Thy breast full nigh,
So thou shalt in mould
Dwell full cold,
Dimly and dark.

Doorless is that house,
And dark it is within;
There thou art fast detained
And Death hath the key.
Loathsome is that earth-house,
And grim within to dwell.
There thou shalt dwell,
And worms shall divide thee.

Thus thou art laid,
And leavest thy friends;
Thou hast no friend,
Who will come to thee,
Who will ever see
How that house pleaseth thee;
Who will ever open
The door for thee
And descend after thee,
For soon thou art loathsome
And hateful to see.

KING CHRISTIAN.

A NATIONAL SONG OF DENMARK.

FROM THE DANISH OF JOHANNES EVALD.

KING CHRISTIAN stood by the lofty mast
        In mist and smoke;
His sword was hammering so fast,
Through Gothic helm and brain it passed;
Then sank each hostile hulk and mast,
        In mist and smoke.
"Fly!" shouted they, "fly, he who can!
Who braves of Denmark's Christian
        The stroke?"

Nils Juel gave heed to the tempest's roar,
        Now is the hour!
He hoisted his blood-red flag once more,
And smote upon the foe full sore,
And shouted loud, through the tempest's roar,
        "Now is the hour!"
"Fly!" shouted they, "for shelter fly!
Of Denmark's Juel who can defy
        The power?"

North Sea! a glimpse of Wessel rent
        Thy murky sky!
Then champions to thine arms were sent,
Terror and Death glared where he went;

From the waves was heard a wail, that rent
Thy murky sky!
From Denmark, thunders Tordenskiol',
Let each to Heaven commend his soul,
And fly!

Path of the Dane to fame and might!
Dark-rolling wave!
Receive thy friend, who, scorning flight,
Goes to meet danger with despite,
Proudly as thou the tempest's might,
Dark-rolling wave!
And amid pleasures and alarms,
And war and victory, be thine arms
My grave![1]

THE HAPPIEST LAND.

FRAGMENT OF A MODERN BALLAD.
FROM THE GERMAN.

THERE sat one day in quiet,
By an alehouse on the Rhine,
Four hale and hearty fellows,
And drank the precious wine.

The landlord's daughter filled their cups,
Around the rustic board;
Then sat they all so calm and still,
And spake not one rude word.

But, when the maid departed,
A Swabian raised his hand,
And cried, all hot and flushed with wine,
"Long live the Swabian land!

"The greatest kingdom upon earth
Cannot with that compare;

[1] Nils Juel was a celebrated Danish Admiral, and Peter Wessel, a Vice-Admiral, who for his great prowess received the popular title of Tordenskiold, or *Thunder-shield*. In childhood he was a tailor's apprentice, and rose to his high rank before the age of twenty-eight, when he was killed in a duel.

With all the stout and hardy men
  And the nut-brown maidens there."

"Ha!" cried a Saxon, laughing,—
  And dashed his beard with wine;
"I had rather live in Lapland,
  Than that Swabian land of thine!

"The goodliest land on all this earth,
  It is the Saxon land!
There have I as many maidens
  As fingers on this hand!"

"Hold your tongues! both Swabian and Saxon!"
  A bold Bohemian cries;
"If there's a heaven upon this earth,
  In Bohemia it lies.

"There the tailor blows the flute,
  And the cobbler blows the horn,
And the miner blows the bugle,
  Over mountain gorge and bourn."

  *   *   *   *   *

And then the landlord's daughter
  Up to heaven raised her hand,
And said, "Ye may no more contend,—
  There lies the happiest land!"

THE WAVE.

FROM THE GERMAN OF TIEDGE.

"WHITHER, thou turbid wave
Whither, with so much haste,
As if a thief wert thou?"

  "I am the Wave of Life,
Stained with my margin's dust;
From the struggle and the strife
Of the narrow stream I fly
To the Sea's immensity,
To wash from me the slime
Of the muddy banks of Time."

THE DEAD.

FROM THE GERMAN OF STOCKMANN.

How they so softly rest,
All, all the holy dead,
Unto whose dwelling-place
Now doth my soul draw near!
How they so softly rest,
All in their silent graves,
Deep to corruption
Slowly down-sinking!

And they no longer weep,
Here, where complaint is still,
And they no longer feel,
Here, where all gladness flies!
And by the cypresses
Softly o'ershadowed,
Until the Angel
Calls them, they slumber!

THE BIRD AND THE SHIP.

FROM THE GERMAN OF MÜLLER.

"The rivers rush into the sea,
By castle and town they go;
The winds behind them merrily
Their noisy trumpets blow.

"The clouds are passing far and high,
We little birds in them play;
And everything, that can sing and fly,
Goes with us, and far away.

"I greet thee, bonny boat! Whither, or whence,
With thy fluttering golden band?"—
"I greet thee, little bird! To the wide sea
I haste from the narrow land.

"Full and swollen is every sail;
    I see no longer a hill,
I have trusted all to the sounding gale,
    And it will not let me stand still.

"And wilt thou, little bird, go with us?
    Thou mayest stand on the mainmast tall,
For full to sinking is my house
    With merry companions all."—

"I need not and seek not company,
    Bonny boat, I can sing all alone;
For the mainmast tall too heavy am I,
    Bonny boat, I have wings of my own.

"High over the sails, high over the mast,
    Who shall gainsay these joys?
When thy merry companions are still, at last,
    Thou shalt hear the sound of my voice.

"Who neither may rest, nor listen may,
    God bless them every one!
I dart away, in the bright blue day,
    And the golden fields of the sun.

"Thus do I sing my weary song,
    Wherever the four winds blow;
And this same song, my whole life long,
    Neither Poet nor Printer may know."

WHITHER?

FROM THE GERMAN OF MÜLLER.

I HEARD a brooklet gushing
    From its rocky fountain near,
Down into the valley rushing,
    So fresh and wondrous clear.

I know not what came o'er me,
    Nor who the counsel gave;
But I must hasten downward,
    All with my pilgrim-stave;

Downward, and ever farther,
    And ever the brook beside;
And ever fresher murmured,
    And ever clearer, the tide.

Is this the way I was going?
    Whither, O brooklet, say!
Thou hast, with thy soft murmur,
    Murmured my senses away.

What do I say of a murmur?
    That can no murmur be;
'T is the water-nymphs, that are singing
    Their roundelays under me.

Let them sing, my friend, let them murmur,
    And wander merrily near;
The wheels of a mill are going
    In every brooklet clear.

BEWARE!

FROM THE GERMAN.

I KNOW a maiden fair to see,
    Take care!
She can both false and friendly be,
    Beware! Beware!
    Trust her not,
She is fooling thee!

She has two eyes, so soft and brown,
    Take care!
She gives a side-glance and looks down,
    Beware! Beware!
    Trust her not,
She is fooling thee!

And she has hair of a golden hue,
   Take care!
And what she says it is not true,
   Beware! Beware!
   Trust her not,
She is fooling thee!

She has a bosom as white as snow,
   Take care!
She knows how much it is best to show,
   Beware! Beware!
   Trust her not,
She is fooling thee!

She gives thee a garland woven fair,
   Take care!
It is a fool's-cap for thee to wear,
   Beware! Beware!
   Trust her not,
She is fooling thee!

SONG OF THE BELL.

FROM THE GERMAN.

Bell! thou soundest merrily,
When the bridal party
   To the church doth hie!
Bell! thou soundest solemnly,
When, on Sabbath morning,
   Fields deserted lie!

Bell! thou soundest merrily;
Tellest thou at evening,
   Bed-time draweth nigh!
Bell! thou soundest mournfully
Tellest thou the bitter
   Parting hath gone by!

Say! how canst thou mourn?
How canst thou rejoice?
   Thou art but metal dull!
And yet all our sorrowings,
And all our rejoicings,
   Thou dost feel them all!

God hath wonders many,
Which we cannot fathom,
   Placed within thy form!
When the heart is sinking,
Thou alone canst raise it,
   Trembling in the storm!

THE CASTLE BY THE SEA.

FROM THE GERMAN OF UHLAND.

"HAST thou seen that lordly castle,
   That Castle by the Sea?
Golden and red above it
   The clouds float gorgeously.

"And fain it would stoop downward
   To the mirrored wave below;
And fain it would soar upward
   In the evening's crimson glow."

"Well have I seen that castle,
   That Castle by the Sea,
And the moon above it standing,
   And the mist rise solemnly."

"The winds and the waves of ocean,
   Had they a merry chime?
Didst thou hear, from those lofty chambers,
   The harp and the minstrel's rhyme?"

"The winds and the waves of ocean,
   They rested quietly,
But I heard on the gale a sound of wail,
   And tears came to mine eyes."

"And sawest thou on the turrets
  The King and his royal bride?
And the wave of their crimson mantles?
  And the golden crown of pride?

"Led they not forth, in rapture,
  A beauteous maiden there?
Resplendent as the morning sun,
  Beaming with golden hair?"

"Well saw I the ancient parents,
  Without the crown of pride;
They were moving slow, in weeds of woe,
  No maiden was by their side!"

THE BLACK KNIGHT.

FROM THE GERMAN OF UHLAND.

'T was Pentecost, the Feast of Gladness,
When woods and fields put off all sadness.
  Thus began the King and spake:
"So from the halls
Of ancient Hofburg's walls,
  A luxuriant Spring shall break."

Drums and trumpets echo loudly,
Wave the crimson banners proudly.
  From balcony the King looked on;
In the play of spears,
Fell all the cavaliers,
  Before the monarch's stalwart son.

To the barrier of the fight
Rode at last a sable Knight.
  "Sir Knight! your name and scutcheon, say!"
"Should I speak it here,
Ye would stand aghast with fear;
  I am a Prince of mighty sway!"

When he rode into the lists,
The arch of heaven grew black with mists,
  And the castle 'gan to rock.
At the first blow,
Fell the youth from saddle-bow,
  Hardly rises from the shock.

Pipe and viol call the dances,
Torch-light through the high halls glances;
  Waves a mighty shadow in;
With manner bland
Doth ask the maiden's hand,
  Doth with her the dance begin;

Danced in sable iron sark,
Danced a measure weird and dark,
  Coldly clasped her limbs around.
From breast and hair
Down fall from her the fair
  Flowerets, faded, to the ground.

To the sumptuous banquet came
Every Knight and every Dame.
  'Twixt son and daughter all distraught,
With mournful mind
The ancient King reclined,
  Gazed at them in silent thought.

Pale the children both did look,
But the guest a beaker took;
  "Golden wine will make you whole!"
The children drank,
Gave many a courteous thank;
  "O that draught was very cool!"

Each the father's breast embraces,
Son and daughter; and their faces
  Colorless grow utterly.
Whichever way
Looks the fear-struck father gray,
  He beholds his children die.

"Woe! the blessed children both
Takest thou in the joy of youth;
    Take me, too, the joyless father!"
Spake the grim Guest,
From his hollow, cavernous breast,
    "Roses in the spring I gather!"

SONG OF THE SILENT LAND.

FROM THE GERMAN OF SALIS.

Into the Silent Land!
Ah! who shall lead us thither?
Clouds in the evening sky more darkly gather,
And shattered wrecks lie thicker on the strand.
Who leads us with a gentle hand
Thither, O thither,
Into the Silent Land?

Into the Silent Land!
To you, ye boundless regions
Of all perfection! Tender morning visions
Of beauteous souls! The Future's pledge and band
Who in Life's battle firm doth stand,
Shall bear Hope's tender blossoms
Into the Silent Land!

O Land! O Land!
For all the broken-hearted
The mildest herald by our fate allotted,
Beckons, and with inverted torch doth stand
To lead us with a gentle hand
Into the land of the great Departed,
Into the Silent Land?

L'ENVOI.

Ye voices, that arose
After the Evening's close,
And whispered to my restless heart repose!

Go, breathe it in the ear
Of all who doubt and fear,
And say to them, "Be of good cheer!"

Ye sounds, so low and calm,
That in the groves of balm
Seemed to me like an angel's psalm!

Go, mingle yet once more
With the perpetual roar
Of the pine forest, dark and hoar!

Tongues of the dead, not lost,
But speaking from death's frost,
Like fiery tongues at Pentecost!

Glimmer, as funeral lamps,
Amid the chills and damps
Of the vast plain where Death encamps.

THE LUCK OF EDENHALL.

FROM THE GERMAN OF UHLAND.

[The tradition, upon which this ballad is founded, and the "shards of the Luck of Edenhall," still exist in England. The goblet is in the possession of Sir Christopher Musgrave, Bart., of Eden Hall, Cumberland; and is not so entirely shattered as the ballad leaves it.]

Of Edenhall, the youthful Lord
Bids sound the festal trumpet's call;
He rises at the banquet board,
And cries, 'mid the drunken revellers all,
"Now bring me the Luck of Edenhall!"

THE LUCK OF EDENHALL.

The butler hears the words with pain,
The house's oldest seneschal,
Takes slow from its silken cloth again
The drinking glass of crystal tall;
They call it the Luck of Edenhall.

Then said the Lord: "This glass to praise,
Fill with red wine from Portugal!"
The gray-beard with trembling hand obeys;
A purple light shines over all,
It beams from the Luck of Edenhall.

Then speaks the Lord, and waves it light,
"This glass of flashing crystal tall
Gave to my sires the Fountain-Sprite;
She wrote in it: *If this glass doth fall,
Farewell then, O Luck of Edenhall!*

" 'T was right a goblet the Fate should be
Of the joyous race of Edenhall!
Deep draughts drink we right willingly;
And willingly ring, with merry call,
Kling! klang! to the Luck of Edenhall!"

First rings it deep, and full, and mild,
Like to the song of a nightingale;
Then like the roar of a torrent wild;
Then mutters at last like the thunder's fall,
The glorious Luck of Edenhall.

"For its keeper takes a race of might,
The fragile goblet of crystal tall;
It has lasted longer than is right;
Kling! klang!—with a harder blow than all
Will I try the Luck of Edenhall!"

As the goblet ringing flies apart,
Suddenly cracks the vaulted hall;
And through the rift, the wild flames start;
The guests in dust are scattered all,
With the breaking Luck of Edenhall!

In storms the foe, with fire and sword;
He in the night had scaled the wall,
Slain by the sword lies the youthful Lord,
But holds in his hand the crystal tall,
The shattered Luck of Edenhall.

On the morrow the butler grope alone,
The gray-beard in the desert hall,
He seeks his Lord's burnt skeleton,
He seeks in the dismal ruin's fall
The shards of the Luck of Edenhall.

"The stone wall," saith he, "doth fall aside,
Down must the stately columns fall;
Glass is this earth's Luck and Pride;
In atoms shall fall this earthly ball
One day like the Luck of Edenhall!"

THE ELECTED KNIGHT.

FROM THE DANISH.

[The following strange and somewhat mystical ballad is from Nyerup
and Rahbek's *Danske Viser* of the Middle Ages. It seems to refer to the
first preaching of Christianity in the North, and to the institution of
Knight-Errantry. The three maidens I suppose to be Faith, Hope, and
Charity. The irregularities of the original have been carefully preserved
in the translation.]

Sir Oluf he rideth over the plain,
    Full seven miles broad and seven miles wide,
But never, ah never can meet with the man
    A tilt with him dare ride.

He saw under the hill-side
    A Knight full well equipped;
His steed was black, his helm was barred;
    He was riding at full speed.

He wore upon his spurs
    Twelve little golden birds;
Anon he spurred his steed with a clang,
    And there sat all the birds and sang.

He wore upon his mail
  Twelve little golden wheels,
Anon in eddies the wild wind blew,
  And round and round the wheels they flew.

He wore before his breast
  A lance that was poised in rest;
And it was sharper than diamond-stone,
  It made Sir Oluf's heart to groan.

He wore upon his helm,
  A wreath of ruddy gold;
And that gave him the Maidens Three,
  The youngest was fair to behold.

Sir Oluf questioned the Knight eft-soon
  If he were come from heaven down;
"Art thou Christ of Heaven," quoth he,
  "So will I yield me unto thee."

"I am not Christ the Great,
  Thou shalt not yield thee yet;
I am an Unknown Knight,
  Three modest Maidens have me bedight."

"Art thou a Knight elected,
  And have three Maidens thee bedight;
So shalt thou ride a tilt this day,
  For all the Maidens' honor!"

The first tilt they together rode,
  They put their steeds to the test;
The second tilt they together rode,
  They proved their manhood best.

The third tilt they together rode,
  Neither of them would yield;
The fourth tilt they together rode,
  They both fell on the field.

Now lie the lords upon the plain,
  And their blood runs unto death;
Now sit the Maidens in the high tower,
  The youngest sorrows till death.

THE TWO LOCKS OF HAIR.

FROM THE GERMAN OF PFIZER.

A YOUTH, light-hearted and content,
   I wander through the world;
Here, Arab-like, is pitched my tent
   And straight again is furled.

Yet oft I dream, that once a wife
   Close in my heart was locked,
And in the sweet repose of life
   A blessed child I rocked.

I wake! Away that dream,—away!
   Too long did it remain!
So long, that both by night and day
   It ever comes again.

The end lies ever in my thought;
   To a grave so cold and deep
The mother beautiful was brought;
   Then dropt the child asleep.

But now the dream is wholly o'er,
   I bathe mine eyes and see;
And wander through the world once more,
   A youth so light and free.

Two locks,—and they are wondrous fair,—
   Left me that vision mild;
The brown is from the mother's hair,
   The blond is from the child.

And when I see that lock of gold,
   Pale grows the evening-red;
And when the dark lock I behold,
   I wish that I were dead.

IT IS NOT ALWAYS MAY.

NO HAY PÁJAROS EN LOS NIDOS DE ANTAÑO.

Spanish Proverb.

THE sun is bright,—the air is clear,
　The darting swallows soar and sing,
And from the stately elms I hear
　The bluebird prophesying Spring.

So blue yon winding river flows,
　It seems an outlet from the sky,
Where waiting till the west wind blows,
　The freighted clouds at anchor lie.

All things are new;—the buds, the leaves,
　That gild the elm tree's nodding crest,
And even the nest beneath the eaves;—
　There are no birds in last year's nest!

All things rejoice in youth and love,
　The fulness of their first delight!
And learn from the soft heavens above
　The melting tenderness of night.

Maiden, that read'st this simple rhyme,
　Enjoy thy youth, it will not stay;
Enjoy the fragrance of thy prime,
　For O! it is not always May!

Enjoy the Spring of Love and Youth,
　To some good angel leave the rest;
For Time will teach thee soon the truth,
　There are no birds in last year's nest!

THE RAINY DAY.

THE day is cold, and dark, and dreary;
It rains, and the wind is never weary;
The vine still clings to the mouldering wall,
But at every gust the dead leaves fall,
　And the day is dark and dreary.

My life is cold, and dark, and dreary;
It rains, and the wind is never weary;
My thoughts still cling to the mouldering Past,
But the hopes of youth fall thick in the blast,
    And the days are dark and dreary.

Be still, sad heart! and cease repining;
Behind the clouds is the sun still shining;
Thy fate is the common fate of all,
Into each life some rain must fall,
    Some days must be dark and dreary.

GOD'S-ACRE.

I LIKE that ancient Saxon phrase, which calls
    The burial-ground God's-Acre! It is just;
It consecrates each grave within its walls,
    And breathes a benison o'er the sleeping dust.

God's-Acre! Yes, that blessed name imparts
    Comfort to those, who in the grave have sown
The seed, that they had garnered in their hearts,
    Their bread of life, alas! no more their own.

Into its furrows shall we all be cast,
    In the shure faith, that we shall rise again
At the great harvest, when the archangel's blast
    Shall winnow, like a fan, the chaff and grain.

Then shall the good stand in immortal bloom,
    In the fair gardens of that second birth;
And each bright blossom, mingle its perfume
    With that of flowers, which never bloomed on earth.

With thy rude ploughshare, Death, turn up the sod,
    And spread the furrow of the seed we sow;
This is the field and Acre of our God,
    This is the place where human harvests grow!

TO THE RIVER CHARLES.

RIVER! that in silence windest
  Through the meadows, bright and free,
Till at length thy rest thou findest
  In the bosom of the sea!

Four long years of mingled feeling,
  Half in rest, and half in strife,
I have seen thy waters stealing
  Onward, like the stream of life.

Thou hast taught me, Silent River!
  Many a lesson, deep and long;
Thou hast been a generous giver;
  I can give thee but a song.

Oft in sadness and in illness,
  I have watched thy current glide,
Till the beauty of its stillness
  Overflowed me, like a tide.

And in better hours and brighter,
  When I saw thy waters gleam,
I have felt my heart beat lighter,
  And leap onward with thy stream.

Not for this alone I love thee,
  Nor because thy waves of blue
From celestial seas above thee
  Take their own celestial hue.

Where yon shadowy woodlands hide thee,
  And thy waters disappear,
Friends I love have dwelt beside thee,
  And have made thy margin dear.

More than this;—thy name reminds me
  Of three friends, all true and tried;
And that name, like magic, binds me
  Closer, closer to thy side.

Friends my soul with joy remembers!
　How like quivering flames they start,
When I fan the living embers
　On the hearth-stone of my heart!

'T is for this, thou Silent River!
　That my spirit leans to thee;
Thou hast been a generous giver,
　Take this idle song from me.

THE GOBLET OF LIFE.

FILLED is Life's goblet to the brim;
And though my eyes with tears are dim,
I see its sparkling bubbles swim,
And chant a melancholy hymn
　With solemn voice and slow.

No purple flowers,—no garlands green,
Conceal the goblet's shade or sheen,
Nor maddening draughts of Hippocrene,
Like gleams of sunshine, flash between
　Thick leaves of mistletoe.

This goblet, wrought with curious art,
Is filled with waters, that upstart,
When the deep fountains of the heart,
By strong convulsions rent apart,
　Are running all to waste.

And as it mantling passes round,
With fennel is it wreathed and crowned,
Whose seed and foliage sun-imbrowned
Are in its waters steeped and drowned,
　And give a bitter taste.

Above the lowly plants it towers,
The fennel, with its yellow flowers,
And in an earlier age than ours
Was gifted with the wondrous powers,
　Lost vision to restore.

It gave new strength and fearless mood;
And gladiators, fierce and rude,
Mingled it in their daily food;
And he who battled and subdued,
    A wreath of fennel wore.

Then in Life's goblet freely press,
The leaves that give it bitterness,
Nor prize the colored waters less,
For in thy darkness and distress
    New light and strength they give!

And he who has not learned to know
How false its sparkling bubbles show,
How bitter are the drops of woe,
With which its brim may overflow,
    He has not learned to live.

The prayer of Ajax was for light;
Through all that dark and desperate fight,
The blackness of that noonday night,
He asked but the return of sight,
    To see his foeman's face.

Let our unceasing, earnest prayer
Be, too, for light,—for strength to bear
Our portion of the weight of care,
That crushes into dumb despair
    One half the human race.

O suffering, sad humanity!
O ye afflicted ones, who lie
Steeped to the lips in misery,
Longing, and yet afraid to die,
    Patient, though sorely tried!

I pledge you in this cup of grief,
Where floats the fennel's bitter leaf,
The Battle of our Life is brief,
The alarm,—the struggle,—the relief,—
    Then sleep we side by side.